# ADVANCE PRAISE FOR *RACE*

"So much tripe has been published and promulgated by the 'we are all equal and race is an illusion' crowd, that to find a coherent, cogent, and penetrating analysis and rebuttal of the PBS approach is a delicious repast! *Race: The Reality of Human Differences* by Vincent Sarich and Frank Miele will represent an important milestone in reducing the millstone of the myths that have accumulated denigrating and/or ignoring our genetic diversity. This book will certainly be a must for my students, and it is surely long overdue!"

> —Dr. Ralph L. Holloway,
> *Professor of Anthropology, Columbia University*

"There are lots of ideas in the book. You probably won't agree with all of them, but you will surely be stimulated to think more deeply."

> —James F. Crow, *Professor Emeritus of Genetics,*
> *University of Wisconsin, Madison*

"Where did we come from? How did we get to where we are? Evolutionary theory is the only viable answer and it requires that we think in terms of populations that differ in their gene frequencies—Mendelian populations. As Sarich and Miele so clearly show, human races are simply Mendelian populations and their study, particularly with modern genetic tools, is yielding fascinating clues, many of which are not widely known, about our origins and the origins of our diversity."

> —Thomas J. Bouchard, Jr., *Professor of Psychology,*
> *University of Minnesota*

"Science investigates how the world works, so passionate debate about how it should or could work better can be informed by facts. Is race a factually meaningless and irrelevant concept for education, medicine, or life success in the twenty-first century? Sarich and Miele think not, and their book drives at the issues head on with a provocative and, at times, disturbing presentation that, in the end, offers hope for a better appreciation of human variability."

—RICH HAIER, PH.D., *Professor of Psychology,*
*Department of Pediatrics, University of California, Irvine*

# RACE

## THE REALITY OF HUMAN DIFFERENCES

Vincent Sarich and Frank Miele

Westview
PRESS

A Member of the Perseus Books Group

Copyright © 2004 by Westview Press, a Member of the Perseus Books Group

Published in the United States of America by Westview Press, A Member of the Perseus Books Group, 5500 Central Avenue, Boulder, Colorado 80301–2877, and in the United Kingdom by Westview Press, 12 Hid's Copse Road, Cumnor Hill, Oxford OX2 9JJ.

Find us on the world wide web at www.westviewpress.com

Westview Press books are available at special discounts for bulk purchases in the United States by corporations, institutions, and other organizations. For more information, please contact the Special Markets Department at the Perseus Books Group, 11 Cambridge Center, Cambridge, MA 02142, or call (617) 252-5298 or (800) 255-1514, or email specialmarkets@perseusbooks.com.

Library of Congress Cataloging-in-Publication Data
Sarich, Vincent.
    Race : the reality of human differences / Vincent Sarich and Frank Miele.
        p.    cm.
"A Member of the Perseus Books Group."
Includes index.
    ISBN 0-8133-4086-1 (hardcover)
    1. Race. 2. Physical anthropology. 3. Human population genetics.
I. Miele, Frank. II. Title.
    GN269.S27 2004
    305.8—dc22
2003017370

The paper used in this publication meets the requirements of the American National Standard for Permanence of Paper for Printed Library Materials Z39.48–1984.

Interior design by Trish Wilkinson

Set in 12-point Goudy by the Perseus Books Group

10  9  8  7  6  5  4  3  2  1

# Contents

# Why Another Book on Race?

While we were preparing the final draft of this book, the Public Broadcasting System (PBS) in 2003 aired a highly acclaimed documentary, *Race: The Power of an Illusion*. The contemporary scientific and ethical consensus in both the media and the social sciences regarding race was concisely summarized in the ten numbered statements that appear at the beginning of the website that accompanies the documentary (http://www.pbs.org/race). The documentary's numbered statements and their elaborations follow; the chapter numbers shown in italics and enclosed in square brackets refer to the chapters of this book that challenge the particular statement.

1. Race is a modern idea. [*Chapters 2 and 3*]
   Ancient societies did not divide people according to physical differences but according to religion, status, class, even language.
2. Race has no genetic basis. [*Chapter 5*]

No one characteristic, trait, or gene distinguishes all members of one so-called race from all members of another so-called race.

3. Slavery predates race. [*Chapter 2*]

Throughout history, societies have enslaved others, often as a result of conquest or war, but not because of physical characteristics or a belief in natural inferiority. In America, a unique set of circumstances led to the enslavement of peoples who looked similar [that is, black skin became associated with slave status in America—our explanatory comment].

4. Race and freedom were born together. [*Chapters 2 and 3*]

When the U.S. was founded, equality was a radical new idea. But our early economy was based largely on slavery. The concept of race helped explain why some people could be denied the rights and freedoms that others took for granted.

5. Race justified social inequalities as natural. [*Chapters 2 and 3*]

As the race concept evolved, it justified extermination of Native Americans, exclusion of Asian immigrants, and taking of Mexican lands.

6. Human subspecies don't exist. [*Chapter 6*]

Unlike many animals, modern humans have not been around long enough, nor have populations been isolated enough, to evolve into separate subspecies or races. Despite surface difference, we are among the most similar of species.

7. Skin color is only skin deep. [*Chapters 5–9, esp. Chapter 6*]

Most traits are inherited independently of one another. The genes for skin color have nothing to do with genes for hair texture, eye shape, blood type, musical talent, or athletic ability.

8. Most variation is within, not between "races." [*Chapter 7*]

Of the small amount of total human genetic variation, 85% exists within any local population, be they Italians, Kurds,

Koreans, or Cherokees. Two random Koreans are likely to be as genetically different as a Korean and an Italian.

9. Race is not biological, but racism is still real. [*Chapter 10*]

Race is still a powerful social idea that gives people different access to opportunities and resources. Our government and society have created advantages to being white. This affects everyone, whether we are aware of it or not.

10. Colorblindness will not end racism. [*Chapter 10*]

Pretending race doesn't exist is not the same as creating equality. Race is more than stereotypes and individual prejudice. To combat racism, we need to identify and remedy social policies that advantage some groups at the expense of others.

The authors of this book, Vincent Sarich, professor emeritus of anthropology at the University of California at Berkeley, and Frank Miele, senior editor of *Skeptic* magazine, disagree with each of these ten points—and that is a remarkable degree of disagreement, given that the first eight points are matters of fact. In *Race: The Reality of Human Differences*, we present the evidence we believe refutes the first eight points and explain why we reject points nine and ten, not only for economic but ethical reasons as well.

We believe the case for the reality of race and of human differences must be presented against the backdrop of time—against the historical time during which the concept developed, against the evolutionary time during which our species developed and racial differences arose, and against the political temper of our times in which the view that race is a mere social construction—that is, a pseudoscientific myth created to justify colonization, slavery, and oppression—has come to be invoked as the justification for public policies based on racial privileges. We present what we believe is compelling evidence to support the propositions that race *is* a valid biological concept, and that human variations—

that is, the differences among individuals and groups, whether in athletic competition, IQ tests, or the competition to lead a satisfying and successful life, however each individual or group may define it——reflect both genetic and environmental factors.

On matters of social policy, we are both individualists. We oppose any governmentally sanctioned benefits or handicaps being applied *solely* on the basis of group membership. Rather, we argue for policies that help each individual do the best he or she can and wants to do. Both of us benefited from programs that foster and reward talent and performance, and we support making them open to anyone who is qualified—Period! Many issues regarding race are yet to be resolved. Denying the reality of race, however, only delays or prevents their resolution.

*Vincent M. Sarich*
Albany, CA
*Frank Miele*
Sunnyvale, CA
*January 2004*

# Acknowledgments

We could not have written this book without the help, encouragement, and patience shown by so many. First, we thank Michael Shermer, publisher and editor-in-chief of *Skeptic* magazine, and its entire staff for inviting us to write and speak freely on so controversial an issue as race, even when our views conflicted with those of others. Thanks also go to Professors Henry Harpending, Richard Lynn, and J. Philippe Rushton for answering our questions and allowing us to summarize those conversations even though, again, there were points of disagreement. We thank Dr. Wilfred T. Gagné, D.V.M., for providing access to the veterinary literature. Ambassador Carl Coon kindly answered our questions about his father's life and work. Our editor, Karl Yambert, project editor Marietta Urban, and the entire staff at Westview Press proved invaluable in making this project a reality.

Any errors or misconceptions in this book, however, are solely ours.

V. M. S.
F. M.

# RACE

# The Case for Race

This book is about what remains America's most taboo four-letter word—R-A-C-E. The link between a biological concept and sociopolitical policy has bedeviled the nation since the Pilgrims landed on Plymouth Rock. For African Americans, the first link was indeed a hard one—the steel chains of slave ships. For blacks, in the words of Malcolm X, "Plymouth Rock landed on us." In American history, race has assumed the role played by the goddess Discord in classical mythology: Invite her and she brings trouble with her; exclude her and she sends it as a reprisal for the slight. The same Thomas Jefferson who wrote "All men are created equal" in the Declaration of Independence also wrote in his *Notes on Virginia* these much lesser known and lesser quoted lines: "In memory they [blacks] are equal to the whites; in reason much inferior, as I think one could scarcely be found capable of tracing and comprehending the investigations of Euclid; and that in imagination they are dull, tasteless, and anomalous." In Abraham Lincoln's debates with Stephen Douglas, "Honest Abe," later to be the Great Emancipator, said, "There is a physical difference between the white and black races which I believe will forever forbid the two races living together on terms of social and political equality. And inasmuch as they cannot so live, while they do remain together there must be the position of superior and inferior, and I as much as any other man am in favor of having the superior position assigned to the white race." In 1905, Progressive-era president Teddy Roosevelt made the very unprogressive statement that "A perfectly stupid race can never rise to a very high place. The Negro, for instance, has been kept down as much by his lack of intellectual development as by anything else." John Ehrlichman has recounted how on two separate occasions Richard Nixon told him that "America's blacks could only marginally benefit from Federal programs because blacks were *genetically inferior* to whites. All the Federal money and programs we could devise could not change that fact. . . . Blacks could never achieve parity—in intelligence, economic success or social qualities; but, he said, we should still do what we could for them, within reasonable limits, because it was 'right' to do so." (emphasis Ehrlichman's). Until relatively recently, believers in the literal equality of the races (or the sexes) in either mental or physical ability have been few and far between, even among the ranks of abolitionists and anticolonialists.

## THE CONTEMPORARY CONSENSUS ON RACE IN THE MEDIA AND THE SOCIAL SCIENCES

These contradictions and the apparent intractability of America's "race problem" (or what some would say is more accurately described as "problem with racism") have led many individuals, perhaps even a majority, in the media and the social sciences to come to the sincere belief that eliminating the word "race," or downgrading it from a biological concept to merely a social construction, is a necessary if not sufficient condition for eliminating racism as well. Denying the biological reality of race and recognizing it as a pseudoscientific myth created to justify white supremacy, they admonish, will produce what biological anthropologist Alan Goodman in the PBS documentary *Race: The Power of an Illusion* terms "an absolute paradigm shift." The resulting realization that "race is not based on biology but race is rather an idea that we ascribe to biology" will cause any thought of genetically based group differences to disappear as well, or at least it will set society on the road to their long-overdue remediation through social and economic policy.

## THE CASE FOR RACE

We present our case for the reality of race in three parts: first, against the backdrop of the historical time during which the concept developed; then, against the evolutionary time during which our species developed and racial differences arose; and finally, against the political temper of our times in which race is viewed as a mere, but nonetheless malignant, social construction that demands remediation through affirmative action, race norming (in which members of different races are measured against differing race-specific standards), and, some have argued, reparations for past inequities.

Chapter 1, "Race and the Law," serves as a prologue to the disputes and debates examined in the chapters that follow. We note that the average person has a clear idea of what is meant by "race," and that even small children more readily classify people on the basis of racial characteristics than on the basis of body build or occupational uniforms. A review of selected court cases demonstrates that such commonsense judgments about race and racial membership are regularly made, without being contested by either party, in the most adversarial aspect of society—the legal system.

For the past fifty years, however, most of the media and the social sciences have rejected the view that race is a biological reality. They have insisted on characterizing "race" as a "social construction," that is, a classification system, developed and maintained to justify European imperialism and white supremacy and, in the pithy title of the 2003 PBS documentary, as "an illusion," rather than what geneticist C. D. Darlington called "part of the imperfect but impartial language of common sense."

The next two chapters review the development of the race concept from its beginning as recorded in the art and literature of ancient civilizations; through the development of anthropology as the science of race, the subsequent reaction against this view, and the individual controversies involved; and the political events that influenced the debate. They conclude by setting the stage for examining research by the senior author, Vincent Sarich, that provided an objective method for dating key events in evolution, including the emergence of our own species.

In Chapter 2, "Race and History," we refute the argument of race as mere social construction, presenting examples from the art of ancient Egypt, China, India, Greece, and Rome as well as the rock art of hunter-gatherers to show that long before the European Age of Exploration, early civilizations and other societies did indeed recognize distinct races based on physical features, and that these correspond quite well to the races recognized by anthropology as late as the 1960s as well as the commonsense view. Drawing on quotations from the literature of ancient civilizations, we demonstrate that these societies also assigned behavioral characteristics (fairly or unfairly) to other racial groups, and tried to explain the cause(s) of race differences given the knowledge of their day. A particularly strong refutation of the social-construct argument comes from the example of the Bushmen of remote areas of southern Africa, who recently and independently made similar racial classifications when they first encountered Asian scientists.

Chapter 3, "Anthropology as the Science of Race," examines how humankind has tried to answer the questions about human origins and human differences from tribal myths, biblical theology, Greek philosophy, and Islamic geography; through to the beginning of anthropology as a science in the Enlightenment; and to the Darwinian revolution, when anthropology emerged as the science of race, and how and why that viewpoint was increasingly marginalized after World War II. Among these questions are

- Monogenesis versus polygenesis: Do the races of humankind have one origin or many?
- Stasis versus change: If the races of humankind had a single origin, how did they come to differ?
- How much time was required for these differences to take place?
- What were the mechanism(s) responsible?
- Do race differences necessarily imply a racial hierarchy?

Chapters 4, 5, and 6 examine race against evolutionary time. Here Vincent Sarich played a seminal role in developing the methodology of comparing the similarities and differences among the proteins and DNA of both living and recently extinct forms, thereby providing us with molecular trees and molecular clocks. This methodology has allowed us to resolve the order in which the branches of the human family tree diverged, calculate their times of divergence, and determine which changes (molecular, morphological, and, to the extent possible, behavioral) took place. These questions could only be debated, without any critically deciding data, in the earlier period of anthropology, described in Chapter 3.

In Chapter 4, "Resolving the Primate (Including Human) Tree," Sarich takes the witness stand and describes how he came to anthropology from biochemistry, and then with his late colleague, Allan Wilson, developed a "molecular clock" that dated the separation of the human lineage from those which led to the modern African apes (chimps and gorillas) at about 5 million years ago, thereby altering forever our view of the human family tree. Sarich describes the revolutionary use of data from living animals to reorder and reinterpret the fossil record. In particular, *Ramapithecus*, a 14-million-year-old fossil previously considered to be the oldest representative of the hominid (humanlike) lineage, was discovered to be obviously far too old to be a hominid, and paleontologists eventually relegated it to the position of an ancestral orangutan, although Sarich has serious reservations about this attribution as well.

In Chapter 5, "*Homo Sapiens* and Its Races," Sarich continues the story of the molecular revolution in anthropology, resolving the relationship (1) among modern humans (*Homo sapiens*) and other hominid species and (2) among races within *Homo sapiens*. The lead-in for this chapter is a mystery novel that indicated that the way to solve this problem was to send genetic samples to Sarich at the University of California at Berkeley! This chapter examines the successes of his UC–Berkeley colleagues Allan Wilson, Rebecca Cann, and Mark Stoneking—and many others—with mitochondrial DNA (mtDNA), and, of first Mike Hammer (also a Wilson student), and then later Peter Underhill with Y-chromosome data. Since 2000 these converging lines of evidence have produced a consistent picture that *Homo sapiens* first arose in Africa only about 50,000 years ago and that no racial divergences predate this time. In short, all living races are very recent and appeared only as ancestral humans migrated out of Africa.

In Chapter 6, "The Two 'Miracles' That Made Humankind," we examine the conundrum this scenario has produced. The combined mtDNA and Y-chromosome data indicate that there was a single out-of-Africa exodus some 50,000 years ago that was ancestral to all recent and extant humans. Since the mid-1990s, many thousands of samples of mitochondrial and Y-chromosome DNA of non-African populations have been analyzed. Yet they have produced no evidence that any of the other human populations around at the time of this African exodus—and there clearly were many, the Neanderthals being perhaps the best known—successfully interbred with the out-of-Africa migrants thereby contributing anything to the modern *Homo sapiens* gene pool.

This new scenario requires what appear to be two "miracles." First, some African population developed a new, genetically based behavioral capability that gave them an advantage over all other human populations—and that none of the other populations could copy. The most popular view is that it involved a quantum leap in linguistic capability, perhaps the augmentation of preexisting gestural language by spoken language. Second, along with this behavioral capability came, directly or indirectly, total reproductive isolation between the new *Homo sapiens* and all other existing hominid species. Matings between them either did not occur or were infertile.

Chapters 7, 8, and 9 examine race against the temper of the times. They form by far the most controversial part of the book. We deny the validity of the contemporary media and social science consensus on the concept of race and reject the need for any race-based policies to right past wrongs. In these three chapters, we discuss how racial variation interacts with the real world, and what cognizance, if any, we should take of that interaction. They present the most important evidence and arguments of the case for race, the gravamen of our countersuit against social-construction theory and our reasons for rejecting the declarations of three distinguished scientists—the late Stephen Jay Gould (race *cannot* exist), Richard Lewontin (race *does not* exist), and Alan Goodman (even if race can and does exist, it *should not be studied*)—that have come to form the scientific cornerstones on which social-construction theory rests.

As we make clear, we accept none of this. If we did, there would be no need to write this book, and good reasons not to. If either Gould or Lewontin is correct, we are wrong, in the sense of being factually in error. If Goodman is correct, it is far worse. Then we are wrong in the sense of being morally evil. The case for race, and with it our defense against the implied charges of incompetence and/or immorality, will be to show that Gould is simply wrong; that Lewontin is, at best, half right with his numbers, but all wrong in the inferences he draws from them; and Goodman unwittingly provides justification for the very hate crime— racism—he so desperately wants to eradicate.

Simply stated, the case for race hinges on recognition of the fact that genetic variation in traits that affect performance and ultimately survival is the fuel on which the evolutionary process runs. If there is no such functional genetic variation, there can be no adaptive evolution. Thus, variation in every relevant domain is the norm, the null hypothesis, the expected condition, and not, as many would have it, the exception in the case of humans. In the study of *Homo sapiens*, the null hypothesis should be that there is genetic variation underlying the variation in performance that is being observed; it should not be assumed that, as has often been claimed, in a fair society, genetic factors can and should cancel each other out.

Strong evidence in the case for race comes from examining the amount of variation actually present in a proper comparative context. The differences in morphology (cranial and facial features) between human races are typically around ten times the corresponding differences between the sexes within a given race, larger even than the comparable differences taxonomists use to distinguish the two chimpanzee *species* from each other. To the best of our knowledge, human racial differences exceed those for any other nondomesticated species. One must look to the breeds of dogs to find a comparable degree of within-species differences in morphology. We also point out other aspects in which human diversity in morphology, pharmacogenetics (body chemistry), and behavior more closely parallels our best friends (the dogs) than our nearest relatives (the apes), and what that reveals about the origin of our species.

Also important is the context of how long it took for human racial differences to evolve. The amount of variation that took approximately one million years to evolve in chimpanzees took only 50,000 years to evolve in humans. *This much shorter time for the evolution of comparatively larger racial differences must mean that these differences are more (not less) significant, and that adaptation, not chance, is the only mechanism capable of explaining this.*

We begin Chapter 7, "Race and Physical Differences," by discussing the nature of variation in our species. Specifically, we address the issues of just how much variation there is and why variation is necessary for evolution to take place.

The most objectively measurable and least culturally bound comparisons involving racial differences can be found in the athletic arena. Just as personal experience confirms that some kids run faster than other kids, so too some groups (women or men; races) contribute disproportionately to one end or the other of the bell curve for any human activity. Just how marked such group differences can be is best illustrated by the fact that over the twelve-year period 1985–1997, one tribe of Kenyans, the Kalenjin, numbering perhaps 3 million people, provided eighteen of the thirty-six medal winners in the World Cross Country Championships. This is about 2,000-fold more than they would have won if the necessary abilities were evenly distributed among the world's populations. There are, of course, many similar examples available, and we present some from sports with which we are most familiar.

We conclude the chapter by presenting evidence from the emerging field of pharmacogenetics, the study of genetic differences in response to drugs. Again there is a parallel to the situation in domestic breeds of dogs—that is, although it is easy to recognize the physical and behavioral differences among breeds, as in human races, the genetic differences as measured by DNA are small.

Chapter 7, "Race and Physical Differences," sets the stage for the more controversial issues discussed in Chapter 8, "Race and Behavior." The two chapters inevitably have some overlap, and similarities to Jon Entine's *Taboo*, but discussions of differences in mind among individuals and groups (especially sexes and races) are far more tabooed than those about bodies.

We begin by describing a classic study of behavioral differences in four dog breeds—and the difficulties the author encountered in publishing a follow-up study that applied the same experimental design to race differences in human neonates. We also deal with the meaning of "racial" from the evolutionary perspective and address the criticisms that have been made of it. We conclude by examining the conundrums of race, brain size, and intelligence; income inequality and intelligence; and the mean sub-Saharan African IQ of 70.

We argue in Chapter 9, "Learning to Live with Race," that it is not only appropriate but important to study race, because it helps us to apply the evolutionary perspective to the analysis of human variation generally. The critical concept here is that variation, in both body and behavior, both within races and between, is the norm, not the exception.

We also address the question of whether the recognition of average race differences must inevitably lead to racist attitudes or policies. In our view, the study of race and racial differences is not racist if people realize that everyone can gain on an absolute basis even as differences between individuals and between groups remain the same or even increase.

In terms of public policy, the best path governments can take is to dispense with the illusory quest for equality of results in favor of the achievable path of promoting equality of opportunity by removing all reference to group identity from both statutory and administrative law, and to focus instead on enhancing the potential for achievement by individuals.

We present three scenarios—termed Meritocracy in the Emerging Global Economy, Affirmative Action and Race Norming, and Rising Resegregation and the Emergence of Ethno-States— and describe what we believe are the costs and benefits, and the dangers and opportunities, of each. In the Ethno-State discussion, we also examine the feasibility of ethnically targeted weapons and the threat they pose.

Finally, we explain our preference for the Meritocracy. We recognize its faults and problems, but it is in keeping with the best (though by no means the only) tradition in our nation's history, is most likely to produce the most good for the most people, and offers our species the  most effective array of options with which to meet the challenges that lie before us.

CHAPTER ONE

# Race and the Law

*In contrast to a recent (2003), highly acclaimed PBS documentary that termed race "an illusion," a myth constructed by Europeans in the Age of Exploration to justify colonialism and slavery, we argue that race is real.*

*We begin the case for race by noting how one of the most contentious facets of our society, our legal system, has no trouble in recognizing either the existence of race or the ability of the average citizen to do so. Further, DNA markers have been used to identified the race of perpetrators.*

*We have an inborn tendency to sort people into groups. The latest evidence shows how this tendency can mirror biological reality.*

Some twenty years ago, coauthor Vincent Sarich received a call from a San Francisco attorney who was serving as defense attorney in a racial discrimination case brought by a man who claimed he had been discriminated against because of his American Indian ancestry. As part of their discussion, the question of legal "standing" arose; that is, did the plaintiff actually have the requisite racial ancestry—was he, in fact, an Indian? Vince naively asked for the legal definition of "race" and was told there wasn't one. Still, in the spirit of scientific inquiry, he observed the proceedings until the first break, at which point he told the attorney that, in his opinion, the attorney's client had no chance of arguing successfully that the plaintiff lacked standing. To Vince's eyes, the plaintiff obviously "looked" Amerindian. End of case.

As we began working on this book, we discussed the issue of the legal definition of "race" and asked the opinion of an attorney who specializes in civil rights law, which touches on this issue. He informed us that there is still no legal definition of "race"; nor, as far as we know, does it appear that the legal system feels the need for one. Thus, it appears that the most adversarial part of our complex society, the legal system, not only continues to accept the existence of "race" but also relies on the ability of the average individual to sort people into races. Our legal system treats "racial identification" as self-evident, whereas an increasing number of anthropologists (the profession, one would think, with the pertinent expertise) have signed on to proclamations that categorically state the term has long ago ceased to have any scientific legitimacy.

Why this clash? To us the answer is simple: The courts have come to accept the commonsense definition of race, and it is this commonsense view that, as we show, best conforms to reality. A look at two recent (2000) cases is illustrative. In both *Rice v. Office of Hawaiian Affairs* and in *Haak v. Rochester School District*, neither side raised any questions about the existence of human races or the ability of the average citizen to make valid judgments as to who belongs to which race (even if the racial categories are euphemistically termed "peoples" or "populations"). No special expertise was assumed or granted in defining or recognizing race other than the everyday commonsense usage, as given in the *Oxford English Dictionary*, that a race is "a group of persons connected by common descent" or "a tribe, nation, or people, regarded as of common stock." The courts and the contending parties, in effect, accepted as givens the existence of race and the ability of the ordinary person to distinguish between races based on a set of physical features.

## RICE V. OFFICE OF HAWAIIAN AFFAIRS—
## RACE BY ANY OTHER NAME IS STILL RACE

In the first case, the United States Supreme Court reversed a judgment of the 9th Circuit Court of Appeals. The petitioner, H. F. Rice, had challenged the State of Hawaii for not allowing him to vote in an election for the nine trustees of the Office of Hawaiian Affairs, an agency that administers programs designed for the benefit of "Hawaiians."

Originally, "Hawaiian" was defined as "any descendant of the races inhabiting the Hawaiian Islands, prior to 1788" [the year the first European, Captain James Cook, reached the islands]. That was later changed to "any descendant of the aboriginal peoples which exercised sovereignty and subsisted in the Hawaiian Islands in 1778, and which peoples thereafter have continued to reside in Hawaii." The term "Native Hawaiian" was defined as "any descendant of not less than one-half part of the races inhabiting the Hawaiian Islands previous to 1778—provided that the definition identically refers to the descendants of such blood quantum of such aboriginal peoples which exercised sovereignty and subsisted in the Hawaiians in 1778, and which peoples thereafter continued to reside in Hawaii."

The tortuous, convoluted text in the Hawaii statutes is not just the usual legalese. Both the drafters of the amendments and the court in its decision admitted that the substitution of "peoples" for "races" was cosmetic, not substantive, and that "peoples" does indeed mean "races." The sole reason for the changes was to banish any mention of the offending word, "race," and substitute a palatable euphemism.

Rice, everyone agreed, was a Hawaiian citizen but without the requisite ancestry to be recognized as "Hawaiian" under state law. The state therefore argued that denying Rice the vote in the OHA election was justified, and the 9th Circuit concurred when Rice challenged.

However, the U.S. Supreme Court reversed the 9th Circuit by a 7-2 margin (Stevens and Ginsburg dissenting), citing in particular the 15th Amendment: "The right of the citizens of the United States to vote shall not be denied or abridged by the United States or by any State on account of race, color, or previous condition of servitude." The Court found the Hawaiian law unconstitutional because it defined voter eligibility on the basis of race.

The 15th Amendment is explicit—race means what the average person thinks it means—and the majority of the Supreme Court read it that way. In the end, the tortuous, convoluted verbiage introduced into the Hawaiian statutes to avoid the offensive term "race" accomplished nothing.

## HAAK V. ROCHESTER SCHOOL DISTRICT— WHAT WE SEE IS WHAT YOU GET

In the other case, the 2nd Circuit Court of Appeals ruled that a white fourth-grade student named Jessica Haak could not transfer from her home district to an adjoining, primarily white district because the transfer program was enacted for the explicit purpose of lessening racial isolation among the six districts involved. The plaintiffs, Haak's parents, challenged on the grounds that denying the right to transfer based upon racial classification violated the clause in section 1 of the 14th Amendment, which makes it unconstitutional for any state to "deny any person within its jurisdiction the equal protection of the law." The district court ruled in Haak's favor, but the 2nd Circuit overturned that decision, noting that although the U. S. Supreme Court had had many opportunities to rule that race could not be used as a factor in deciding who attended which school, it had never taken the opportunity to establish a precedent by doing so.

In *Haak*, neither side even raised the issue of who belonged to which group (race or ethnicity). A "minority pupil" was defined as "a pupil who is of Black or Hispanic origin or is a member of another minority group that historically has been the subject of discrimination." Interestingly, however, neither the application to transfer under the program, the program brochures, nor the acknowledgment letter sent to parents who apply provides any standard by which to establish a student's race or ethnicity. Parents are expected to self-screen their children. Once the applicant is met in person by a program administrator, a question may be raised as to the student's race as a result of the student's "name, manner of speaking and phrasing, and personal appearance during an interview or orientation." Even so, it seems that Haak, who is white, was accepted into the program by the school's assistant principal and sent an official letter of acknowledgment. That acceptance was revoked after a second administrator saw Haak in person and verified her race as Caucasian/White according to the school district's records, therefore making her ineligible for the transfer program.

The critical points here are that in both *Rice* and *Haak*, neither side raised any questions about the existence of human races or the ability of the average citizen to make valid judgments as to who belongs to which race. No special expertise was assumed or granted in defining or recognizing race other than the everyday usage of the term. In *Rice*, the court, in effect, took judicial notice of the commonsense definition of race. In *Haak*, the court accepted physical appearance as a valid means by which the average citizen can recognize races and distinguish among them.

The Hawaii statutes at issue in *Rice* were inventively drafted to include the word "ancestry" for fear that the term "race" would be grounds to strike down the law. Notwithstanding the convoluted definition of having Hawaiian "ancestry," the definition maps quite well to the commonsense definition of "race." In short, the courts accepted the existence of race, even if the legislature was afraid to use the offending word. The Supreme Court struck down the Hawaii law because its definition of being Hawaiian based on ancestry was for all intents and purposes the equivalent of the commonsense definition of race and so was expressly prohibited by the 14th Amendment.

In *Haak*, the plaintiffs did not dispute that the school administrator (or anyone else, for that matter) correctly identified or was able to identify Haak's race. Rather, they contested the constitutionality of a law that discriminates on the basis of race. The ability to determine race was assumed and accepted by both parties and by the court.

## SHOULD THE CRIMINAL JUSTICE SYSTEM RECOGNIZE THAT RACE IS REAL?

A critical question is whether the courts recognize the existence of race as a mere social construct or as an underlying biological reality. In taking statements from witnesses and in courtroom testimony, the criminal justice system routinely, and with little or no complaint, accepts statements such as "The perpetrator was identified as a male, Caucasian, about twenty-five years old," or "The little girl I saw abducted in the parking lot looked like she was Hispanic or a fair-skinned African American." But consider a re-

cent example in which accepting the existence of race as a biological reality, rather than "race" as a social construct of Western
society, became a matter of life and death.

Throughout 2002 and the first half of 2003, Louisiana police
were hunting for a serial killer who had murdered at least five
women in the Baton Rouge area. Relying on tips and two eyewitness accounts of a white male allegedly driving a white pickup
truck containing the body of a slumped, naked white female on the
night of one of the murders, police focused the search on white
males. A host of experimental research has demonstrated that eyewitness testimony of an unexpected event that is viewed only
briefly is notoriously unreliable in far more than racial identification. Perhaps the best-known real-life example is the number of
observers who report planes bursting into flames before they crash;
later examination of the wreckage shows that there was no in-flight
explosion. However, in the Louisiana serial-killer case, another
eyewitness, a neighbor of one of the victims, frustrated that the police were restricting their search to whites, circulated a flyer with a
composite sketch of the perpetrator the neighbor thought he saw—
a black male who it turned out closely resembled Derrick Todd Lee.

The state police crime lab had linked all five cases to the same
perpetrator by using the minimum of thirteen DNA markers required by the FBI forensic crime lab for individual identification.
(DNA markers are sequences in the complete human genome
that can identify a person's ancestry or parentage.) If the thirteen
markers in samples taken either from two of the victims or, more
likely, from a victim and a suspect, are the same, the probability
that they come from the same individual is virtually certain,
about the same probability as flipping a coin thirteen times and
getting the same result or verifying a thirteen-digit credit card or
bank account number. The odds of misidentification are effectively about one in a billion.

In the Baton Rouge case, samples of the perpetrator's DNA (probably from semen, though not specified in the reports we read) were taken from the victims' bodies. Holding firm in their belief that almost all serial murderers are white, the police swabbed the cheeks of more than 600 white male suspects for DNA analysis to see if they matched the samples taken from the victims.

We should note here that this method of individual DNA matching, sometimes called "DNA fingerprinting," has also cleared suspects and provided grounds for appeal. Since 1992, the Innocence Project at Yeshiva University's Cardozo School of Law, headed by Barry Scheck and Peter Neufeld (best known as defense attorneys in the O. J. Simpson criminal trial), alone has freed over thirty-five people wrongly convicted, including a number of African Americans. DNA is also used in paternity testing; evaluating kinship in inheritance disputes; and missing-persons cases, especially in identifying kidnapped children who may be unable or afraid to speak to the police on their own behalf. In 1993 a two-year-old was returned to his parents two years after being kidnapped only after police established scientifically who the child was by using genetic fingerprinting. DNA profiling is so accurate that it is highly recommended by law enforcement departments around the United States to protect individuals in the event of abduction or kidnapping.

Thirteen markers are sufficient to determine a reliable individual match, but more are needed to sort individuals by race correctly. Technically, the thirteen markers used by the FBI for individual DNA fingerprinting are termed "short tandem repeats" (STRs). They are repetitions of the same sequence of base pairs in junk (noncoding) DNA. Junk DNA is just that. It is not responsible, to the best of our knowledge, for any trait or variation within a trait. There is more junk DNA than one might think. The current estimate is somewhere over 90 percent of the total. However, it is possible that science has yet to determine the function of some so-called junk DNA. The particular thirteen STRs used in the FBI Combined DNA Index System, or CODIS, were selected because they can be rapidly determined from very small amounts of DNA, using commercially available kits; more important to the discussion here, laboratories worldwide are contributing to the analysis of STR allele frequencies in different human populations.

The seventy-three genetic markers used in the DNAPrint methodology (commercialized by DNAPrint Genomics), on the other hand, are termed "single nucleotide polymorphisms" (SNPs, pronounced "snips"). Each SNP is a specific place on the DNA molecule that can have one or more of the variant nucleotides (adenine, guanine, cytosine, or thymine [A, G, C, T]) in the population, termed "alleles." Certain alleles are more common in some races than in others, and sometimes, much more so. These have been called "ancestry informative markers" (AIMs). Just one or two or six AIMs are not enough to establish a person's race, that is, genetic ancestry. The more AIMs examined, the greater the probability of accurately determining the person's race. (The same holds true for physical racial characteristics and for blood groups—the more predictors, the greater the accuracy of the prediction—but AIMs are much more powerful). Repeatable, independent academic research has established that with 100 genetic markers, it is possible to sort people whose known ancestors are from Africa, Europe, Asia, or the Americas with almost 100 percent accuracy. DNAPrint Genomics has reduced the number of AIMs required to seventy-three and extended the methodology to determine the percentage of racial background in people of mixed ancestry.

After examining seventy-three DNA markers, Tony Frudakis of DNAPrint Genomics told the Baton Rouge serial-killer task force in the first week of March 2003 that it should shift its focus from

white suspects to an African American of average skin tone, because his analysis indicated the perpetrator had 85 percent sub-
Saharan African and 15 percent Native American ancestry. The
seventy-three-marker DNAPrint, which became sufficiently developed for this type of investigation only in early 2003, deter-
mines an individual's proportion of East Asian, Indo-European,
Native American, and sub-Saharan African ancestry and then
compares these proportions against a database of 300 to 400
people already typed to produce a comparable skin tone. A suspect
fitting the racial profile, thirty-four-year-old Derrick Todd Lee of
St. Francisville, whose DNA matched that found at the crime
scenes and who was indeed recognizably black, was arrested and
charged with first-degree murder, rape, kidnapping, and burglary.

The methods of behavioral profiling that have been highly pro-
moted in both blockbuster movies and "real crime" TV shows mis-
led the police in the Baton Rouge case, because their compilation
of cases supposedly solved showed the vast majority of serial killers
to be white males ages 25–35. The DNAPrint methodology is correct at a rate as high as that for the individual DNA fingerprinting
that is accepted as legally valid. As of mid-2003, there had been
no independent confirmation of the DNAPrint methodology, but
Frudakis told ABC News in June 2003 that in 3,000 blind tests (in
which each person's self-reported race was unknown to techni-
cians doing the DNA analysis), there was not a single error.

The Baton Rouge case is not the first time police have used
DNA samples to identify or narrow the list of potential suspects.
For over a year, Britain's Forensic Science Service (FSS) has em-
ployed what the agency terms "DNA photofitting," in which the
genetic markers in the suspect's DNA found at a crime site are
compared against a database of DNA markers that are more common in one race than in others. FSS even tests the suspect's
sample for a gene associated with red hair.

If "race" were a mere social construction based upon a few highly visible features, it would have no statistical correlation with the DNA markers that indicate genetic relatedness. The maximum degree of genetic relatedness an individual has is with himself or herself—or with an identical twin (or two identical triplets, and so on). There is also a certain amount of "family resemblance" in facial features and the like, especially in groups that tend to marry among themselves. If the commonsense recognition of races based on a relatively small set of physical features reflects an underlying biological reality, then those visible features should be correlated with genetic resemblance (as measured by DNA markers) as well as with self-reported ancestry.

Unless race is a biological reality that gives important information about an individual's degree of genetic resemblance to the various human populations and the sequence in which those populations evolved by separating from other populations, it would be inconceivable to achieve the level of accuracy obtainable through the DNAPrint methodology. Indeed, given a sufficient number of markers, such analysis is capable of not only identifying race but predicting skin tone as well. To say the least, it also calls into question the "experiment" in the PBS *Race* documentary, in which students of different racial appearance were surprised to find that the similarity among them in mitochondrial DNA (mtDNA, which is inherited only along the maternal line) did not agree with either physical features or ancestry.

"Episode One: The Difference Between Us" of the PBS program showed an experiment in which students of different racial backgrounds obtained a buccal swab (a tissue sample collected by wiping the inside of the cheek with a cotton swab) to get a sample of their mtDNA. Then the students examined six selected mtDNA markers and used them to guess which other students' DNA would be most like theirs. They made their picks based upon the usual set of physical features and ancestry used in the commonsense definition of race. If race has any biological reality, their guesses should have been fairly on target. The students registered surprise when the two methods of racial sorting—physical features and ancestry on the one hand, and mtDNA markers on the other—did not agree. The transcript concluded: "If human variation were to map along racial lines, people in one so-called race would be more similar to each other than to those in another so-called race. That's not what the students found in their mtDNA."

The program's take-home message is that straightforward experimental evidence reveals "race" is a mere social construct, a snare and delusion, and that race has no real substance in biology. This unwarranted conclusion is clearly contradicted by the DNAPrint methodology previously described (see also Chapters 4 through 9). The PBS experiment, in effect, stacked the deck. First, the number of markers used in the experiment was below the standard of thirteen required by the FBI crime labs for even individual identification. A good analogy would be political-opinion polling. In order to get a valid result, the pollster must sample enough people.

Second, the experiment relied solely on mtDNA, which is inherited only along the maternal line. There is no reason physical racial markers should necessarily be inherited along only one of the two parental lines. To use the political-polling analogy, interviewing only women does not produce a valid sample of all voters. Males and females differ, on average, in that men tend to vote for conservative candidates, and women to support more liberal ones.

With enough markers and comparison of mtDNA and Y-chromosome DNA (which traces only the paternal line), scientists can even obtain biological verification of history. In India, for example, the Y-chromosome DNA reflects the Aryan invaders, whereas the mtDNA shows a greater presence of females from the indigenous population. Among Ashkenazi Jews, the Y-chromosome DNA reflects a Middle Eastern component; the mtDNA shows that these Jewish males interbred with local European women. The same is true for the Lemba, an African tribe that follows certain Mosaic practices and whose traditions have long professed a Jewish origin. The Y-chromosome data showed the male Jewish ancestry of the Lemba, and the mtDNA revealed their African maternal roots. Another example comes from Latin America, where there is a greater contribution of European Y-chromosome DNA versus Amerindian mtDNA. The usual pattern found in recorded history is that a small number of intruding males in a dominant position, either as powerful conquerors or rich merchants, mate with a much larger number of indigenous females. The top prize in this regard, perhaps, goes to Genghis Khan and his Mongol Golden Horde. One Y-chromosome study has shown that one in every 200 males alive today, mostly in Asia, is descended from the Great Khan.

## HOW—AND WHY—DO WE KNOW RACE?

The fact is that the latest genetic technologies are, for the most part, confirming the classification schemes of not only traditional anthropology but also the commonsense understanding of race. Ordinary people can and do divide *Homo sapiens* into a number of reasonably discrete groups on the basis of reasonably objective criteria. No special expertise is required. A series of experiments in cognitive psychology carried out by social anthropologist Lawrence Hirschfeld showed that as early as age three, children readily classify people on the basis of racial characteristics, without having to be taught to do so. He presented the children with a series of drawings. Each drawing consisted of the figure of an adult (termed the target figure) and two figures of children, each of which shared one of three characteristics—race, body build (light or heavy build), and occupational uniform (postal or medical worker)—with the target. They were asked which of the two figures looked like the target did as a child; which of the two figures looked like it was the target's offspring; and which of the two figures looked most similar to the target. In the minds of the children being tested, race was predominant over the other two categories. The children "expected that race was more likely to be inherited and to remain unchanged over the life span than either occupation or body build." After almost fifteen years of such research, Hirschfeld concluded that children do not have to be taught to believe in the reality of race, nor do they believe it is just some superficial quality. Rather, they believe that "race is an intrinsic, immutable, and essential aspect of a person's identity," and "they come to this conclusion on their own."

Why can we do this? Why, in fact, are we so good at it? The reason is no mystery, or at least it shouldn't be. *Homo sapiens* is a socially interactive species and was so even before we became quite so sapient. The common ancestor we share with chimpanzees and all our ancestors along the way must have been able to recognize the members of their social group as individuals and, by extension, tell the difference between any of them and members of another group. So can baboons, wolves, dogs, killer whales, and lions (but not the other big cats, who are solitary) make such distinctions. The evolution of interactive sociality strongly selects for individuals who are able to recognize other similar individuals and adjust their behaviors with respect to who else is involved. The physical evidence for the evolutionary importance of this ability can be seen in the large amount of brain tissue devoted to these tasks at the base of our brains. As Hirschfeld concluded, "Because human groupings (i.e., collectivities of people based on gender, race, native language, or kinship status) are integral parts of nearly all social environments, acquiring knowledge of such groupings is a necessary part of the child's early development."

When they discuss evolution and social behavior, philosophers and ethicists never seem to tire of warning their readers against falling into what is known as "the Naturalistic Fallacy," namely that if some scientific research were to prove (or, at least, seem to imply) that there is a natural tendency for humans to be aggressive or rapacious, or even prejudiced, therefore we ought to be that way and consequently either approve of or ignore such behavior. The same ethical philosophers have shown much less interest in disabusing their readers of "the Moralistic Fallacy," that is, arguing that since, according to many moral codes, humans ought not be aggressive, rapacious, or prejudiced, therefore, we *are* not—the scientific evidence be damned. We have already noted the recent tendency of proceeding from what one thinks ought to be to what is. One corollary of the Moralistic Fallacy has been the argument that since "race" is merely a social construction, and a very evil one at that, used to justify European colonialism and the enslavement and extermination of native peoples, the study of "race" inherently leads to the justification of "racism" in both thought and deed. And that did happen. In this realm *Homo sapiens* has hardly justified the species name *sapiens*—the "wise ones"—and one can depressingly wonder when, if ever, the species will become wise in this realm.

The race problem, or as social constructionists would prefer to put it, the "problem of race," will yield only through a broader and deeper historical and evolutionary perspective. We lay the groundwork for the broader view in the next chapter by discussing how earlier, especially non-European cultures and civilizations dealt with human differences in their literature and particularly their art.

## CHAPTER TWO

# Race and History

*The consensus view in the media and the social sciences is that "race" was constructed by Europeans in the Age of Exploration to justify colonialism and slavery. Our review of the art and literature of ancient Egypt, China, India, Greece, and Rome contradicts this social-constructionist view.*

*The early civilizations clearly depicted the distinctive physical features of the major races with which they were familiar. Their literature shows that they also attributed behavioral characteristics (fairly or unfairly) to the different races and explained them according to the knowledge of their day.*

"Race," says science historian Evelynn Hammonds in the PBS documentary *Race: The Power of an Illusion*, "is a human invention. We created it, we have used it in ways that have been, in many, many respects, quite negative and quite harmful. And we can think ourselves out of it. We made it; we can unmake it."

Is it true, as the PBS documentary website tells viewers, that "ancient societies did not divide people according to physical differences, but according to religion, status, class, even language?" We considered this question when we first began working on this

book, and Vince suggested that I (Frank Miele) search the anthropology library at the University of California–Berkeley for
examples of the way ancient civilizations, non-European civilizations, and hunter-gather societies depicted and described themselves and other races in their art, their literature, and their oral
tradition. Did they distinguish races, groups of people, sorting
them on the basis of skin color, hair form, and facial features as
we do today? The answer is an unequivocal yes.

Examination of the art and literature of non-European civilizations shows that race was not suddenly "constructed" out of thin
air by Europeans in the Age of Exploration to justify dispossessing
and oppressing people of color. Contrary to the claims of the PBS
documentary and the consensus view of contemporary social science, the art of the ancient civilizations of Egypt, Greece, Rome,
India, and China, and the Islamic civilization from AD 700 to
1400 shows that these societies classified the various peoples they
encountered into broad racial groups. They sorted them based
upon the same set of characteristics—skin color, hair form, and
head shape—allegedly constructed by Europeans when they invented "race" to justify colonialism and white supremacy. Not
surprisingly, each civilization thought of itself as superior to all
others and regarded its characteristics as being the ideal. Some attempted to explain the origin of race differences given the knowledge of their time, and at times, even made racial classification a
basis of political policy.

Of course, it could be that the artists in these various societies
were simply depicting individuals as realistically as possible.
However, corroborating evidence of their belief in race, that is,
their tendency to sort the many different peoples they encountered into a smaller number of basic categories, comes from the
record of what ancient civilizations wrote about other groups, or,
in the case of contemporary hunter-gatherers, what they say

about them. Again, it is evident that they relied upon a set of observable features (skin color, hair color and form, body build, facial features) quite similar to those used in the commonsense notion of race and the racial classifications of nineteenth-century anthropology to sort the many diverse groups they encountered into a smaller number of categories.

They also commented on the behavior of these groups. In the vast majority of cases, their opinions of other peoples, including the ancestors of the Western Europeans who supposedly "invented" the idea of race, are far from flattering, at times matching modern society's most derogatory stereotypes. In this chapter, we bolster our argument that race is not a recent European social construction by providing examples from both the art and the literature of the ancient civilizations of Egypt, India, China, and classical Greece and Rome.

Research in cognitive psychology supports this interpretation of the art and literature of these societies. A series of studies have shown that race acts as a prepotent cue. As noted in Chapter 1, by age three children can recognize the existence of race and racial differences without having to be taught to do so, and they think of the characteristics as being unchangeable. The emerging discipline of evolutionary psychology provides further evidence that there is a species-wide module in the human brain that predisposes us to sort the members of our species into groups based on appearance, and to distinguish between "us" and "them." Racial differences are emphasized, exaggerated, and stereotyped to the benefit of the in-group that is doing the sorting and to the detriment of the out-groups being sorted.

These converging lines of evidence disprove the claim that race is a mere social construction developed only recently by white Europeans. Although the evidence implies that humans have this innate sorting tendency, it does not prove that our concepts of race, racial differences, or racial stereotypes—no matter how consistent across time or geography—reflect any biological reality. It could be that the human tendency to categorize people into different races says more about cognitive processes than it does about the way the world really is. It could be that the human mind evolved to categorize some things as having intrinsic, unchangeable properties—the sorts of things that lead different cultures around the world to have in their vocabulary essentially the same list of color terms (even though the visible light spectrum is continuous) or to recognize and name the animal and plant species as the same set of discrete kinds.

However, these racial categories match those produced by the DNA methods that did not come into existence until the senior author's work and its extensions (described in Chapters 4 and 5). Ancient civilizations and early anthropology would have had to have been clairvoyant to produce such agreement if there was no underlying biological reality to race.

In the case of race, the consensus view in contemporary social science is that Western European culture, and it alone, falsely and self-servingly constructed such a view of human variation and then imposed it on the rest of humanity until our minds were liberated with the advent of deconstructionism. An outgrowth of postmodernist philosophy, deconstructionism denies that any science can establish ultimate meaning. It "deconstructs" scientific statements, claiming to reveal their hidden, underlying racial, sexual, and political biases.

In this chapter, we present evidence to show that all cultures that have been studied have categorized people into essentially the same set of races recognized by the average person and that being a member of one race means the individual can't change into a member of another race. Further, we show that race is associated with not only physical but behavioral traits as well. In later chapters, we show that these statements are strongly supported by modern scientific research.

## ANCIENT EGYPT

The civilization of ancient Egypt (circa 3000–300 BC) is a good place to start our survey, first because of its antiquity, and second because of its central location with regard to two of the three major races (whites, or Caucasoids, versus blacks, or Negroids) recognized by nineteenth-century European anthropology.

The walls of the royal tombs of the Egyptians are decorated with "representations of the four races of mankind, among whom the Egyptians of the nineteenth dynasty supposed the world to be partitioned—(1) The Egyptians, whom they painted red; (2) the Asiatics or Semites, yellow; (3) the Southerns or Negroes, black; and the Libyans, Westerners or Northerners, white, with blue eyes and fair beards." The Egyptian monuments are not mere "portraits, but also an attempt at classification," and "this facility for race discrimination was still earlier exhibited in the prehistoric or early historic palettes." As early as the latter part of the third millennium BC, the Egyptians depicted "blacks with broad noses, thick lips, and tightly coiled or woolly hair," the same characteristics by which European anthropologists of the nineteenth century would define the Negroid race.

The Egyptians considered their Pharaoh to be the master of the earthly world and decorated their temples with reliefs of peoples conquered or subjugated by him. The Egyptian conquerors appear larger than their enemies and with a ruddy complexion. The vanquished foe is usually shown in profile, arms tied behind the back, grouped racially, with the name of the conquered country written in hieroglyphics. The example from the tomb of Seti I shown in Figure 2.1 is just one of many such works. Captives from

FIGURE 2.1    Egyptian tomb painting showing four races.

the northern countries (Asiatics) are shown with beards and aquiline noses and light skins. Those from southern countries (Nubians or black Africans) are shown as dark-skinned with flat noses and thick lips.

Further evidence of the Egyptian awareness of racial differences can be found among the undisturbed treasures of the tomb of Tutankhamen (1379–1361 BC). A wooden chest shows the king slaughtering white Syrians on one side, while a corresponding massacre of his black African foes appears on the other. A footstool is decorated with alternating Asiatic (that is, Levantine white) and Kushitic (black African) captives, while a ceremonial throwing stick has at its top two heads facing in opposite directions, one a black African made of ebony, the other a bearded white Asiatic carved in ivory.

Are these and the many other similar examples evidence of racial sorting on the part of Egyptian artists, or were they adept at recording the differences in their art but not assigning them any cognitive importance? Here they can testify through their written hieroglyphic record. The *Great Hymn to Aten* documents the earliest written account of both the origin of race differences (initial differences in climate) and their subsequent inheritance:

> *O sole god, like whom there is no other:*
> *Thou didst create the world according to thy desire,*
> *. . .*
> *The countries of Syria and Nubia, the land of Egypt,*
> *Thou settest every man in his place . . .*
> *Their tongues are separate in speech,*
> · *And their natures as well;*
> *Their skins are distinguished,*
> *As thou distinguishest the foreign peoples.*

The Egyptians also attributed behaviors to the different groups, some favorable, some derogatory and stereotyped. For example, a stele (an inscribed stone column that serves as a marker and looks somewhat like a tombstone) from Twelfth Dynasty Pharaoh Sesostris III (circa 1887–1849 BC) ridicules black Africans: "The Nubian [black African] obeys the man who puts him down. When you oppose him he turns tail; when you give ground he becomes aggressive. They are not a people of might, they are poor and faint-hearted."

Another stele records history's first color bar, forbidding blacks from entering Pharaoh's domain: "Southern Boundary. Raised in the eighth year of the reign of Sesostris III, King of Upper and Lower Egypt, to whom be life throughout all ages. No Negro shall cross this boundary by water or by land, by ship or with his flocks, save for the purpose of trade or to make purchases in some post."

Clearly, the Land of the Nile distinguished among broad racial categories, characterized their behavior (however accurately or inaccurately), and even based social policy on those classifications. All this sorting happened many millennia before Columbus sailed the oceans or slaves loaded barges along the Mississippi.

## THE ASSYRIANS AND THE ISRAELITES

Black Africans also appear in monuments from 7th century BC Assyria that depict its battles with 25th Dynasty Egypt. A victory stele shows two prisoners, one black, one white, kneeling and lifting their hands in supplication to the figure of King Esarhaddon (680–669 BC), who towers over them. A bas-relief from the palace of King Ashurbanipal (669–626 BC) depicts a procession of black captives. The captives are similar to representations of black Africans seen in earlier Egyptian art at a time when they were enemies rather than a part of the Egyptian army. The Assyrian artists "correctly observed the physiognomy of men from the Sudan" and distinguished their facial appearance from that of whites.

The ancient Israelites, who were forbidden from making graven images, left no visual record. However, the prophet Jeremiah's rhetorical question "Can the Ethiopian change his skin or the leopard his spots?" shows that they considered skin color to be a permanent, inherited, racial characteristic. Its use as a literary device is comparable to the cliché "to wash an Ethiopian white," used in Greek and Roman literature to signify "futile labors or to illustrate the unchangeability of nature."

## ANCIENT INDIA

India's caste system is well known, as are attempts to rid the country of it. The English word "caste" is not derived from Hindi but from the Portuguese word *castas*. This is not, however, evidence that the Portuguese, who were the first Europeans to colonize India, constructed its caste system. The Hindi word for caste is *varna*. It means color (that is, skin color), and it is as old as Indian history itself.

The earliest civilization on the Indian subcontinent existed along the Indus valley between 2500 and 1750 BC at Harappa and Mohenjo-daro. The race and language of its people are not known. However, the Vedas, the sacred texts of the Indo-Europeans (also known as Aryans) who overran the Harrapan civilization between 1500 and 900 BC, describe how "under the banner of their God, Indra, lord of the heavens and 'Hurler of the Thunderbolt,' fierce Aryan warriors stormed the ancient 'cities' of the hated 'broad-nosed' Dasas, the dark-skinned worshippers of the phallus." According to one scholar, "dasa" originally meant simply "enemy," but the term suffered a shift of meaning later, when it came to mean "dark-faced" and subsequently "slave."

Further evidence for the recognition of racial differences in India comes from the *Bhagavad Gita* (The Song of the Lord), a part of the *Mahabharata* (the Hindu analogue to the Homeric poems). In it Lord Krishna assumes the disguise of the charioteer of the warrior-prince, Arjuna. In Sanskrit, *arjuna* means silver or white, cognate to the Greek *argos* or the Latin *argentum* (as in Argentina, the land of silver).

When Alexander the Great's army reached India, the Greeks described the people they met as being blacker than all other peoples except the Ethiopians (black Africans). They also noted that those north of the Ganges were lighter in skin color, more like the Egyptians. Foreshadowing nineteenth-century anthropologists' racial classifications, the Greeks recognized that black Africans' hair form differed from that of even the darkest-skinned Indians. In other words, the Greeks believed in race and did not believe it was just "skin deep."

Over the course of history, the various racial groups in India have intermixed. Trying to guess the caste background of Indians by skin color is a dicey proposition. Today there are many dark-skinned Brahmans. And whereas dark-skinned Dravidian-speaking peoples from the south of India are extremely successful in high-tech industries not only in India but also in the United States, fair-skinned groups in the Northwest Frontier are primarily concerned with the use of high technology for weapons of war. In sum, the sacred texts of ancient India confirm the evidence from ancient Egypt that racial differences were recognized and that race was used as a concept and as a basis for policy long before the European Age of Exploration.

## ANCIENT CHINA

Because of its large, relatively homogeneous population and its geographic location, China would seem an unlikely place to look for evidence of the recognition of race and race differences. However, important new evidence has come to light from mummies found in the remote Tarim Basin of Central Asia that date to around 2000 BC, long before the Silk Road, the famed artery of commerce linking China and Rome. The mummies have been remarkably well preserved because of the dry desert conditions. They are not Chinese or Asian but rather have Caucasoid facial features and auburn hair. DNA analysis of a later mummy (circa 1000 BC) matches that of Europeans more closely than it does any Asian (Mongoloid) group. Graves excavated just north of Beijing contain depictions of typical Caucasoid, rather than Mongoloid, faces. Art and literature from a later period show that when the Chinese encountered descendants of the Tarim Basin people, they recognized them as being a different race.

As Buddhism spread from India northward into China, its sacred texts were translated into the written languages of the local inhabitants. Two scrolls found at one site turned out to be in previously unknown Indo-European languages, now called Tocharian A and B. Whereas the Tarim Basin mummies from 2000 to 1000 BC are "completely Caucasian in their features," the paintings of religious acolytes found accompanying the Tocharian scrolls from the later period of AD 600 to 1000 (see Figure 2.2) depict clearly distinguishable "devotees of many races—Chinese, Indian, Mongol, and Turkic types, as well as fair-haired, blue-eyed, white-cheeked Caucasians."

Like other civilizations, the ancient Han Chinese regarded other groups they came into contact with as barbarians. They were especially taken aback by the odd appearance of one group, the Yuezhi,

FIGURE 2.2    Buddhist painting showing
European and Asian faces.

because of their hairy, white, ruddy skin and their prominent noses, which the Chinese likened to those of monkeys. (Compare the Romans' use of the term "simas" (monkeylike) to disparage black Africans, another example of a group seeing its racial features as being the ideal and those of other groups as not fully human.)

The Han Chinese applied the term "Hu" to barbarians like the Yuezhi who had "deep eye sockets, prominent noses, and beards." But they did not apply it to the Qiang, another barbarian group, who had a Mongoloid appearance and among whom some of the Yuezhi lived. Both groups were denigrated as uncivilized and inferior to the Chinese, but the Qiang were deemed to belong to the same racial stock, whereas the Yuezhi were viewed as being part of a very different stock, not only barbarian but ugly and monkeylike to boot.

From the Tarim Basin mummies of 2000 BC to the Buddhist cave paintings of a century to a century and a half later, the art and writings of Chinese civilization show that these people too recognized races and racial differences. Like the ancient Egyptians and Indians, the Chinese used the same set of physical features (skin color, hair, and facial form) as classical physical anthropology and the contemporary man-in-the-street used to sort people into groups. All this sorting came long before the arrival of European colonialism. Naturally, the Chinese considered their characteristics the ideal and often belittled people (in this case, Caucasians) who looked different.

## ANCIENT GREECE AND ROME

Greek and Roman depictions and descriptions of the black Africans to their south and the Scythians and Celts to their north provide further evidence that racial classification predated the advent of European colonialism. The classical artists and authors contrasted the black skin, frizzy hair, flat noses, and thick lips of the Africans with the straight, often yellow or red hair and the pale white skin of the peoples to the north of them, while regarding their own features as ideal. Citing the opposite characteristics of the Scythians and the black Africans in appearance and behavior, the classical authors developed the first naturalistic explanation of the origin of racial differences: the decreasing intensity of sunlight as one moved from the southernmost to the northernmost regions of the world as they knew it. They used similar names for both the offspring of interracial marriages and for transitional populations with intermediate racial characteristics; this labeling shows that they also recognized that once these traits had been acquired, they were hereditary and transmitted from parents to children.

The first black Africans to appear in Mediterranean-area art outside of Egypt show up in Cretan frescoes from the early second millennium BC. "A procession of coal-black warriors appears in a fresco from Knossos (circa 1550–1500 BC) and another fresco of approximately the same period from the island of Thera carries the profile of a black whose Negroid traits are somewhat re-duced—wavy hair, rather thick lips, and medium-broad nose."

Greek, Roman, and Etruscan artistic representations contrast-ing the skin color, facial features, and hair form of Africans with those of Europeans are plentiful. One striking type (Figure 2.3), of which there are many variations and examples, is a rhyton (jug) with the face of a Caucasoid on one side and that of a black African on the other.

The genitalia of black Africans were also deemed noteworthy to the Greek and Roman artists. Within the same art piece, black males are depicted with penises larger than those of white figures, and in others are shown as being erect.

The Barberini mosaic, a late Hellenistic (circa AD 200) copy of an earlier Ptolemaic original, is a racial map of the Nile region

FIGURE 2.3    Graeco-Roman jug with black and white faces

of Africa as the river flows to the Mediterranean. The people in the foreground are white, but the hunters shown on mountains at the top (the background), which represents the uppermost (southern) origin of the river, are black.

## Greek and Roman Racial Classifications

In an early first century AD poem on astrology, Manilius classified the peoples known to the classical world according to skin color: Ethiopians, the blackest; Indians, less sunburned; Egyptians, mildly dark; and the Mauri (Moors), whose name derived from the color of their skin, mulatto. Xenophan in describing the flat noses of Africans was "the first European to apply to Africans a physical characteristic other than color." To this Herodotus added that the hair of blacks was the "woolliest" of all mankind. Diodorus combined this suite of physical characteristics, noting that Africans were black-skinned, flat-nosed, and woolly haired. Petronius rejected the view of most of today's social scientists and PBS's *Race* documentary that "race is only skin deep." The satirist gibed that the idea that "a white man could pass for an Ethiopian merely by blackening his body was ridiculous, because color alone does not define the group. The white man would also have to change his hair, lips, and add facial scars" (the last being a purely cultural feature—our explanatory note).

The most detailed surviving description of the racially defining characteristics of black Africans from the classical world appears in *The Moretum*, a poem attributed to Virgil (circa 1st century AD). A female character named Scybale is described as "African in race, her whole figure proof of her country—her hair tightly curled, lips thick, color dark, chest broad, breasts pendulous, belly somewhat pinched, legs thick, and feet broad and ample." In his book *Blacks in Antiquity: Ethiopians in the Greco-Roman Experience*, Frank M. Snowden compared that description with portrayals by twentieth-century anthropologists E. A. Hooton and M. J. Herskovits (Table 2.1). For example, Hooton described the "outstanding features of the ancient and specialized Negro division of mankind" as "narrow heads and wide noses, thick lips and thin legs, protruding jaws and receding chins, integument rich in pigment but poor in hairy growth, flat feet and round foreheads, tiny curls and big smiles."

Snowden concluded: "While the author of *The Moretum* was writing poetry, not anthropology," his description of the distinguishing racial characteristics of black Africans "is good anthropology; in fact, *the ancient and modern phraseology is so similar that the modern might be considered a translation of the ancient*" (emphasis added). In his survey of the depiction of black Africans in

TABLE 2.1 Comparison of racial traits of black Africans in the Roman poem *The Moretum* with observations by anthropologists E. A. Hooton and M. J. Herskovits

| Racial Trait | Virgil's *The Moretum* (circa 1st century AD) | E. A. Hooton's *Up from the Ape* (1946) | M. J. Herskovits in *Encyclopedia Britannica* (XVI, 1960) |
|---|---|---|---|
| Skin color | Dark (*"fusca colore"*) | Integument rich in color | Reddish-brown to deep brownish-black |
| Hair | Tightly curled (*"torta comam"*) First described by Xenophan and Herodotus | Tiny curls | Hair wiry, tightly curled, and lying close to the scalp |
| Lips | Puffy (*"labro tumens"*) | Thick lips, puffy, everted | Lips thick |
| Shoulder or pectoral area | Broad (*"pectore lata"*) | Omitted | Broad shoulders |
| Waist | Belly somewhat pinched (*"compressior alvo"*) | Omitted | Narrow waist |
| Legs | Thin (*"cruribus exilis"*) | Thin legs | Arms and legs slender and long in proportion to stature |
| Feet | Broad and ample (*"spatiosa prodiga planta"*) | Flat feet | Omitted |
| Breasts | Pendulous (*"iacens mammis"*) Also noted by Roman writer Juvenal | Omitted (but mentioned in J. H. Lewis, *The Biology of the Negro*, 1942) | Omitted |
| Other | Omitted (but mentioned by other classical writers and depicted in classical art) | Wide noses, narrow heads, round foreheads, protruding jaws and receding chins, integument poor in hairy growth | Broad nostrils, high cheekbones; prognathous faces, with an acute facial angle; short stocky build and heavily muscled, triangular-shaped torso |

SOURCE: Frank M. Snowden, *Blacks in Antiquity: Ethiopians in the Greco-Roman Experience* (Cambridge, Mass.: Harvard University Press, 1934).

Egyptian, classical Greek, and Roman art in a second book, *Before Color Prejudice*, Snowden noted how "the ancient artists have furnished vivid pictorial definitions of blacks, a kind of anthropological 'carte d'identité.'"

## Greek and Roman Theories of the Origin of Racial Differences

Beginning with Hippocrates, the principal theory used to explain the origin of these differences was climate. Blacks to the south were scorched by the sun, whereas people like the Scythians who lived to the north were subjected to frost. Diodorus, for example, concluded that because of differences in climate, "both the fare and the manner of life and the bodies of the inhabitants [of the other regions] should differ very much from such as are found among us." Sextus Empiricus stated that black Africans aged early because their bodies were aged by the scorching sun, and Britons aged later (a clearly exaggerated 120 years) because their natural heat was maintained longer.

Once formed, however, racial differences were considered to be inherited and not easily changed. For example, Herodotus cited the dark skin and kinky hair of the inhabitants of Colchis (in the Caucasus) as support for the tradition that they were descended from the African soldiers of the Egyptian Pharaoh Sesostris.

The classical writers also noted that the gradations of color and other physical features found among peoples as one traveled north or south were the same as those found in the children of black-white crosses, and they made the connection in attributing an origin to intermediate groups such as the Mauri (Mauretanians, or Moors). Black-white crosses were described as "neither *nigri* [black] nor *fusci* [dark], but *decolores*, corresponding perhaps to the modern usage of the word 'mulattoes.'" Aristotle made the first reference to mixture between a Greek woman and an Ethiopian: He noted that the descendants of such unions were "mulattoes," and that should such intermarriage continue, the lines distinguishing the parental races would become blurred.

The reduced African features in the "brown babies," most probably the offspring of black soldiers in the army of the Persian emperor Xerxes that invaded Greece in 480 BC, attracted the eye of artists in the next century and were cited as evidence for the transmission of racial features, as were mixed children from Elis and Sicily.

## Race and Slavery in Greece and Rome

The Greek and Roman descriptions and depictions of blacks were not uniformly negative. Slavery was not associated with a particular skin color or race. Many Greek slaves were better educated than their Roman masters, and some black Africans achieved distinction. The fact that the classical authors and artists identified races based on the same traits, on occasion engaged in some derogatory stereotyping, and called attention to the breasts and genitals of black Africans, however, shows once again that these practices long predated European colonialism or American slavery.

## ISLAMIC CIVILIZATION

Islamic civilization offers yet another test of whether the race concept arose only with European colonialism in order to justify white supremacy. The Islamic scholars provide descriptions of the physical and behavioral characteristics of the black Africans to their south and the Europeans to their north. Like the Greeks and Romans, they typically attributed these differences to climate, especially the effects of varying amounts of sunlight.

Despite the Koranic prohibition on graven images, some Islamic art provides further evidence of the portrayal of racial groups. More valuable is the literature. The Koran itself provides no sanction for racial prejudice. Only two verses directly address the race question. Chapter 30, verse 22, echoes the much earlier Egyptian *Great Hymn to Aten*, quoted earlier. It states: "Among God's signs are the creation of the heavens and of the earth and the diversity of your languages and of your colors. In this indeed are signs for those who know."

Later, chapter 49, verse 13, makes it clear that piety and obedience to Allah are more important than any racial, ethnic, or tribal difference: "O people! We have created you from a male and a female and we have made you into confederacies and tribes so that you may come to know one another. The noblest among you in the eyes of God is the most pious, for God is omniscient and well informed."

Authors as diverse as historian Arnold Toynbee and Malcolm X have therefore praised Islam for its inclusiveness, tolerance, and absence of race prejudice. A more detailed study by Bernard Lewis, however, shows that this judgment may be true only in comparison to its European Christian counterpart. Even then, a careful examination reveals derogatory characterizations of other races, especially black Africans, and an increasing tendency to demean their intellectual abilities. Slavery in the Islamic world was not restricted to blacks. However, over time, it became less common among whites, and those who were slaves could rise to higher positions, whereas blackness became increasingly associated with the most menial and abject forms of servitude.

In *The Arabian Nights*, for example, blacks, whether free or slave, are rarely shown in roles above those of porters, household servants, cooks, bath attendants, and the like. They are also attributed great sexual prowess and appetites. One tale characterizes the sexuality of black slaves as so primal and irresistible to the wife of King Shahriyar and the other women in his harem that the king was possessed of "sexual fantasies, or rather nightmares" that Lewis goes so far as to say have "an Alabama-like quality."

## Islamic Racial Classification

As the religion of the Prophet spread from its origin in Arabia, it remained confined to peoples of a similar Middle Eastern racial background. The Islamic conquest of parts of Asia, Africa, and Europe brought very different peoples into the fold. Arabic literature originally used color terms on a personal, within-group basis, much as "Philip the Fair" or "Edward, the Black Prince" referred to complexion or armor rather than race. With the Islamic world eventually spreading from the Atlantic coast of Africa to the Pacific, the only color terms to remain were black, red, and white, each denoting racial, not personal, characteristics. Arabs, along with Persians, Greeks, Turks, and Slavs, were classified as being white or light red, though sometimes the European peoples to the north were described as bright red, pale blue, or dead white. Sub-Saharan Africans were termed "black," and that term was only rarely applied to Indians.

In the earliest Arabic references, Lewis noted,

> black Africans are called either Habash or Sudan, the former designating the Ethiopians and their immediate neighbors in the Horn of Africa, the latter (an Arabic word meaning black) denoting blacks in general. It sometimes includes Ethiopians, but never Egyptians, Berbers, or other peoples north of the Sahara. Later, after the Arab expansion into Africa, other and more specific terms are added, the commonest being Nuba, Bujja (or Beja), and Zanj. Nuba, from Nubia, usually designates the Nilotic and sometimes also Hamitic peoples south of Egypt, i.e., roughly in the present area of the republic of the Sudan; the Bujja were nomadic tribes between the Nile and the Red Sea; Zanj, a word of uncertain origin, is used specifically of the Bantu-speaking peoples in East Africa south of the Ethiopians, and sometimes, more loosely of black Africans in general. The term Bilad al-Sudan—"land of the blacks"—is applied

to the whole area of black Africa south of the Sahara, from the Nile to the Atlantic, and including such West African black states as Ghana and Songhay.

As evidence that the Greeks and Romans also recognized the subgroups of black Africans, Snowden cited two plates. The first shows the striking similarity between a fifth century BC terracotta head and a contemporary photo of a Shilluk from the Sudan, whom traditional anthropologists considered representative of the "pronounced Negroid or 'pure' type." The second shows the remarkable resemblance between a bronze head-vase from the third or second century BC and a Somali from east Africa, considered representative of the mixed or intermediate type by racial anthropologists. (The photographs are taken from Carleton Coon's books *The Origin of Races* and *The Living Races of Man*. We discuss Coon and his critical role in the post–World War II debate over the reality of race at the end of Chapter 3.)

Together with the specialization and fixing of color terms, Lewis noted, "comes a very clear connotation of inferiority attached to darker and more specifically black skins." Citing a poem in which one character begs for mercy even though "My color is pitch-black, my hair is woolly, my appearance repulsive" [that is, his facial features were typically Negroid rather than Semitic], Lewis pointed out that this reveals the association of "blackness, ugliness, and inferior station" in Islam. It had become the convention by medieval times "to use different words for black and white slaves. White slaves were normally called mamluk, an Arabic word meaning 'owned,' while blacks slaves were called 'abd. In time, the world 'abd ceased to be used of any slaves but black ones and eventually of a black man, irrespective of whether he was slave or not."

Mas'udi (d. AD 956) quoted Galen as allegedly having listed "ten specific attributes of the black man, which are all found in him and in no other; frizzy hair, thin eyebrows, broad nostrils, thick lips, pointed teeth, smelly skin, black eyes, furrowed hands and feet, a long penis and great merriment. Galen says that merriment dominates the black man because of his defective brain, whence also the weakness of his intelligence." In fact, only two of these traits, black skin and woolly or frizzy hair, can be found in any existing text of Galen. More likely, Mas'udi was simply summarizing the consensus views of the Islamic writers of his time.

The non-European author of this derogatory portrait of black Africans, which for disparagement matches anything to be found in tracts defending slavery in the American South in the days of slavery or Jim Crow, died in AD 956. Given this evidence, one would have to argue that the European colonizers did not construct "race" as a justification for slavery, but picked up an earlier social construction of Islam, which took it from the classical world, which in turn took it from ancient Egypt. Either that, or each of these civilizations independently "constructed" the same worldview, and the civilizations of ancient China and India independently "constructed" similar worldviews, even though they were looking at different groups of people.

## Islamic Theory of Racial Origins and Race Differences

The Islamic physician and philosopher Avicenna in a poem offered a racial-classification scheme that took into account both physical and behavioral characteristics, which he explained in terms of climate:

> Do not draw inferences from the color of the skin
> if it is conditioned by the country.
> Among the Zanj [black African] heat has
> transformed their bodies

*until blackness covers their skins.*
*While the Slav have become so pale*
*that their skins are soft and white.*
*If you define the seven climates*
*you will know their various temperaments.*
*The fourth climate is balanced and temperate*
*and their color depends on temperament.*

The jurist Sa'id al-Andalusi (AD 1029–1070) named the Indians, Persians, Chaldeans, Greeks, Romans, Egyptians, Arabs, and Jews as the only peoples who have produced science and learning, and conceded certain accomplishments to the Chinese and the Turks. Following the climatic-zone theory of racial origins and race differences, he dismissed the races of the far north and far south as barbarians "more like beasts than like other men":

For those who live furthest to the north between the last of the seven climates and the limits of the inhabited world, the excessive distance of the sun in relation to the zenith line makes the air cold and the atmosphere thick. Their temperaments are therefore frigid, their humors raw, their bellies gross, their color pale, their hair long and lank. Thus they lack keenness of understanding and clarity of intelligence, and are overcome by ignorance and dullness, lack of discernment, and stupidity. Such are the Slavs, the Bulgars, and their neighbors. For those peoples on the other hand who live near and beyond the equinoctial line to the limit of the inhabited world in the south, the long presence of the sun at the zenith makes the air hot and the atmosphere thin. Because of this their temperaments become hot and their humours fiery, their color black and their hair woolly. Thus they lack self-control and steadiness of mind and are overcome by fickleness, foolishness and ignorance. Such are the blacks, who live at the extremity of the land of Ethiopia, the Nubians, the Zanj, and the like.

Sa'id reserved his greatest contempt for the latter people, whom he dismisses as "rabble," "savages," and "scum," barely part of the human order, lacking any semblance of government or religion.

The fourteenth-century geographer and historian Ibn-Khaldun noted that unlike the Arabs, the Greeks and Romans did not apply a special term based on skin color to describe the northern European peoples with whom they came in contact because "whiteness was something usual and common (to them) and they did not see anything sufficiently remarkable in it to cause them to use it as a specific term."

The Islamic scholars also followed the Greek and Roman philosophers in believing that once racial differences were caused by the differing amounts of sunlight, they were inherited (an early form of Lamarck's theory of the inheritance of acquired characteristics). For example, Ibn Habib, the ninth-century jurist from Islamic Spain, wrote that "A black woman may be repudiated if there is no blackness in her family; likewise a scald-head [that is, scabrous], because such things are covered by kinship." Since according to strict Muslim practice, a woman is to remain veiled and unseen by her prospective groom until they are married, the meaning of Habib's ruling is that a husband may repudiate a new wife (that is, annul the marriage) if, upon removing her veil he finds her to be black or scabrous, because both conditions were considered not only undesirable but hereditary as well.

## Islamic View of Black Africans

The poet and satirist Jahiz of Basra (circa AD 776–869), in a manner not unlike that of the white defenders of slavery and colonialism who allegedly invented "race," described Africans (termed Zanj) as "the least intelligent and the least discerning of mankind, and the least capable of understanding the consequences of actions." Like his later counterparts, Jahiz credited black Africans, "despite their dimness, their boundless stupidity, their crude perceptions and their evil dispositions," with the ability to "make long speeches."

Ibn Khaldun had this view: "The only people who accept slavery are the Negroes, owing to their low degree of humanity and their proximity to the animal stage. Other personas who accept the status of slave do so as a means of attaining high rank, or power, or wealth, as is the case with the Mameluke Turks in the East and with those Franks and Galicians who enter the service of the state [in Spain]."

In addition to the pejorative of not knowing their own fathers, practicing cannibalism, and having little understanding or intelligence, Maqdisi (circa tenth century AD) described the Zanj as "people of black color, flat noses, kinky hair." Similarly, the geographer Idrisi disparaged black Africans as having "stinking sweat" as well as a "lack of knowledge and defective minds such that men of learning are almost unknown among them." The thirteenth-century Persian writer Nasir al-Din Tusi went even further, claiming that the Zanj differed from animals only in walking on two rather than four feet, and that "Many have observed that the ape is more teachable and more intelligent than the Zanji." In addition to lack of culture and intelligence, Islamic writers also disparaged black Africans as being hypersexual, yet also filled with simple piety and carefree, happy, and with a natural sense of rhythm. Without knowing the source, one could easily believe such characterizations came from the Cotton South of the United States.

The Arabs, "like all other conquerors before and since, were reluctant to concede equality to the conquered, and for as long as they could they maintained their privileged position." In short, white European society was not the first to apply abusive stereotypes to black Africans.

## Islamic Black Slavery Preceded
## Slavery by White Europeans

Although there were black slaves, as well as slaves of other races, in ancient Egypt, Greece, and Rome, "the massive development of the slave trade in black Africa," according to Lewis, dated "from the Arab period." He further noted: "The total identification of blackness with slavery which occurred in North and South America never took place in the Muslim world. There were always white slaves as well as black ones. Nevertheless, the identification of blackness with certain forms of slavery went very far—and in later centuries white slaves grew increasingly rare."

Anticipating the claims of Southern slave holders, one Muslim legend attributed the servile status of blacks to their being descended from Ham, one of the three sons of Noah. Ham and his descendants, it was claimed, were cursed because of his skin color rather than for his having looked on his father's drunken nakedness, as offered in the much later biblical rationalizations for black slavery.

Ibn Hazm (AD 994–1064) at the beginning of a treatise on genealogy stated, "God has decreed that the most devout is the noblest even if he be a Negress's bastard, and that the sinner and unbeliever is at the lowest level even if he be the son of prophets." As Lewis commented, "The sentiment is impeccably pious and egalitarian—yet somehow does not entirely carry conviction." Another story tells of a black African king who is kidnapped by his Muslim guests and then sold into slavery. When he meets them years later he shows no resentment, because they brought him to Islam.

Similar moralistic, patronizing remarks are easy enough to find in the writings of abolitionists, anticolonialists, and Christian missionaries. According to Lewis, "At no time did the Islamic world ever practice the kind of racial exclusivism . . . which has persisted until very recently in the United States," but he also noted that

"Even now, members of the comparatively small number of recognizably black families in the Middle East tend on the whole to marry among their own kind." He cogently warned against "the illogical assumption that the reprobation of prejudice in a society proves its absence. In fact, of course, it reveals its presence." For example, one utopian Islamic group, the Carmathians, established a community in Bahrain. Although it abolished many of the distinctions of persons and property that had arisen in Islam, all hard manual labor was performed by 30,000 black slaves.

Nor was the treatment of black African slaves necessarily better in the Islamic world. A British observer in Egypt in the 1840s estimated that a generation of slaves would die from disease and overwork every five to six years. Even allowing for exaggeration, these conditions, though by no means typical of the Islamic world, equal the worst found in the European colonies in the New World or the antebellum South. The utopian view of race relations under Islam is contradicted by the ironic and tragic fact that when the American Civil War cut off the supply of cotton to Britain, the compensating boom in Egyptian cotton provided the funds for increased purchase of black African slaves to work the Egyptian cotton fields.

Neither the nexus of race and slavery nor opposition to it was a unique construction of Western society. "It is the fashion here, as well as in our colonies, to consider the negroes as the last link in the chain of humanity, between the monkey tribe and man; but I do not believe the negro is inferior to the white man in intellect; and I do not suffer the eloquence of the slave driver to convince me that the negro is so stultified as to be unfit for freedom." So wrote an Englishman, R. R. Madden, traveling in Egypt in 1825— more than three decades before Charles Darwin wrote *Origin of Species by Means of Natural Selection or the Preservation of Favored Races in the Struggle for Life* and before any European invoked his theory to support a racial hierarchy in which whites were at the top and black Africans at the bottom.

Eschewing any attempt to "argue the relative wickedness of Muslim and Western practice," Lewis concluded that his review of the evidence served "to refute the claims of exclusive virtue and exclusive vice, and to point to certain common failings of our common humanity."

## HUNTER-GATHERER SOCIETIES

In all of the civilizations noted here, their art and literature sorted peoples into races based on characteristics such as skin color, hair form, and nose shape. Each group described itself as superior to the others, which is perhaps understandable given that its level of technological complexity was higher than that of the different-looking peoples whom they encountered. If, as we have argued, race is not a construction of European colonialism, then perhaps the notion of superiority is a tendency of expanding civilizations when they encounter less complex societies. Even this attitude, however, does not seem to be the case.

Rock paintings from Africa show that the artists distinguished between the Bushmen (the people who today live in the Kalahari and are well known from the movie *The Gods Must Be Crazy*). At one time the Sahara was a fertile area inhabited by elephants and rhinos, rather than the desert it is today. It also apparently was home to at least two different human populations, Pygmies and Bushmen. A trail of rock art, depicting the animal life and the two races, suggests their migration from the north down to their present refuge in southern Africa.

The reaction of the Bushmen upon first seeing Asians provides not only another example but one that also comes as close as possible to a natural experiment to test whether racial sorting is a social construction or a human universal that occurs wherever and whenever there are visible differences among peoples. Further, this example demonstrates that such sorting is done by both the dominant group that possesses the technologically complex society and by the technologically less sophisticated, subordinate group.

Henry Harpending, professor of anthropology at the University of Utah and a member of the National Academy of Sciences, has done extensive research among the Bushmen of the Kalahari desert of southern Africa. Modern DNA analysis sorts the Bushmen with the other peoples of sub-Saharan Africa. Traditional anthropology, however, did not. Their yellowish rather than black skin, high cheekbones, folded eyelids, the occurrence of "shovel-shaped" (versus flat) incisor teeth, and what was then termed "the Mongolian dark spot" that appears on the lower back of newborns led anthropologists to believe that Bushmen were more like Asians than other Africans. And so, interestingly, do the Bushmen today. They sort all mammals into three mutually exclusive groups: "*!a*" (the exclamation point represents the "clicking" sound for which their language is well known) denotes edible animals such as warthogs and giraffes; "*!oma*" designates an inedible animal such as a jackal, a hyena, a black African, or a European white; the term "*zhu*" is reserved for humans, that is, the Bushmen themselves. When they first encountered Asian researchers, the Bushmen immediately classified them as "*zhu*," even though they had never seen members of that racial group before.

## RACE IS AS OLD AS
## HISTORY OR EVEN PREHISTORY

The surveys presented here of the art and literature of non-European civilizations and the art and oral record of the Bushmen lend no support to the view that the race concept was "constructed" by Europeans. What is novel was that Western European civilization was the first to describe race and race differences using the grammar and lexicon of science rather than of religion or philosophy or protoscience. But not until the European Age of Exploration did the tradition that led to modern science begin. In the next chapter, we trace the development of anthropology as the science of race. It too was subject to all the prejudices and stereotyping of the nonscientific approaches to understanding human diversity. The unique feature about science, however, is that it is a self-correcting process.

CHAPTER THREE

# Anthropology as the Science of Race

*Two groups have been engaged in an ongoing debate on the issue of race. On one side are those termed polygenists, who look at the obvious differences in appearance between races and doubt that they could have a common or at least recent common origin. Others, termed monogenists, note how readily members of any race can interact, mate, and form societies with members of any other race when given the opportunity to do so.*

*During the Renaissance, the polygenist view was championed by freethinking minds, often at great personal risk. Had there been a desire to "construct" a view of human origins and race differences that would dehumanize the peoples of the New World and Africa, the European power structure should have embraced the polygenist view. It did not. Nor did America's Southern states in the debate over slavery that led to the Civil War.*

*Anthropology first emerged as the science of race, with researchers measuring fossil skulls and attempting to determine their race and antiquity. That approach was increasingly abandoned. We highlight three critical junctures in which science, politics, and personality interacted:*

*the disputes between Ernst Haeckel and Rudolf Virchow, between Franz Boas and Madison Grant, and finally between Carleton Coon and Ashley Montagu.*

The Bible says God created man. In fact, the Torah, which Christians have adopted (and some scholars would argue have reinvented) as their Old Testament, says God created Adam. Who, or what, is meant by the Hebrew word "Adam"? Eve's companion in the Garden of Eden, who fathered the entire human race? That has been the usual interpretation, but it isn't necessarily correct. The Hebrew word *adam* appears 106 times in the Torah but refers to the character "Adam" only fourteen times. The other ninety-two occurrences "translate as *man* or *men*, usually referring to Israelites generally, as distinct from designating gender." The door has always been open—and often entered—by any individual or group wanting to confine "adam" to "us" and to exclude "them." In this, the ancient Israelites and their later Jewish, Christian, and Muslim successors have been neither unique nor uniquely guilty.

The Europe of the Middle Ages was far more restricted in perspective than the ancient classical world. It had only limited contact with distant places and different races. The majority of medieval scholastics were more theologians than philosophers. There were, however, individuals who did make important contributions by weakening the pillars of faith through questioning dogma and laying the foundation for the later development of modern science.

In his 1265 *Opus Maius* (Major Work), Roger Bacon identified the causes of error as authority, custom, popular prejudice, and the concealment of ignorance with the pretense of knowledge. According to Bacon, there were two methods of acquiring knowledge, argument and experience, but "the strongest argument proves nothing so long as the conclusions are unverified by experience." William of Occam provided what would become one of science's sharpest tools, Occam's Razor, also known as the Law of Parsimony. Called the Invincible Doctor because of his unbeatable skill in logical argumentation, he wrote that essences should not be multiplied beyond necessity. Thus, a guiding principle of modern science is to prefer the theory or hypothesis that requires the fewest variables and the simplest mechanism to explain the phenomenon being studied or the question being asked. Neither Occam nor his razor was so welcomed in his own time. In 1323 he was imprisoned by the Pope for four years and censured by the Paris Faculty of Arts in 1339. (Now, over seven centuries later, we urge readers to consider both Bacon's call for empirical verification and Occam's demand for parsimony as guiding principles in examining the case for race.)

Unlike Bacon or Occam, the Scholastics were dedicated to the preservation of existing knowledge, not the ongoing, unbridled pursuit of the new. All that needed to be known about human origins and racial differences had been spelled out, by the Almighty himself, in Genesis. Adam was created on the sixth day in the image and likeness of God. All men descended from Adam and his helpmate, Eve; all possessed souls and were therefore uniquely distinct from the animals. Any differences in language and appearance arose as part of mankind's punishment for Nimrod's building the Tower of Babel.

This theory of human origins, termed "monogenesis" (that is, single origin), was not called into question until the Renaissance and the Age of Exploration. But the challenge to monogenesis, termed "polygenesis" (multiple origins), did not come from the power establishment bent on dehumanizing the other races that Europeans began to encounter as the Age of Exploration started. Rather, it came from independent thinkers who dared to cast off the intellectual shackles imposed by biblical theology. They did so in a number of areas and often paid a price for it.

Paracelsus (1493–1541), the pseudonym of Phillippus Aureolus Theophrastus Bombast von Hohenheim, was born in Switzerland in 1493, one year after Columbus's first voyage to the New World. A contemporary of Copernicus, Martin Luther, and Leonardo da Vinci, he was a prime mover in the intellectual transition from the Middle Ages to the Renaissance. His works were responsible for more of the scientific debates that took place in the late sixteenth century than was Copernicus's assertion that the earth revolved around the sun, not vice versa.

In 1520 the Renaissance humanist wrote that the people in far-off islands were the descendants of a different Adam. According to Paracelsus, the book of Genesis was not philosophy or science but theology, written "according to the faith, for the weaker brethren." Andreas Vesalius (1514–1564) revived the experimental study of human anatomy and physiology by dissecting cadavers. In *De humani corporis fabrica* (1543), he pointed out the similarities between humans and apes (or more likely, monkeys) and noted racial differences in head shape, which he believed were due to artificial deformation. The Inquisition charged Vesalius with having dissected the living and sentenced him to death, but the sentence was commuted to making a pilgrimage to the Holy Land, from which he never returned. Similarly, the Italian philosopher Lucilio Vanini (1585–1619) was persecuted for his freethinking ideas and driven from one European country to another. When he wrote in 1616 that some people entertained the belief that man was descended from or related to monkeys, he aroused suspicion. Vanini was condemned and burned at the stake in Toulouse, France, for atheism and witchcraft.

The Calvinist Isaac de la Peyrère of Bordeaux, France, questioned whether Moses could have authored the first five books of the Bible. For example, he noted that the phrase "across the Jordan," which appears at the beginning of Deuteronomy, implies that it was written by someone who was in Israel or on the west side of the Jordan River. But a major point of the Bible is that Moses never made it across the river into the land of Israel. In 1655 de la Peyrère argued that the Bible's Adam and Eve were not the first human beings on Earth but a later and special creation. The Gentiles who peopled the rest of the world, including the newly (to Europeans) discovered peoples of the New World, were created along with the other animals. De la Peyrère based his argument upon the biblical passages recounting Cain's fear of being killed, his flight, his marriage, and his building of a city as evidence of the existence of people other than Adam and Eve. He also asserted that ancient Jewish and Mohammedan tradition supported his theory. De la Peyrère's *Prae-Adamitae* (pre-Adamites, or those who lived before God created Adam) was not published in Catholic France but in Protestant Amsterdam. The Catholic Church placed the book on its index of prohibited works, and the tome was publicly burned by the parliament of Paris. The forbidden-fruit effect made *Prae-Adamitae* a sixteenth-century bestseller, but de la Peyrère enjoyed no royalties. The Inquisition forced him to recant both his Calvinism and polygenism, and he died in a convent in 1676.

Giordano Bruno was even less fortunate. In 1591 he declared that "no sound thinking person will refer the Ethiopians to the same protoplast as the jewish one." Like Vanini before him, Bruno was burned at the stake, for espousing not polygenism but another biblical doctrine—that the earth was the center of the universe around which the sun and all other celestial bodies revolved.

The European discovery of the Americas caused many to wonder if the native Indian peoples were true descendants of Adam and Eve and thus possessed souls as did their European conquerors. Or, if not, the question was whether they could be treated as beasts of burden, not men. The issue of monogenesis versus poly-genesis was heatedly debated within the Church.

In 1435, almost sixty years before Columbus reached the Americas, Pope Eugene IV condemned the enslavement of the inhabitants of the Canary Islands, ordering that they be freed in fifteen days or that their enslavers would face excommunication.

In 1537, Pope Paul III issued his bull (decree) *Sublimis Deus*, which proclaimed that Indians "as true men not only capable of receiving the Christian faith but, as we have been informed, eagerly hurry to it . . . we command that the aforesaid Indians and all other nations which come to the knowledge of Christians in the future must not be deprived of their freedom and the ownership of their property."

The papal bull decreed that Genesis could only be read to mean monogenesis. This granting of common humanity, at least at a spiritual level, in no way guaranteed the American Indians or sub-Saharan Africans humane treatment on the part of Europeans. It certainly did not spare the Native Americans of North America from dispossession at the hands of the English, nor those of Central and South America from servitude on the *encomiendas*, nor black Africans from enslavement throughout the New World by all the colonial powers. In the eighteenth and nineteenth centuries, "bringing the Gospel to the heathens" to save their souls could and did provide a rationalization for "the white man's burden." But if "race" was constructed by whites to justify slavery, Europeans missed a golden opportunity to dehumanize people of color by failing to put their seal of approval on some form of polygenesis. At the time of first contact, social conscience was weak or nonexistent, but rather than embrace a theory of multiple origins, the power structure rejected it.

Then, in summer 1550, Hapsburg Emperor Charles V convened a council in Valladolid, Spain, to debate whether the colonization of the New World was justified. The Aristotelian scholar

Juan Gines de Sepulveda argued that the civilizing mission of Spain justified the conquest, so long as it was done humanely. Describing the Native Americans as "inhumane barbarians who thought the greatest gift they could offer to God was human hearts," he said that they fit Aristotle's definition of "natural slaves." Rejecting the argument that their majestic art and architecture were proof that they were civilized and equal to their European conquerors, Sepulveda countered, "Do not even bees and spiders make works which no human can imitate?"

A Dominican friar, Bartolome de Las Casas, answered Sepulveda by presenting a vast dossier filled with firsthand reports of the atrocities committed by the conquistadores against the Indians. Las Casas concluded his case for the equality of the Indians with the impassioned proclamation "All the world is human."

After carefully listening to both sides, the emperor ordered that the conquests be suspended so that the issue could be explored further. The halt was short-lived. Power politics soon won out over moral argument, and the conquests resumed. The critical point for discussion here, however, is that the highest levels of ecclesiastical and temporal authority each declined easy opportunities to put their seal of approval on polygenesis and the full power of their office behind dehumanizing people of color.

Voltaire was another supporting voice for polygenism. Unlike de la Peyrère, Voltaire did not build his case on the Bible, but he couldn't resist yet another chance to mock Scripture. He argued that the races were so different in appearance, behavior, and even sexual anatomy that they should be regarded as distinct species. In his 1774 book *Sketches of the History of Man*, Henry Home, Lord Kames, tentatively raised the possibility of polygenesis. Arguing that climate alone (the consensus nontheological theory of the origin of racial differences since the Greeks) could not have effected the obvious differences between races, he raised the question of whether the different groups might have been made

for different climates. Kames pointed to the difficulties that Europeans had in adapting to warm climates of the areas they were
colonizing as support for polygenism. Unlike de la Peyrère, Kames
argued that the Native Americans were not pre-Adamite but
post-Adamite.

The question of whether other races originated before, at the
same time as, or after Europeans, and its implications for the issue
of equality or inequality, would remain a matter of contention
within and between both the polygenist and the monogenist
camps for the next two centuries. If the races had separate origins,
which (if any) was superior—the first or the last? If they all originated at the same time, how did they come to be so different?
Whatever might be responsible for creating race differences, did
it affect only their bodies or their minds as well? Would Europeans change their appearance as they inhabited the different
parts of the world? Would colonizing sub-Saharan Africa turn
successive generations of Europeans black?

## EQUALITY, THE DECLARATION OF
## INDEPENDENCE, AND THE CONSTITUTION

In the United States, where people of European (overwhelmingly
British), American Indian, and sub-Saharan descent lived side by
side but by no means equally, "every man became an anthropologist." Whatever interracial mating took place, it was white males
with black, and less often Indian, females. Few of these mixed-
race children were accepted into the white race.

As previously noted, Thomas Jefferson wrote "All men are created equal" in the Declaration of Independence, but he expressed
a very low opinion of the intellectual ability of blacks in his
*Notes on Virginia*. The PBS *Race* documentary cited this contradiction as support for its fourth point, "Race and freedom were

born together. When the U.S. was founded, equality was a radical new idea. But, our early economy was based largely on slavery. The concept of race helped explain why some people could be denied the rights and freedoms that others took for granted."

This contradiction is noted by historian Paul Finkelman in the transcript of *Race*, "Episode Two: The Story We Tell": "Jefferson is the first person to truly articulate a theory of race in the United States, and in effect, he has to do so." Fellow historian Robin Kelley explains that Jefferson and the other founders faced the intellectual dilemma of how they could "promote liberty, freedom, democracy on the one hand, and a system of slavery and exploitation of peoples who were non-white on the other." A third historian, James Horton, provides the answer: "The way to do that is to say 'Yeah, but you know, there is something different about these people. This, this whole business of inalienable rights, ah, that's fine, but it only applies to certain people." Finally, historian George M. Fredrickson makes it clear that this intellectual volteface was not necessarily a conscious strategy but instead could have well been "the result of a number of unthinking decisions."

This whole line of reasoning is suspect, however. First, Jefferson was not the sole author of the Declaration of Independence. His role was more that of secretary of the drafting committee. Like any committee product, it reflected a compromise.

Second, the document is not legally binding. It can't be used even to beat a parking ticket (though it is astounding to hear how many people in casual conversation believe that "All men are created equal" is in the Constitution, which is the supreme law of the land, or that any law of any land could produce physical or intellectual equality rather than equality before the law). The Declaration of Independence was a piece of propaganda meant to win support for the rebellion both at home and abroad. Domestically, it was meant to convince average colonists to form the rank and file and to be led into combat by the upper class, who had a large personal stake in throwing off British rule and taxation. Internationally, it was meant to win the sympathy of the *philosophes* in their Paris salons in the hope they would help push Louis XVI into aiding the Americans against France's traditional enemy. (He did, for which he was rewarded with the guillotine, and France with a true, bloody revolution rather than a mere change of leadership.)

The third point arguing against the interpretation given in PBS's *Race* is to see what the founders said regarding the question of equality in *The Federalist Papers*, which laid the foundation for the Constitution. Written under the pseudonym "Publius" by James Madison, Alexander Hamilton, and John Jay, the essays originally appeared in a number of New York City newspapers. (Scholars have since identified the respective authors.) Unlike the *cri de couer* of the Declaration of Independence, Publius's words, by his own admission, were "reasonable and responsible"—meant only for "established men" like himself. In *Federalist* number 10, Madison, who would become the principal author of the Constitution, wrote:

> The diversity in the faculties of men, from which the rights of property originate, is not less an insuperable obstacle to a uniformity of interests. The protection of these faculties is the first object of government. From the protection of different and unequal faculties of acquiring property, the possession of different degrees and kinds of property immediately results; and from these on the sentiments and view of the respective proprietors ensues a division of the society into different interests and pursuits.

Notwithstanding the somewhat stilted eighteenth-century prose, the passage states unambiguously that individuals differ in mental ability (faculties), that these differences result in their being able to acquire different amounts of wealth (property), and that the protection of these differences in ability is government's most important job (first object). There is no fixation on equality.

The final objection to the interpretation offered by the PBS documentary that race helped explain why some people could be free while others were held in slavery is that it credits the human mind, not just the minds of the founders, with far too great a need for intellectual consistency. Why was it necessary to concoct some theory of biological racial supremacy when that "peculiar institution" could more easily be justified on some religious basis (which, as we explain later, it was), or the contradiction simply ignored? *The Federalist Papers* do not attempt to justify (or condemn) slavery. The only references are to the barbarism of the slave trade in number 42, and numbers 54 and 55 (all three by Madison), which attempt to justify the three-fifths compromise under which every five slaves would count as three for purposes of apportioning seats in the House of Representatives based on population.

## THE AMERICAN SCHOOL OF ANTHROPOLOGY AND THE DEBATE OVER SLAVERY

Another line of argument that the belief in the biological reality of race and racial differences arose as rationalizations for slavery concerns what has been called the American School of Anthropology. The principal advocates of polygenism were Samuel G. Morton, George R. Gliddon, Josiah C. Nott, and George Squier.

Samuel George Morton (born 1799) was the son of an Irish immigrant father who died when he was six, and whose mother then married a Quaker. A lifelong resident of Philadelphia, Morton became a physician and professor of anatomy. He has been described as "gentle and courteous," with an "astonishing ability to inspire loyalty among his associates," and "completely dedicated to his scientific interests." His book describing the fossils collected by the famous Lewis and Clark expedition established Morton as the founder of invertebrate paleontology in the United States, and he was also elected secretary of the Academy of Natural Sciences. For these accomplishments Morton would still be hailed as one of the major figures in American science had he not also turned to the subject of the origin of races and of race differences in brain size and intellectual ability.

Around 1820, Morton became interested in studying skulls because he could find no information on the subject while preparing for his anatomy lectures. He began accumulating skulls and received collections sent to him by his fellow scientists in the United States and around the world, often obtained at great personal risk. Eventually he amassed at the Academy of Natural Sciences what was called "the American Golgotha," the largest collection of skulls in the world. Morton began measuring their size and shape and eventually published his results in a massive tome, *Crania Americana*.

Morton's principal argument was for polygenism. If one accepted (as most people did at that time) the short biblical chronology calculated by Archbishop Usher, the Creation occurred in 4,004 BC. The oldest pictorial representations known, the Egyptian monuments and paintings (see Chapter 2), show the different races exactly as they appear now. This would mean that if the races had a common origin, all the observable racial differences were produced in a mere thousand years, but no further change took place in the much longer period that followed. This, Morton concluded, was "a physical impossibility." Rather than the races having a single origin, he arrived at what he termed "a reasonable conclusion," that an all-wise Creator had "at once" created each race for "the physical, as well as to the moral circumstances" in which they were to live.

By "moral circumstances" Morton meant what today is termed intelligence and intellectual accomplishment. Thus he believed the white race had the "highest intellectual endowments"; Mongolians (northeast Asians) were "ingenious, imitative, and highly susceptible of cultivation"; the Malays (southeast Asians), "active and ingenious" but also "predaceous"; the Americans (American Indians), "averse to cultivation, and slow in acquiring knowledge; restless, revengeful, and fond of war"; and the Ethiopians (black Africans), "joyous, flexible and indolent" but diverse in "intellectual character," some tribes constituting "the lowest grade of humanity."

Morton's derogatory characterizations of blacks should be compared against those written by Islamic scholars Mas'udi and Jahiz a thousand years earlier (see Chapter 2). Since Morton relied on information as well as crania supplied to him by others, one might best dismiss his remarks as armchair speculations, in keeping with the temper of his times but highly biased from that of the twenty-first century. The point is that Americans were not the first to apply these characterizations. It is, of course, possible that every dominant group tries to heighten the difference between itself and subordinate groups, painting itself in the best light possible while painting the others in the worst.

A more serious charge against Morton concerns his measurement of racial differences in average cranial capacity and its implications for intellectual ability. He reported that the 52 Caucasian skulls he measured had the highest average cranial capacity (87 cubic inches); his 10 Mongolians were next at 83; then 18 Malays at 81; 147 American (Indian) at 80; and finally 29 Ethiopian skulls at 78 cubic inches.

The PBS documentary states that in his measurements Morton "made systematic errors in favor of his assumptions" that whites should have "decided and unquestioned superiority over all the nations of the earth." The accusation that Morton, consciously or unconsciously, finagled his measurements gained popularity in

Stephen Jay Gould's book *The Mismeasure of Man*, and an accompanying video features an animated Gould showing how Morton could have skewed his results. A final accusation concerning Morton is that he also dabbled in the pseudoscience of phrenology (reading personality not from astrological signs but from bumps on the skull).

Three points should be made in defense of Morton's craniological work, though not his off-the-cuff descriptions. First, in the most detailed study of the American School of Anthropology, author William Stanton quoted Morton's detailed description of his measurement methodology and concluded that Morton's technique was "painstaking" and taken with "great care" to "insure accuracy." Wherever the condition of the skull made it possible, Morton measured thirteen different quantities, of which cranial capacity was only one. He then repeated each of the thirteen.

Still, it is possible that Stanton was awed by Morton's prose and failed to consider the possibility of unconscious bias. The obvious way to resolve the issue would be to measure the skulls in Morton's collection. This has, in fact, been done. The results show that any errors were Gould's, not Morton's; Gould, though made aware, simply ignored them in his second edition. Newer evidence, with larger samples and more standardized techniques, should also be considered. The most extensive study of race differences in cranial capacity to date measured 20,000 skulls from around the world and reported East Asians, Europeans, and Africans had average cranial volumes of 1,415, 1,362, and 1,268 cubic centimeters, respectively. East Asians and Europeans (Morton's Mongolians and Caucasians) have swapped places, with Asians now slightly on top, but the average cranial capacity of Africans remains significantly below them. Other methods, such as magnetic resonance imaging (MRI), have produced the same results. Of course, what average racial differences in cranial capacity may reveal about racial differences in intellectual ability as measured by IQ tests is another question.

The final accusation against Morton's *Crania Americana* is that it is based on the pseudoscience of phrenology. This charge is totally unjustified. Morton himself wrote nothing about phrenology, a subject that was still open to debate at that time. He did, however, allow the well-known phrenologist George Combe to contribute an essay on the subject. All measurements and all interpretations for that chapter were by Combe, not Morton. Combe wanted it to appear at the front of the book, but Morton refused, insisting it could appear only at the back. Anders Retzius, who developed the cephalic index (the ratio of the width of the head to its length), wrote that Morton's *Crania Americana* was "the strongest argument" against phrenology.

Even before publication of *Crania Americana*, Morton had been corresponding with the next member of the American School of Anthropology, George R. Gliddon, the U.S. vice-consul to Egypt. Born in England in 1809, Gliddon had a temperament closer to P. T. Barnum's than to Samuel Morton's. A classic bipolar personality, his disposition swung from that of "a name-dropper, a sponger, a swinger on the shirttails of the great, a braggart, pretender, and scatologist" to being "courageous, generous, warmhearted and loyal." When Gliddon came to America, he toured the country, giving lectures to accompany his traveling road show of Egyptian antiquities and crania. His driving passion lay in baiting Bible believers, not belittling blacks. Pointing out that Usher's dating of the Creation was contradicted by the age of the Egyptian civilization, he told his audience, "The charge of heresy cannot destroy hieroglyphic facts." Usher's chronology, and the biblical exegesis on which it was based, had to be abandoned.

Gliddon also presented Morton with twenty embalmed Egyptian heads. The racial differences were just as clear in the oldest specimens then available as in Morton's contemporary collection. The Caucasian crania had the highest cranial capacity, mulattoes intermediate, and pure Negroid types the lowest. The results were published by Morton in *Crania Aegyptica* (1844). He noted that slavery was "among the earliest of the social institutions of Egypt" and that the social position of blacks was the same as that in the nineteenth century, that of servants and slaves, but he also pointed out that slavery was imposed on "all conquered nations, white as well as black."

The third member of the American School of Anthropology was Josiah C. Nott of Mobile, Alabama, also a physician. Walter Reed credited Nott with being the first to suggest that yellow fever was spread by an intermediate host such as mosquitoes, noting that the incidence of the disease subsided with first frost. Like Voltaire, Nott pointed derisively to the contradictions of the Genesis account and noted what Egyptology had revealed about the antiquity of human races. Nott also offered a reply to the strongest argument advanced for monogenesis—that members of all the races could interbreed and produce fertile offspring—by pointing to crosses of male goats with ewes and goldfinches with canaries.

The final member of the American School was Ephraim George Squier (born 1821). After working for various newspapers, he accepted an editorial position in Chillicothe, Ohio, over one in Baltimore because, as he wrote his parents, "I will not live where there are slaves." Once in the Buckeye State, Squier became interested in the large, rounded earthworks, known as "the mounds," found throughout the countryside. He later wrote Morton, as everyone then interested in the subject did, asking if he would compare those he unearthed from the mounds with crania from Mexico and Central and South America.

Squier's book, *Ancient Monuments of the Mississippi Valley*, would eventually appear in 1848 as the first volume of the Smithsonian Museum's Contributions to Knowledge series. Despite claims that the Mound Builders were the lost tribes, Tartars, or some other nonindigenous race, Morton's measurements showed that the

Mound Builders were indeed American Indians. Further, Morton concluded from his cranial analysis that the American Indians of North, Central, and South America all belonged to one race, so the same differences in climate that monogenists offered as the causal mechanism for racial differences in the Old World apparently didn't work in the New. (This issue also becomes relevant in our discussion of racial differences and the development of the molecular clock in Chapter 5.)

Squier's excavations and Morton's analysis of the crania joined that of Gliddon on the Egyptians in establishing that the civilizations and the differences between the races who built them were ancient. If the Caucasian, Negro, and American Indian races had not changed in over 4,000 years, either the biblical chronology was far too short to account for the racial differences, or the races were created separately, or something far more than linguistic division took place with the fall of the Tower of Babel, though the Good Book tells nothing about it. Either that, or Phillippus Aureolus Theophrastus Bombast von Hohenheim was centuries ahead of his time when he claimed that Genesis was written "according to the faith, for the weaker brethren."

The polygenists of the American School of Anthropology argued that there was insufficient time in which to produce the observed racial differences. On the other side, the monogenists staked their case on the fact that all humans can, and quite readily do, mate and produce fertile offspring, despite their observable physical differences; this implies that all humans are of a single kind, deriving from a single origin. Neither side had a specific mechanism to account for the differences, as the debate raged before Darwin had supplied the answer, natural selection, in *Origin of Species* (as did Alfred Russell Wallace).

Charles Lyell, whose *Principles of Geology* sounded the death knell for the short biblical chronology and greatly influenced the development of Darwin's thinking before he wrote *Origin*, cogently noted that the support for monogenesis was increased by "every investigation which forces us to expand the duration of time past." Even after Darwinian evolution became established as the basis of the biological sciences, the size of racial differences, on the one hand, versus the ability of all members of all races to produce fertile offspring, on the other, would remain anthropology's overriding and most divisive issue for more than 100 years. Until there was an accurate clock with which to measure evolutionary change, however, the issue would remain no more than a debate, though a scientific rather than a theological one. The development of the molecular clock (see Chapter 4) at last provided hard numbers against which the origin of racial differences could then be computed (see Chapter 5).

But Lyell was on to something, something even more significant than he (or anyone) could have realized at the time. Dispensing with the ridiculously short chronology that Paracelsus correctly noted was "written according to the faith, for the weaker brethren," and replacing it with one grounded in the hard sciences of geology and biology, an enigma would still remain. The shorter the time allowed for the origin of racial differences, the more Darwin's mechanism of natural selection would have to do to produce them.

## POLYGENISM AND
## THE ISSUE OF SLAVERY

What part did the anthropologists of the American School play in the debate over slavery? Were they sympathetic to that issue? Did polygenism provide the South with a scientific basis for its "peculiar institution"? Did the abolitionists feel obliged to reject polygenism because it seemed to provide aid and comfort for slavery?

The most extensive analysis of the American School of Anthropology has shown that it actually had little effect on nineteenth-

century America's most divisive issue. For the North and for all opponents of slavery, the issue was one of morality, not science. Uni-
tarians found a certain sympathy with any opponents of bibliolatry,
but that could not outweigh what they felt were the demands of
conscience.

Nor did the South embrace polygenism as a scientific defense
for keeping blacks in servitude. Southerners relied instead upon
tradition and religion. It was easy enough to use the curse laid on
Ham to explain the inferiority (in their view) of black Africans,
or to cite St. Paul's request that the slave Onesimus be returned as
support for the fugitive-slave law. There was no need to measure
skulls or examine ancient buildings, especially if they called into
question the chronology of Genesis.

In 1854 the editor of the secessionist Richmond (Virginia) *En-
quirer* considered the question of whether polygenism provided a
scientific foundation for slavery. He concluded that it could not,
because the price of accepting the doctrines of infidels like Gliddon and Nott was abandoning the Bible. The Scriptures, he
wrote, were "the grand object of attack from the Abolitionists." If
you destroy the Bible, he went on, "you lay bare the very citadel
of our strength." Historian William Stanton concluded in his in-
depth study of the American School that "the South turned its
back on the only intellectually respectable defense of slavery it
could have taken up."

And what of Morton, Gliddon, Nott, and Squier? Morton
showed no interest in any political implications of his work, and
Gliddon denied any. Only Nott, the Alabamian, used the research of the polygenists to support a political cause. Squier, who
early in his professional life had written his parents that he refused to work in Baltimore because it permitted slavery, may have
spoken most truthfully, not only for himself but for many in the
North, including a number of abolitionists. With the Civil War
at hand, he wrote his parents again, this time saying he had "a

precious poor opinion of niggers, or any of the darker races," but he had "a still poorer one of slavery."

Nor did the monogenists necessarily hold a higher opinion of people of color. If the environment produced racial differences, many believed it produced a degradation—in the darker races, of course, as whites were the people doing the writing. If the races (or individuals) were created equal, that did not mean they remained equal. Any change in the ability and status of blacks, if possible, may have required an indeterminable amount of time. Jefferson's self-evident truth meant only that all men were born equally men.

William T. Hamilton may have come as close as any monogenist in arguing for not only the unity but also the equality of all mankind in an abolitionist sermon he preached before the American Colonization Society (which repatriated freed slaves to the African nation of Liberia). In *The Friend of Moses*, a defense of the Genesis account against polygenist skeptics, he wrote that he had been unable to find "in comparison with the white man, any essential inferiority of intellect native to the negro." But he did not invoke monogenism to support emancipation in that book. In fact, he made no mention of slavery at all.

Historian John S. Haller Jr. concluded his analysis by summarizing the debate between the monogenists and the polygenists and its implications for the slavery issue that divided the country by noting: "Almost the whole of scientific thought in both America and Europe in the decades before Darwin accepted race inferiority, irrespective of whether the races sprang from a single original pair or were created separately. Whether for or against slavery, anthropologists could not escape the inference of race subordination."

## THE IMPACT OF DARWIN

In *Origin of Species* (1859), *The Descent of Man* (1871), and *The Expression of the Emotions in Man and Animals* (1872), Charles

Darwin changed forever the way people look at themselves. Rather than "made in the image and likeness of God," Darwin argued, man shared a common origin with other creatures and had evolved from the apes. The explanation for human nature and human differences, both between individuals and groups, was therefore to be found by studying what man shared with other species.

Key to Darwin's theory of evolution by natural selection was the underlying variation within the species. Nonetheless, the *Origin* subtitle, *The Preservation of Favored Races in the Struggle for Life*, is much less frequently cited today. In *The Descent of Man*, the sage of Down House made his position clear: "It is not my intention here to describe the several so-called races of men; but I am about to inquire *what is the value of the differences between them under a classificatory point of view and how they have originated"* (emphasis added).

In 1859, the same year as the publication of Darwin's *Origin*, Paul Broca, best known for discovering the special role played by the frontal area of the dominant side of the brain in speech, founded the Anthropological Society of Paris. This was followed by the founding of the Anthropological Society of London in 1863, the Berlin Society for Anthropology, Ethnology, and Prehistory in 1869, the Anthropological Society of Vienna in 1870, and the American Anthropological Association and the American Association of Physical Anthropologists in 1921.

Between 1859 and 1945, the evolutionary perspective was the central principle of anthropology. It required the combination of Darwin's theory of evolution by natural selection with Mendel's laws of inheritance, in what is often called the synthetic theory of evolution, to provide a coherent theory for the study of human origins and variation. This occurred in biology between 1936 and 1947 in the work of Theodosius Dobzhansky, Sir Julian Huxley, Ernst Mayr, George Gaylord Simpson, Bernhard Rensch, and G. Ledyard Stebbins. With World War II intervening, however, the synthetic theory did not penetrate anthropological thinking until the 1950s, which we discuss later in the chapter.

## CHARLES DARWIN'S
## SMARTER YOUNGER COUSIN

One of the first to seize on the implications of human variation was Darwin's younger cousin, Sir Francis Galton (1822–1911). Dubbed "a Victorian genius," Galton authored over 300 publications, founded differential psychology (the scientific study of human differences), developed the first weather maps, pioneered the use of fingerprints as a means of identification, originated the twin method of genetic analysis and the use of correlational statistics, invented a myriad of devices for scientific measurement, and explored then little-known Southwest Africa (now Namibia).

Galton used Shakespeare's "alliterative antithesis" in the titles of his book *English Men of Science: Their Nature and Nurture* (1874) and his article in *Fraser's Magazine*, "The History of Twins, as a Criterion of the Relative Powers of Nature and Nurture" (1875). He wrote that the "nature and nurture" phrase "provides a convenient jingle of words, for it separates under two distinct heads the innumerable elements of which personality is composed. Nature is all that a man brings with him into the world; nurture is every influence from without that affects him after birth."

Galton believed his research had strong implications for education, criminology, economics, medicine, and many other aspects of life. He was particularly concerned that the more intelligent and those with stronger moral character had begun to have fewer children than those less gifted. (Interestingly, his own long marriage produced no offspring.) He therefore coined the word and inaugurated the science of "eugenics," derived from the Greek *eugenes*, for "good in stock, hereditarily endowed with noble qualities." Galton described two types of policies: Positive eugenic programs would give financial support to those deemed to be more intelligent to encourage them to have children. Negative eugenics aimed to reduce the fertility of those with severe intellectual, health, or character problems; to put it bluntly, to sterilize them.

In 1908 (three years before his death), while reflecting on his life and work, Galton wrote: "Man is gifted with pity and other kindly feelings; he has also the power of preventing many kinds of suffering. I conceive it to fall well within his province to replace Natural Selection by other processes that are more merciful and not less effective. This is precisely the aim of Eugenics."

Galton also believed that there were race differences in intelligence. He estimated them by counting the number of eminent individuals they produced. His method was based on the statistical properties of the bell curve. A race that produced a high proportion of highly gifted individuals had a high level of intelligence. Using this method, which certainly has its problems, Galton constructed a sixteen-category scale of intellectual ability, ranging from the mentally retarded to genius. He estimated that sub-Saharan Africans scored two categories below the English, and Australian aborigines one category below Africans. Each category corresponds to approximately ten IQ points on a standard intelligence test. So, if the English were allocated an average IQ of 100, sub-Saharan Africans would have a mean IQ of about 80 and Australian aborigines about 70.

Some of the problems with Galton's method are obvious: How accurate were his counts of eminent men? Does eminence mean the same thing in different cultures? Do all cultures even promote eminence as opposed to equality? In fairness to Galton, his method reveals average differences and considerable overlap between races. In this respect, it was more modern than the typological race theories of the early anthropologists. And for whatever it is worth, Galton's estimates of mean racial differences are not inconsistent with the results obtained with modern IQ tests. Nor was he out to prove that his fellow Victorian Englishmen were the pinnacle of evolution. Rather, he concluded the Athenians of the fifth century BC achieved the highest intelligence rating, two full grades above his contemporary countrymen (which equates to an average IQ of 120). He wrote:

> This estimate, which may seem prodigious to some, is confirmed by the quick intelligence and high culture of the Athenian commonality, before whom literary works were recited, and works of art exhibited, of a far more severe character than could possibly be appreciated by the average of our race, the calibre of whose intellect is easily gained by a glance at the contents of a railway bookstall.

One can only imagine what Galton might have thought of today's tabloid TV, dumbed-down textbooks, and sound-bite political campaigns. A good guess comes from his less than flattering description of contemporary Americans: "Enterprising, defiant and touchy; impatient of authority; furious politicians; very tolerant of fraud and violence; possessing much high and generous spirit, and some true religious feeling, but strongly addicted to cant."

## MONISM: EIN VOLK, EIN REICH, EINE PHILOSOPHIE

Darwinism in Britain, whether in the early days or today, has focused on individuals, with groups emerging from them. British evolutionism has always had the shopkeeper's sober obsession with keeping a good set of books. In Germany, however, Darwinism took on a collectivist, romantic tone. There the great apostle of Darwin, Ernst Haeckel (1834–1913), imbued the theory of natural selection with the spirit of German Romanticism. The latter is hard to define but easy to experience—just study some paintings by Caspar David Friedrich while listening to a Wagner opera.

Haeckel and all he came to champion were opposed by his former professor, the distinguished biologist Rudolf Virchow (1821–1902). The conflict between them was both personal and political. The two men were polar opposites in appearance, ancestry, and temperament. Haeckel was tall, blond, German in name and appearance, with a strong love of the out-of-doors, and a generalist looking for one grand theory to account for everything. Virchow, whose name and appearance betrayed a Slavic ancestry, was a detail man and a pedantic laboratory taskmaster. Haeckel was charismatic and developed a huge, almost religious following; Virchow was respected, even feared, but rarely liked. Haeckel was a strong supporter of the German Volk and Reich; Virchow was a radical advocate of social reform who fought at the barricades in the revolution of 1848. Virchow was a member of the German Progressive Party and opposed Bismarck's policies. The Iron Chancellor, having already dispatched or intimidated earlier opponents with saber or pistol, challenged the professor to a duel. Virchow declined—unless they agreed to fight with scalpels.

In 1860, Haeckel translated Darwin's *Origin* into German. His own masterwork, *Die Welträthsel* (The Riddle of the Universe), used natural selection as the master key to explain all existence, from inanimate objects through a progression of animals to human races. It was translated into twenty-five languages and sold over 100,000 copies in the first year alone and eventually over half a million in Germany alone. Haeckel later termed the book's doctrine "monism." It was proeugenic, Nordicist, nationalist, secularist, and hierarchical. In 1906 he founded the German Monist League to further the political application of its principles. According to historian Daniel Gasman, Haeckel's monism was a direct precursor to National Socialist and Fascist ideology. In fairness it should be noted, however, that many monists were liberals, drawn to the philosophy by its anticlerical aspects, and that the league "disbanded in 1933 rather than become 'coordinated' into the Nazi state."

Between 1863 and Virchow's death in 1902, Haeckel and his former professor clashed at scientific conferences and in print. Haeckel's evolutionism was progressive, moving from lower to higher forms. Without any physical evidence, Haeckel went out on a limb and predicted fossil hunters would soon discover a creature he dubbed *Pithecanthropus*, the ape-man or missing link. Inspired by Haeckel's prediction, one of his disciples, Eugène Dubois, found the fossil he termed *Pithecanthropus erectus* (now classified as *Homo erectus*) in Java in 1891. For Virchow this finding entailed pointless speculation. He rejected the fossils, saying they were the result of pathological degeneration. As his repugnance grew at what he saw as the associations and implications of monism, Virchow came to reject evolution altogether. Any change in individuals or species that could be observed rather than hypothesized, he argued, was evidence of degeneration, not progress.

When Haeckel died in 1913, monism had taken firm root in German soil. In the view of anthropologist Pat Shipman, "Between them, Virchow and Haeckel defeated empirical science in Germany altogether. By using science as the weapon of political reform, the one [Virchow] was led to deny the existence of evolution apparent to his eyes and the other [Haeckel] to mutate, expand, and wrench Darwin's poor theory out of all recognition." Indeed, the Haeckel-Virchow dispute would not be the last time an in-group—out-group clash lurked beneath the surface of the anthropology wars.

## AND THEN ALONG CAME BOAS: GOOD-BYE RACE, HELLO CULTURE!

When Galton died in 1911, eugenics was widely accepted not only in Britain and Germany but in the United States as well. Raymond Pearl, professor of biology at Johns Hopkins University (then a supporter of eugenics but later an opponent), noted that by 1912, "eugenics was catching on to an extraordinary degree with radical and conservative alike." Enthusiasts included literary giants H. G. Wells, George Bernard Shaw, and H. L. Mencken; crusaders for reproductive rights and sexual freedom Margaret Sanger and Havelock Ellis; scientists Harold Laski, J.B.S. Haldane, Alexander Graham Bell, and Luther Burbank; conservationist Gifford Pinchot; Winston Churchill (one of the English vice presidents of the First International Congress for Eugenics held in London in 1912); socialist organizer Emma Goldman; Stanford University president David Starr Jordan; and American Museum of Natural History president Henry Fairfield Osborn. In 1918, Osborn joined biologist Charles Davenport and Madison Grant in founding the Galton Society for "the promotion of study of racial anthropology, and of the origin, migration, physical and mental characters, crossing and evolution of human races, living and extinct."

In 1927, Supreme Court Justice Oliver Wendell Holmes, arguably America's most brilliant jurist and by no means a conservative icon, supported state-mandated sterilization of the mentally retarded in *Buck v. Bell*. Writing for an 8-1 majority that included noted civil libertarian Louis Brandeis, Justice Holmes penned the immortal line "three generations of imbeciles are enough." *Buck v. Bell* has never been overturned by any subsequent Supreme Court decision, though the issue appeared before the court again in 1942 in *Skinner v. Oklahoma*. It was even cited by Justice Thurgood Marshall, as liberal a justice as ever to sit on the high bench, as "the initial decision," then reaffirmed by the famous *Roe v. Wade* abortion decision, that the Constitution provided no special protection for procreation.

At the start of the twentieth century, most American anthropologists came from wealthy Brahmin families and were educated at Harvard University. They were solidly in the eugenics camp, agreeing with Galton on both individual and race differences. And then, as one author put it, *Along Came Boas*. His name is hardly a household word, but it is no exaggeration to say that Franz Boas (1858–1942) remade American anthropology in his own image. Through the works of his students Margaret Mead (*Coming of Age in Samoa* and *Sex and Temperament in Three Societies*), Ruth Benedict (*Patterns of Culture*), and Ashley Montagu (innumerable titles, especially the countless editions of *Man's Most Dangerous Myth*), Boas would have more effect on American intellectual thought than Darwin did. For generations, hardly anyone graduated from an American college or university without having read at least one of these books. They all drew their inspiration from Boas's *The Mind of Primitive Man*.

Franz Boas came from a German Jewish home, steeped in the "sentiment of the barricades" of the 1848 revolutions that swept across Europe. He originally obtained his doctorate in physics but later turned to geography. After fieldwork with the Greenland Eskimos, he took up anthropology—Virchow's brand, not Haeckel's. Virchow, in the words of one biographer, "had perhaps the greatest influence on Boas."

Although not religious, Boas was highly sensitive to anti-Semitism. His admiration for Virchow did not prevent him from fighting duels, including one that arose from an anti-Jewish slur. Repulsed by the rising tide of anti-Semitism in Bismarck's unified Germany, Boas left the fatherland he no longer felt to be his own and went to America.

Appointed chairman of the department at Columbia University in 1899, Boas transformed anthropology from the leisure study of a few well-to-do WASPs into a highly credentialed discipline that pumped out Ph.D.'s. By 1915 his students had a two-thirds controlling majority on the executive board of the American Anthropological Association. In 1919, Boas could boast that "most of the anthropological work done at the present time in the United States" came from his former students at Columbia. By 1926 they headed every major department of anthropology in America.

Before Boas, anthropology was the study of race. After Boas, anthropology in America became the study of culture, defined as "personality writ large," that is, "how a given temperamental approach to living could come so to dominate . . . that all who were born in it would become the willing or unwilling heirs to that view of the world." In *Sex and Temperament in Three Primitive Societies*, Margaret Mead described how very different sex roles were among the Arapesh, the Mugdugumor, and the Tchambuli, three peoples that lived within 100 miles of each other on New Guinea. She concluded that "many, if not all, of the personality traits which we have called masculine or feminine are as lightly linked to sex as are clothing, the manners, and the form of head-dress that a society at a given point assigns to either sex." Ruth Benedict's *Patterns of Culture* contrasted what she dubbed the "Apollonian" (sober, egalitarian, and cooperative) Zuni Indians of New Mexico with the "Dionysian" (excessively emotional, individualistic, and megalomaniacal) Kwakiutl of British Columbia and the "paranoid" (intensely jealous, suspicious, and resentful) Dobuans of New Guinea. These differences were cultural because "the biological bases of behavior in mankind are for the most part irrelevant." As "Papa Franz" (as his students called him) had written in the foreword to Mead's *Coming of Age in Samoa*, "much of what we ascribe to human nature is no more than a reaction to the restraints put upon us by our civilisation." (Subsequently, critics challenged not only the conclusions of Mead and Benedict but also the reliability of the data upon which they were based.) In innumerable editions of *Man's Most Dangerous Myth: The Fallacy of Race*, Ashley Montagu waged a campaign to replace the term "race" with "ethnic group," arguing that human biological differences were minimal. Culture was what made groups different in all but the simplest physical features.

Historian Carl Degler emphasized the essential role Boas played in decoupling social sciences from biology: "Boas's influence upon American social scientists in matters of race can hardly be exaggerated." Boas engaged in a "life-long assault on the idea that race was a primary source of the differences to be found in the mental or social capabilities of human groups. He accomplished his mission largely through his ceaseless, almost relentless articulation of the concept of culture."

Like his mentor Virchow, Boas was skeptical of evolutionary explanations, genetic or cultural. He even entertained a sympathy for Lamarckism. What turned him into the godfather of cultural determinism in America, however, was the growing popular appeal and political power of the eugenics and anti-immigration movements. Standardized intelligence tests had recently been developed and administered to military recruits in World War I. Armed with results that showed large race differences in IQ, books like Madison Grant's *The Passing of the Great Race* argued that the survival of America depended on limiting immigration to those of northwestern European descent; southern and eastern Europeans, and especially Jews, need not apply.

Franz Boas was a dark-haired Jewish immigrant from a leftist milieu, educated at German universities steeped in the ideals of the Enlightenment. Madison Grant, an archetypal Nordic, was a lawyer turned amateur biologist and a pillar of America's WASP establishment. Grant claimed that his fellow American Nordics were committing racial suicide, allowing themselves to be "elbowed out" of their own land by ruthless, self-interested Jewish immigrants, who were behind the campaign to discredit racial research. Yogi Berra's words would have been apt: "It was déjà vu all

over again." Haeckel's monism had driven Virchow from skepticism into rejecting biological evolution. Nativist, proeugenic,
elitist tracts such as Grant's drove Boas from skepticism into rejecting the evolutionary perspective on culture and even linguistics (which he had earlier advocated).

In his book *In Search of Human Nature* (1991), which is subtitled *The Decline and Revival of Darwinism in American Social
Thought*, Degler concluded that Boas's substitution of cultural for
genetic determinism was not the result of

> a disinterested, scientific inquiry into a vexed if controversial ques-
> tion. Instead, his idea derived from an ideological commitment
> that began in his early life and academic experiences in Europe
> and continued in America to shape his professional outlook. To as-
> sert that point is not to say that he fudged or manufactured his evi-
> dence against the racial interpretation—for there is no sign of that.
> But, by the same token, there is no doubt that he had a deep inter-
> est in collecting evidence and designing arguments that would
> rebut or refute an ideological outlook—racism—which he consid-
> ered restrictive upon individuals and undesirable for society.

Although the Boasians considered the views of the eugenicists
and evolutionists to be value-laden (which is true), the works of
Mead, Benedict, and the others were hardly value-neutral. Rather,
what lurked below the surface were moral indictments of contemporary Western society, especially its sexual mores.

The Boasians were outsiders. Papa Franz and many of his students were Jews, though "the preponderance of Jewish intellectu-
als in the early years of Boasian anthropology and the Jewish
identities of anthropologists in subsequent generations has been
downplayed in standard histories of the discipline." Some, like
Boas himself, were immigrants to boot. Montagu was born Israel

Ehrenberg in the working-class East End district of London, England. He was so leery of anti-Semitism ("If you're brought up as a Jew, you know that all non-Jews are anti-Semitic . . . It's a good working hypothesis") that he reinvented himself as Montague Francis Ashley-Montagu from London's well-to-do West End financial district, complete with a posh public school accent. When he came to the United States, Montagu played the role of the British headmaster, lecturing American audiences before a receptive media on the foolishness of their prejudices. Later he dropped the hyphen and became simply Ashley Montagu.

Mead and Benedict could point to WASP pedigrees as pure as Madison Grant's, but Mead was bisexual and Benedict a lesbian. At that time, those sexual orientations were far more stigmatized than they are today. Their sexual preferences are relevant, because developing a critique of traditional American values was as much a part of the Boasian program in anthropology as was their attack on eugenics and nativism. In this, Mead's *Coming of Age in Samoa* and *Sex and Temperament in Three Societies* succeeded to a degree neither she nor Boas could have imagined at the time. As required reading in college and university social science courses, the books laid the groundwork for the view that society, neither God nor evolution but society, created sex differences and sex roles.

Whatever their individual origin, the Boasians felt deeply estranged from mainstream American society and the male WASP elites they were displacing in anthropology. Gene Weltfish, another student of Boas, epitomized this sense of alienation when she said she felt that her generation had only three choices—go live in Paris, sell *The Daily Worker* (the U.S. Communist Party newspaper) on street corners, or study anthropology at Columbia.

The Boasians shared an out-group sensibility, a commitment to a common viewpoint and a program to dominate the institutional structure of anthropology. Through it they successfully dethroned "the moral and political monopoly of an elite which had justified its rule with the claim that their superior virtue was the outcome of the evolutionary process." The cultural determinism of the Boasians served as a corrective to the genetic determinism of racial anthropology, emphasizing the variation within races, the overlap between them, and the plasticity of human behavior. The price, however, was divorcing the science of man from the science of life in general. The evolutionary perspective was abandoned, and anthropology began its slide into the abyss of deconstructionism.

According to Degler, "Boas almost single-handedly developed in America the concept of culture, which, like a powerful solvent, would in time expunge race from the literature of social science." In fact, Boas achieved his goal only with help, including a great deal from a most unwelcome source—Hitler and the Holocaust. After World War II, "race" and "eugenics" became very dirty words. The University of London's Department of Eugenics changed its name to the Department of Genetics; the Eugenics Society became the Galton Institute; the *Annals of Eugenics* was renamed the *Annals of Human Genetics*; and *Eugenics Quarterly* became *Social Biology*. In 1949 the United Nations Educational, Social, and Cultural Organization (UNESCO) was called upon to adopt "a program of disseminating scientific facts designed to remove what is generally known as racial prejudice." For the drafter of the first UNESCO statement, Ashley Montagu, this was an opportunity to deny the reality of race.

## ASHLEY MONTAGU
## VERSUS CARLETON COON

The preliminary match in anthropology's fight over race was Virchow versus Haeckel. Then there was Boas versus Madison Grant.

The final match in anthropology's dispute went the distance. It was almost as lengthy as the names of its participants—Montague Francis Ashley-Montagu versus Carleton Stevens Coon.

Again there was a personal element to the clash. Coon was from a New England family that could trace its roots to colonial times and before that to Cornwall, ancestral home of the legendary King Arthur. Coon was quite proud of his ancestry. Those sympathetic to Coon believed his personal dislike of Montagu was because he thought everyone else should dislike him as well. Why the need to pass oneself off as something one is not? Montagu, as already noted, had his "good working hypothesis" about non-Jews and anti-Semitism.

Coon, with his Harvard B.A. and Ph.D., has been likened to Lawrence of Arabia and Indiana Jones. He conducted extensive fieldwork in Albania, Arabia, Ethiopia, Afghanistan, and North Africa, all of which at that time were quite hard to access. He served as an undercover agent with the OSS (predecessor to the CIA) during World War II and was even accused of having a part in the assassination of Admiral Darlan, the Vichy French commander in North Africa.

Coon believed that race was a central issue and his job as an anthropologist was to study race; Montagu felt his was to banish race to the periphery and replace it with the concept of "ethnic group." He began his effort to have the word "race" replaced by "ethnic group" in his 1942 book, *Man's Most Dangerous Myth: The Fallacy of Race*. When he was selected to draft the initial (1950) UNESCO Statement on Race, Montagu was given a platform from which to present his view to a much larger, nonacademic audience.

The UNESCO statement was subsequently revised in response to criticisms that it went too far in Montagu's direction. There was almost unanimous agreement with the points stating that all humans belonged to a single species, though German medical geneticist Fritz Lenz (whose reputation had been tarnished by his association with the Third Reich) disagreed, as did British geneticist R. Ruggles Gates.

The truly contentious question, and one that would not go away, was whether the mental ability of all ethnic groups (or races) was the same. Some pointed to the IQ test data showing average group differences, and the renowned quantitative geneticist R. A. Fisher argued that this implied there was some genetic factor involved. German anthropologist Hans Weinert even went so far as to ask a variation on a familiar question: Which of the signers was prepared to have his daughter marry an Australian aborigine?

Montagu also presented his argument for replacing "race" with "ethnic group" at a 1950 symposium, Quantitative Biology on the Origin and Evolution of Man. Evolutionary biologist Ernst Mayr provided the most cogent response when he pointed out that having a proper concept of race was far more important than terminology. The typological conception, in which every individual could be placed in a specific racial pigeonhole, had to be replaced by a statistical one that examined populations.

Early anthropology was just that—an exercise in typology. Race was considered to be the primary, Platonic essence, or type; culture (tools, pottery, and customs), language, and sometimes mental traits were regarded as the manifestations of each type. With this approach, anthropologists were able to gather vast amounts of data and neatly catalog the results. However, it lacked both an empirically testable theory of race and a method of validating its results. Without these tools, early anthropology relied upon speculations about migrations, conquests, hybridization between races, and degeneration to describe its alternative to the biblical account of human origins. This was the predominant view when Coon published his 1939 book, *The Races of Europe*.

Attempts to fit the various racial-classification schemes to the synthetic theory proved forced, if not impossible. One problem was that most anthropometric traits (e.g., head shape) depend on a number of genes. Although clearly inherited, head shape does not follow the rules of simple Mendelian inheritance. Further, early genetic theory assumed that the anthropometric traits, no matter how many genes each one depended on, were inherited independently. Given that premise, why spend so much time taking all those different measurements of skulls? Increasingly, it was argued that a much cleaner picture could be obtained by examining single gene traits such as blood type, for which the mode of inheritance was known. Later, the underlying DNA fingerprints would provide an even more precise measure of human variation. From the 1940s on, many voices increasingly questioned the utility, and eventually the reality, of the concept of race. In the vanguard of this movement was Ashley Montagu.

The most important of Coon's books for this discussion is *The Origin of Races*. When it came out in 1962, we were either in the anthropology department at the University of California–Berkeley (Sarich) or high school in New Jersey (Miele) and became intrigued with the subject. *The Origin of Races* was praised by some but damned by others. What made the book and its author the center of a raging controversy was that Carleton Putnam, a former president of Delta Airlines, used it in support of his campaign against the U.S. Supreme Court's *Brown v. Board of Education* decision. Putnam's book, *Race and Reason*, was denounced as a work of racist pseudoscience by many in anthropology, but the times were different then, and it was actually endorsed by the American Bar Association, an indication that the turnover in the ABA was slower than in anthropology. Coon and Putnam shared a distant relative back in colonial days, General Israel Putnam, and Coon's brother was named Maurice Putnam Coon. The timing suggested to some that Putnam had advance notice of Coon's *Origin of Races*. Some even suspected Carleton Putnam was Coon's pseudonym. Once again, political events became interlocked with the debate about race.

Coon was elected to a two-year term as president of the American Association of Physical Anthropologists (AAPA) in 1961. He replaced his friend, W. Montague Cobb, an African American from Howard University who would later become the first black president of the NAACP. Largely in response to works like Putnam's, a resolution was proposed that the AAPA declare that there were no race differences in intelligence. Cobb agreed with Coon that the honest scientific position was agnosticism and so no vote should be taken.

In his autobiography, *Adventures and Discoveries*, Coon explained how younger members wanted a special meeting at the 1961 AAPA convention, supposedly to discuss new business but in fact to censure Putnam's book. In Coon's view, "This of course was the usual trick that minorities used to get their way." The word "minorities" is ambiguous, allowing as many interpretations as interpreters. Since there were only two black members of AAPA at that time, Coon could not have been referring to them. The passage does fit the way a small number of dedicated hard-core extremists were taking control of organizations and fits with Coon's comments on the affair. Given Ashley Montagu's rule of thumb, however, many might suspect that Coon was really referring to Jews.

For his part, Coon fell back on his OSS training and instructed the maintenance crew to cut the electricity in the conference hall when he raised his hand so that "the conspirators would stumble out in confusion." According to Coon's account, he never gave the signal because the room contained not only the young agitators he expected but many of his old friends.

It turned out that the resolution condemning Putnam was not proposed by a young agitator unknown to Coon but by Stanley Garn, Coon's student and coauthor of *Races*. (This would not be the last time Coon would be somewhat naive about how his colleagues would react to the race issue and his books on the subject.) Coon asked for a show of hands on how many attendees present had read the book they were about to censure. Only one. Then he asked how many had even heard about it before the session. Only a few. Nonetheless, the resolution condemning *Race and Reason* passed.

In Coon's words, "The Communists did not need to fight us. They could rot us from within. I could see it all as in a horrid dream." (Remember, this was 1961 when both the Cold War and the civil rights movement were at their peaks.) He refused to have his name appear on the resolution as president of AAPA and resigned. The next day he fell into what he described as a "partial coma" but still managed to pack and leave. He also took a terminal sabbatical from the University of Pennsylvania and began working on the page proofs of what he believed would be his crowning achievement, *The Origin of Races*. Coon again showed a strange naïveté for a person so widely traveled and experienced.

*The Origin of Races* offered a definitive statement of the polygenic view. Coon argued that human fossils could be assigned not only a date but also a race (which correlated to a large degree with geographic location) and an evolutionary grade (how far the race had advanced toward becoming thoroughly modern humans, which he defined largely in terms of cranial capacity). Coon identified five major races, which he termed the Caucasoid (Europeans), the Mongoloid (Asians), the Congoid (usually called Negroid or Africans), the Capoid (the Bushmen of South Africa, whose physical features, both to anthropologists and themselves, more closely resemble those of neighboring black Africans), and

Australoids (Australian aborigines and the peoples of New Guinea and the surrounding islands). Each race had ascended the ladder of human evolution at different rates. Caucasoids and Mongoloids had reached the *Homo sapiens* goal line earliest; Congoids, Capoids, and Australoids only later.

All of this was welcome news to Carleton Putnam. Had *The Origin of Races* appeared before the civil rights movement and the reaction against it had gotten into high gear, the book might have elicited only an academic debate, if a heated one. But given the times, it produced a furor in which the book was denounced by Montagu, geneticist Theodosius Dobzhansky, anthropologist Sherwood Washburn, and many others. In his 1962 presidential address to the American Anthropological Association, Washburn said that the subject matter of physical anthropology became more and more "the things that have caused the evolution of all mankind, not races . . . which are minor." Coon's theory of the "great antiquity of human races," Washburn told his audience, was "supported neither by the record nor by evolutionary theory." (This wording appears in the written transcript published in *American Anthropologist*. According to those who attended, Washburn in his remarks ripped into Coon far more harshly.)

The AAPA had never accepted Coon's resignation, and he had prepared a response to deliver in his second presidential address. Neither Coon nor Washburn spoke at the meeting, however. The conference organizer decided there was no need for a repeat of the previous fray.

*The Origin of Races* is not without its defenders, even if begrudging ones. Anthropologist Milford Wolpoff, who still championed a theory of regional continuity of traits (but not of races), described it as both "an excellent and a terrible book" that provided the most comprehensive one-volume study of human evolution published to that date. It covered the existing research on humans as social animals, the relationship between social and biological evolution, the primates, human growth, development, adaptation, and archaeology, with thirty-two plates, eighty-four drawings, thirteen maps, and thirty-five tables.

Dobzhansky, though highly critical of Coon's theory, made the same points, calling it a "painstaking description of the available hominid fossils" and noting that "no other work in English, nor as far as I know any in another language, gives as complete and up-to-date an account of the matter." Not so Ashley Montagu. In his review, which was paired in the same 1963 issue of *Current Anthropology* with Dobzhansky's, he wrote that "it could be written off as the failure it is, were it not for the fact that Coon delivers himself of opinions as if they were facts, and these in an area where they are likely to be misunderstood by the unwary, or rather understood for what they are not, and misused by racists, and others."

Coon, answering in kind, replied that "Montague Francis Ashley Montagu must have felt some overweeningly powerful compulsion to smash my book or he would not have begged Alfred Knopf & Co. [Coon's publisher] for a free review copy and then written the present diatribe for *Current Anthropology*. Were it not for the possibility that some readers who do not know him might take him seriously, I would not bother to answer."

"So far as Coon is concerned," Montagu wrote, "Dobzhansky and Montagu need never have written their paper on 'Natural Selection and the Mental Capacities of Mankind.'" Coon fired back that this was the one statement with which he agreed, "at least concerning the junior author." Like the conference organizer, the editor of *Current Anthropology* decided to cut off the debate on *The Origin of Races* then and there.

In a footnote in the final chapter of *The Origin of Races*, Coon noted that two younger anthropologists, Frank Livingstone and C. Loring Brace, had "independently of myself and each other" arrived at a similar theory of human evolution. As its title alone shows, Livingstone's 1962 paper in *Current Anthropology*, "On the Nonexistence of Human Races," couldn't have been further from Coon's point of view. Brace did write a paper, "The Fate of the 'Classic Neanderthals,'" that, like Coon's *Origin*, argued they were ancestral to living Europeans. He was, however, an ardent opponent of anything suggestive of any race differences in behavior and ability.

Coon had initially planned *The Origin of Races* to cover both fossil and living humans. Given the length, the book was split in two. The second part, *The Living Races of Man*, appeared in 1975, written by Carleton S. Coon with Edward Hunt Jr. Coon had promised to discuss racial differences in both blood groups and the anatomy of the brain in that volume, but decided to avoid the latter because it was a subject "so laden with emotion that its mere mention evokes unsolicited acclaim and feverish denunciation."

*The Living Races of Man* was given a multiple review in *Current Anthropology* with both favorable and critical commentaries. Coon again proved somewhat naive. His coauthor, who dealt primarily with the sections on racial differences in blood groups, disease resistance, and physiology, joined the critics.

As the years passed, Coon became increasingly embittered and isolated. In his 1981 autobiography he attempted, somewhat self-servingly and not very convincingly, to put the blame for what some saw as the racist implications of *The Origin of Races* on his copy editor, explaining how he had to make corrections in a later edition. Oddly, he directed most of his wrath at Dobzhansky, convinced that he and Montagu would quarrel no more. Wrong again. Even after Coon died in 1981, Montagu took a final shot at him in a 1992 letter to the *New York Times*.

When Montagu died in 1999, it was to much greater acclaim. Few would have wagered it would turn out that way when Carleton

Stevens Coon was born in Wakefield, Massachusetts, in 1904 and Israel Ehrenberg the following year in London's East End.

## THE NEXT PHASE

In all three of the disputes we have discussed here—Virchow versus Haeckel, Boas versus Madison Grant, and Montagu versus Coon—political events, personality, class background, and ethnic identity became intertwined with science. As in the abortion debate even, the evolution-creation "debate" involves the argument of what it means to be human and who is or is not fully human.

After the Coon affair, anthropology increasingly drew away from the subject of race. First, in 1969 psychologist Arthur Jensen returned the question of the nexus between intelligence, race, and genetics to the mainstream of behavioral science in his famous article "How Much Can We Boost IQ and Scholastic Achievement?" in the *Harvard Educational Review*. Then in 1995 another psychologist, J. Philippe Rushton, published *Race, Evolution, and Behavior*, which one reviewer in *Nature* described as "a frank attempt to rehabilitate the concept of race as a primary descriptive category." Rushton presented a matrix of not only intelligence and brain size but also sixty life-history variables that measure maturation, personality, reproduction, and social organization. Both in the United States and around the world, he reported, Asians and blacks fell at the opposite ends of a continuum with whites in between. He explained these differences in terms of sociobiology's $r/K$ theory in which there is a tradeoff between reproductive effort (having many offspring, symbolized by $r$) and parental care (having fewer offspring but investing heavily in their survival, symbolized by $K$). In Rushton's race-behavior matrix, Africans fall at the $r$ end of the scale and Asians at the $K$ end.

Another factor that led to the decline of the study of race and evolution in anthropology is that the debates were just that— debates. There was no objective clock with which to date any of the fossils. Sherwood Washburn, who had so vigorously denounced Carleton Coon, was the most important figure behind research conducted in the anthropology department at the University of California in Berkeley during the 1960s that would lead to the de- velopment of such a clock, about which there is more to come.

## CHAPTER FOUR

# Resolving the Primate Tree

*This chapter provides an insider's view of the molecular revolution in anthropology. Rather than examining and attempting to date human fossils, the senior author (Sarich) and his late colleague Allan Wilson measured the differences among the various versions of proteins found in the bloodstreams of different species and found that these could be used to date the time of divergence of the branches of any evolutionary tree.*

*After initial resistance, the molecular approach won the day. The date of separation of our ancestral species from those of the African apes (that is, the chimpanzees and the gorillas) was reduced from 20 million years before the present to only about 5 million years before the present. This meant that none of the many fossils that various anthropologists had championed as putative human ancestors could have been anything of the kind.*

How do we determine the human pedigree? In this (as in so much else), we follow Darwin, who did not call his process "evolution" but the precisely descriptive "descent with modification by means of natural selection." The task, then, was to develop the genetic linkages among the forms we were interested in (that is, the branching order) and then the times of separation among those lineages. Once you have the tree with dates on it, you can start worrying about what happened, when it happened, and how and why it happened, always using the tree as a framework within which to interpret such evidence as we glean from the fossil record, the comparative anatomy of living forms, and, more recently, their biochemistry (DNA and proteins). One might have thought, given our fascination with and intimate knowledge of the subject, that we would have long ago settled these matters about ourselves. But therein lies a tale.

As fate would have it, back in 1961 or so, I (Sarich), as a disaffected chemist, began, at first rather informally, my studies in anthropology at the University of California at Berkeley, where Sherry Washburn, as he was known, was perhaps the leading physical anthropologist of the century and, fortunately, became my adviser. His main research interest was the course of our evolution, both physical and behavioral, and he had long strongly argued, against the consensus, for a brachiating ape phase in our ancestry. He also saw clearly that Darwin's approach to such questions, as previously described, was the correct one, and in fact organized a 1972 conference with that orientation at the Wenner-Gren Foundation castle in Austria, which resulted in the classic, pioneering volume *Classification and Human Evolution*. That book made me aware of just how empty was the limb Sherry was perched on, and I often wondered, sometimes uneasily, why I thought his view made so much sense. After all, he was almost the last of the holders of that view. The increasing consensus on whether our species had ever gone through any phase resembling modern apes was "no." In other words, if we were able to look into a family album in which we could see our parents, and their parents before them, and their parents before them, we would never set eyes on an ancestor whose appearance would cause us to exclaim "that's a chimpanzee," or "that looks an awful lot like a chimpanzee." Expert opinion in the field increasingly came down in favor of the view that all the living apes were no more than distant cousins of ours (a refrain we still hear often), and that our ancestry never included a phase when we looked like any of the living apes.

I found this very hard to believe, especially when I would visit the zoo, look seriously at one or the other of them, and get the feeling (as multitudes have) that looking into the eyes of a chimpanzee or gorilla made me think I was looking into the eyes of a basal human being. But that was a judgment call in what, for many, was the more squishy realm of the mind (it's called anthropomorphizing and considered a dangerously unscientific reaction, one best left to writers of fiction). Thus, anatomy and what the apes did with it provided more substance for discussion.

The following derived characteristics are shared by both us and the apes: no tail; a broad, shallow chest; shoulder blades on the back rather than the sides; ability to hang with arm and body in one vertical line or to pull the left earlobe with the right hand from behind the neck; or, holding the upper arm still, to rotate the forearm 180 degrees at the elbow; or, with right hand held toward the face, to bend the wrist much more to the left (little-finger side) than the right (thumb side). All of these abilities are readily seen as representing an adaptation known as "brachiation," the technical term for being able to swing, with arm fully extended, underneath the limbs of trees.

I took it for granted that this meant that humans, chimps, gorillas, orangutans, and gibbons shared a common ancestor with those structures and concomitant abilities and was, to say the least, surprised to find that in fact this was very much the minority view, and that Washburn, who had recently come to Berkeley,

California, from the University of Chicago, was one of the very few authorities who still had a place for a brachiating phase in human ancestry. I found myself uncommonly fortunate to have landed in a place where what eventually became the reality else-where was already the norm. Of course, the Berkeley of the 1960s came to lead the way, for better and worse, in many other matters (but that merits a book of its own).

As the decade went on, Washburn and I became even more isolated in championing the brachiator hypothesis. Paleontolo-gist Elwyn Simons put *Ramapithecus* from India on the hominid line, and Louis Leakey did the same for *Kenyapithecus*. Simons's student, David Pilbeam, argued that two African forms, *Proconsul major* and *Proconsul africanus*, were respectively, a proto-gorilla and a proto-chimpanzee. *Pliopithecus* from Austria had long been seen as a proto-gibbon, and some years later, *Sivapithecus* from In-dia came to be seen as a proto-orangutan.

The problem for me was that none of these or any other fossils showed the least indication of those upper-body features that we and the living apes shared with one another. So if one accepted those fossils as being ancestral to the living apes, one had either to deny the reality of those upper-body similarities or to place a good deal of faith in either parallel, or convergent, evolution. Or, of course, one could argue that the absence of those features in the fossil record was far more parsimoniously explained by posit-ing that they had not yet evolved, and that the last common an-cestor of living apes and humans in fact postdated most of the fossils. If so, then those fossils simply would revert to being, at least for the purposes here, irrelevant Old World monkeys.

I saw no hope that this quandary could be convincingly re-solved if we limited ourselves to arguing about the evolutionary significance of various pieces of the anatomy. If experts from Huxley and Darwin to Washburn hadn't carried the day here, I didn't see how it could be done; and I certainly wasn't going to try to do it myself—not using anatomy, that is.

## A NEW SOURCE OF INFORMATION

By 1963, however, Morris Goodman at Wayne State University in Detroit, Emile Zuckerkandl and Linus Pauling at Stanford, and Emmaneul Margoliash and Emil Smith at Armour Labs in Chicago had given us the bits and pieces of a new approach. Here I was doubly fortunate—first, bright enough to comprehend how it could resolve this apparent conundrum between the anatomies of living forms and their putative ancestors in the fossil record, and, second, that none of the scientists just mentioned, or anyone else anywhere, thought to do it before me.

In 1961, Zuckerkandl and Pauling, working with some very fragmentary hemoglobin data, had suggested that genes and proteins appeared to have accumulated mutational change in a clocklike fashion. If that was true, one might be able to count the number of such differences between the same protein in different species and deduce how long it had taken to produce them—that is, how long ago they had shared a common ancestor.

Then, Margoliash and Smith had compared the amino acid sequences of a number of cytochromes c across the taxonomic span from tuna to human. Their results confirmed Zuckerkandl and Pauling and showed how to test the molecular clock hypothesis directly.

The implication was that if we could find a protein, or proteins, that evolved at an appropriate rate, and a way of comparing their various incarnations in ourselves, apes, monkeys, other primates, and mammals in general, we might be able to say, no, X could not be ancestral to Y, as compared to Z, because the separation between the Y and Z lineages had not yet occurred when X was alive. In other words, a putative ancestor had to be older than a putative descendant.

In fact, we didn't even have to do the protein work, because Morris Goodman already had. Beginning in 1959, Goodman had been generating a large body of data from comparisons of various primate serum proteins. From this database, Goodman was able to tell us that the serum proteins of gibbons, for example, were roughly one-fifth as different from ours as from those of a lemur. He had found that humans, chimpanzees, and gorillas were equidistant from one another at the serum protein level. In short, the two African apes had no period of common ancestry that wasn't also shared with us. This remains the single most surprising finding of the forty-plus years of the molecular enterprise. The idea that chimpanzees and gorillas are *not* more closely related to one another than either is to us is a result no one foresaw, and which would not, even today, some forty years later, have been suggested prior to the coming of the molecular data and perspective. This despite the general flavor that the famous American paleontologist G. G. Simpson caught perfectly long ago: "(T)he student of classification is likely to feel that almost *all* arrangements for which there is any reason, and a good many for which there is none, have been proposed."

Furthermore, Goodman had even explicitly considered the temporal implications of his data. Not only were we, chimps, and gorillas equidistant from one another, but the serum protein differences among the three were also minimal. Nor did they increase markedly when orangutan and gibbon sera were added to the mix of comparisons. When Goodman asked himself why the serum protein differences among the apes and us were so small, he found two possible explanations: They were so small (1) either because they hadn't had time to get bigger—that is, we and the living apes shared very recent common ancestry, or (2) there had

been a slowdown of protein evolution among their lineages relative to those of other primates.

So by 1961 Goodman was way ahead of the game, measuring
genetic distances with an ingenious yet simple technique and
contemplating the time scale they implied. Then he made an understandable yet fatal error. With reasonable but flawed logic, he
proposed:

Genetic distance (here, degree of difference between the same
protein in different species) = (time of separation) × (rate of genetic change)

All right. Goodman could measure genetic distance in the lab but
could not measure either of the other two factors. He could get
time of separation only by asking someone who was supposed to
know—a paleontologist. Then, rate of genetic change would be
genetic distance divided by whatever the paleontologist told him
was the time of separation.

He asked the paleontologists, who told him that the human
line was probably at least some 20 million years old. Their line of
reasoning went like this: *Ramapithecus* at 13 million years of age
was a direct human ancestor; *Proconsul africanus* and *major*, at
about 18 million years, were direct ancestors of, respectively,
chimps and gorillas. And because virtually everyone accepted
that the human line split off from that putatively led to the two
African apes, that split had to be at least 20 million years ago.
Then the paleontologists needed to peg the orang, and even earlier, gibbon splits, and put the latter at, probably, more than 30
million years.

If one accepted the paleontologists' account, the evolution of
us and our closest relatives would comprise a substantial portion
of the primate history of perhaps 60 million years. But, as already

noted, the serum protein distance between gibbons and other hominoids doesn't begin to get to half that to lemurs. Nor are those among the three African forms nearly a third of that to lemurs. So if one accepted the paleontologists' judgments, and Goodman did, there had to have been a slowdown in serum protein evolution (that is, change over time) in the higher primates, and he developed an elaborate theory to explain that slowdown:

1. Increased maternal-fetal transplacental contact, which
2. Had the effect of selecting against mutational input because this would increase the likelihood that fetus and mother would differ chemically, and would
3. Increase the likelihood that maternal-fetal incompatibilities would develop, and
4. Thus make it more likely that fetal rejection would occur.

Goodman didn't realize that this exercise was unnecessary. He could have answered his question about rate entirely in his laboratory, where he already had all the requisite data. He didn't need to measure *rates* of change, which did require known dates, but only to compare *amounts* of change, which did not. Take, for example, the human line, for which Goodman posited a major slowdown relative to, say, that for a spider monkey or tarsier. To test that proposition, he needed only to measure the genetic distance from each of the three to a lemur. To posit a slowdown was to say that there was less change along the human line, which would then make human proteins more similar to those of a lemur than would be those of a spider monkey or tarsier. But when those comparisons were done, they did not come out more or less similar but simply equally similar—no slowdown by direct test. All of that was in Goodman's notebooks, and a good bit of it had already been published.

It is of interest here that Washburn had organized a conference in 1962 at the Wenner-Gren Foundation castle in Austria at which the implications of the molecular data were discussed extensively. Both Goodman and Zuckerkandl presented papers, but nobody could get beyond the fact that use of the term "rate" meant that two variables, amount of change and amount of time, had to be measured, and the only way to get amount of time was directly from the fossil record. Once one started thinking that way, it was apparently very nearly impossible to stop thinking that way. It was frustrating but eventually enlightening over the years to ask our graduate students at their oral examinations to explain how one tested the slowdown hypothesis, and to find that they simply couldn't do it, even though virtually every one of them had been a teaching assistant in the introductory physical anthropology course where the matter had been extensively discussed and, often, exam questions asked about it. The topic seemed to come accompanied by its own mental glitch (comparing rates required measuring rates), and they found it very hard to see the point even when it had been repeatedly presented to them.

The dénouement was somewhat anticlimactic. A New Zealander named Allan Wilson had taken his graduate degrees in zoology at Washington State and biochemistry at UC–Berkeley and gone on to postdoctoral work at Brandeis in comparative biochemistry. In fall 1964, Allan was beginning his first academic year as a beginning professor of biochemistry at Berkeley. That same fall I (Sarich) by chance was taking my one and only course in biochemistry, and I had many questions for the instructor about how the material he was presenting tied in with the evolutionary process. I was also enrolled in a seminar being given by Washburn and another distinguished anthropologist, F. Clark Howell. I volunteered to handle one of the sessions on the state of affairs in the molecular evolution realm. It went well, and

Washburn and Howell liked the paper I produced. My biochemistry professor also told me about a new faculty member I should talk to—which I did, also bringing along a copy of that seminar paper. Things went well with him, too. Allan liked the paper, and Washburn called me in (I assume after he talked to Allan) and asked what I thought about turning this stuff into a doctoral dissertation. I thought it was a great idea, and Allan invited me to come and help him set up his lab and see if I could sort some of these problems related to human evolution.

The rest is history.

## THE BERKELEY HUMAN
## EVOLUTION NARRATIVE

I repeated some of Goodman's comparisons in Allan's laboratory using a single serum protein (albumin—584 amino acids long with the sequences varying from species to species) and a somewhat more sensitive measuring tool that Allan had learned about at Brandeis, and found that human albumin had changed to much the same degree as had the albumins of most other primates over their time on earth. For example, human, baboon, spider monkey, and tarsier albumins were pretty much equally different from those of a loris, a lemur, a dog, or a bear. In other words, they had changed in a clocklike fashion over the 60-plus million years that separated them from the latter. This came to be called the Relative Rate Test, in which the latter four served as "out-groups." We could then make productive use of the fossil record to determine the time that primate lines began to diverge from one another.

One might quibble here about using certain dates from the fossil record to, as it came to be, challenge others. The justification is that once one demonstrated the existence of a molecular clock, its calibration was fairly straightforward. I would put it very simply. You're welcome to place the human-chimpanzee split at the date of

20 mya (millions of years ago) on the basis of data you deem relevant, rather than the 5 mya that I prefer on the basis of data I deem
relevant—provided that you are also willing to have the lorises and
lemurs at roughly 250 mya (that is, if you're going to increase the
human-chimp date by a factor of four, you must do the same for
lorises and lemurs). Of course, that is a reductio ad absurdum—250
mya was long before dinosaurs, never mind mammals. You could
pick a calibration, fine, but, as I would put it, it had to be one that
made the largest number of paleontologists the least unhappy—
and they could live much more easily with humans and chimps at 5
mya than with lorises and lemurs at 250 mya.

Allan and I originally used 30 million years ago between Old
World monkeys (for example, baboons) and apes as the most conservative figure we felt our data could support. Given that, and the
fact that the human-chimp-gorilla differences were about one-
sixth of those between any of the three lines and baboons, we argued that the three African forms had shared common ancestry as
recently as 5 million years ago, with orangs at about 8 mya, and gibbons at 10. In my most recent assessment of these dates, they still
don't look at all bad—an outcome that owes something to good
fortune and something to ingenuity and intelligence, and let's not
worry about precisely how much of each. I now estimate we shared
our last common ancestor with chimps probably at 4.5 mya, with
gorillas around 5 mya, with orangs around 9 mya, and with gibbons,
where technique betrayed Allan and me to some extent, around 13
mya. The date for Old World monkeys has come down to 20 mya;
and for New World monkeys, a bit more than 30 mya. But the precise numbers were originally not all that important; the important
thing was to get the descent-with-modification discussion into
something resembling a realistic framework. No more 30-million-
year-old gibbons; no more 14-million-year-old hominids; no more
proto-chimps and proto-gorillas 18 million years ago in Kenya.
And that framework has come to be (see Figure 4.1).

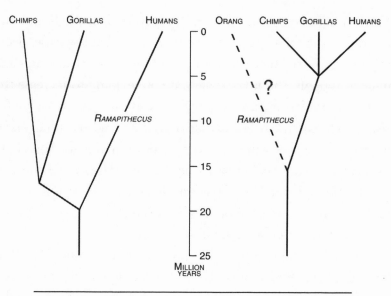

FIGURE 4.1     Family trees before and after Sarich and Wilson

Allan and I made the purpose of our effort clear in the penulti-mate paragraph of our 1967 *Science* article, where we first put for-ward in print our new time scale for ape and human relationships:

> If the view that man and the African apes share a Pliocene ances-tor and that all of the living Hominoidea derive from a late Miocene form is correct, a number of the problems that have trou-bled students of this group are resolved. The many features of morphology present in the thorax and upper limbs, which man and the living apes share in varying degrees, but which were not present in the Miocene apes . . . are then seen as due to recent common ancestry and not, as generally accepted, to parallel or convergent evolution.
>
> We suggest that the living apes and man descend from a small member of the widespread Miocene dryopithecines, which became uniquely successful due to the development of the locomotor-

feeding adaptation known as brachiation. The adaptive success of this development and the subsequent radiation of the group possessing it may have made this group the only surviving lineage of the many apes present throughout the tropical and subtropical Miocene forests of the Old World. Possibly the African members of this radiation, in the middle Pliocene . . . began varying degrees of adaptation to a terrestrial existence. The gorilla, chimpanzee, and man appear to be the three survivors of this later radiation. According to this hypothesis, some 3 million years are allowed for the development of bipedalism to the extent seen in the earliest fossil hominid, *Australopithecus*.

Now, it shouldn't be thought that Allan and I lit the lamp, and everyone immediately, or even upon measured contemplation and consideration, saw the light. Not exactly. One colorful but not unrepresentative comment from that era came from a well-known physical anthropologist, John Buettner-Janusch:

Sarich and Wilson have suggested that hominids and pongids were part of a common population about 5 million years ago. If Sarich and Wilson had looked more carefully at paleontological investigations, they would have found their suggestion is unwarranted. . . . There are some things that cannot be done with molecular data and some things that cannot be done with fossils, and I object to careless assumptions and thoughtless statements about evolutionary processes in some of the conclusions drawn from the immunological data mentioned.

Unfortunately there is a growing tendency, which I would like to suppress if possible, to view the molecular approach to primate evolutionary studies as a kind of instant phylogeny. No hard work, no tough intellectual arguments. No fuss, no muss, no dishpan hands. Just throw some proteins into a laboratory apparatus, shake them up, and bingo!—we have answers to questions that have puzzled us for at least three generations.

Also weighing in was a leading primate paleontologist, Elwyn Simons:

> If the immunological dates of divergence devised by Sarich are cor‑ rect, then paleontologists have not yet found a single fossil related to the ancestry of any living primate and the whole host of species which they have found are all parallelistic imitations of modern higher primates. I find this impossible to believe. Some fossil pri‑ mates do exhibit evolution parallel to modern forms, as is particu‑ larly well demonstrated in the case of the subfossil Malagasy lemurs, but it is not presently acceptable to assume that all the fossil pri‑ mates resembling modern forms are only parallelisms, that highly arboreal apes wandered hundreds of miles out of Africa across the Pontian steppes of Eurasia in search of tropical rain forests, or that *Australopithecus* sprang full‑blown 5 million years ago, as Minerva did from Jupiter, from the head of a chimpanzee or gorilla.

At the time, Allan and I had a good deal to say in response. The flavor of those responses is best typified by this comment of mine:

> As might be expected, then, it is not particularly difficult to inter‑ pret the available paleontological and anatomical evidence in terms of the short time scale protein phylogeny. . . . I have yet to see any suggestion as to how a twenty‑million‑year date can possi‑ bly be used to explain the molecular evidence. To put it as bluntly as possible, I now feel that the body of molecular evidence on the *Homo‑Pan* [human‑chimp] relationship is sufficiently extensive so that one no longer has the option of considering a fossil specimen older than about eight million years as a hominid *no matter what it looks like* (emphasis in original).

I meant every word of that last sentence when I wrote it in 1970, even though Washburn was later quoted as saying that it was the dumbest thing I had ever written. There is no doubt that Roger Lewin got it right in his book *Bones of Contention*: "In other words he did not care whether *Ramapithecus* looked like *Australopithecus* or even *Homo sapiens*. It was simply too old. Period. A statement more calculated to raise the blood pressure of paleoanthropologists could hardly be imagined."

Since those words were written, the paleontologists themselves have come to the conclusion that, however impossible to believe it seemed at the time, those serum albumin dates of divergence have proved out, and the fossils that had been put on existing lineages no longer are. *Ramapithecus/Sivapithecus* is no longer a proto-hominid or a proto-orang; *Proconsul* is neither a proto-chimp nor a proto-gorilla; *Pliopithecus* is no longer a proto-gibbon. Furthermore, no other fossils have come along to be put in their places, and 5 million years for the human-chimp split is the current standard figure. History has vindicated Allan and me, but need it have? Did we have a better reason for turning out to have been right, than Simons and most others did for turning out to have been wrong? More important, is there a lesson in this?

Yes, and that's the point. The original puzzle had been in the anatomy—the fossils the paleontologists had placed on those existing ape lineages did not have (presumably, because they had not yet developed) those hallmark characteristics that all the modern apes and we share and that differentiate us from monkeys. Had the paleontologists been reading the anatomy lessons correctly, they would have realized the molecules were simply making the same point in another, independent way. The point was that all the lines of evidence ought to be interpretable within one evolutionary scenario—one phylogenetic framework—because in real time for real animals, there had been only that one scenario, and all the bits and pieces being studied were, ultimately, parts of a single puzzle.

As previously mentioned, Goodman's discovery that chimpanzees and gorillas were not each other's closest relatives proved a great surprise; to the extent of his then-limited resolving power, he showed that the human lineage and those of the two African apes formed a trichotomy. Much later work suggests that in fact the gorillas are the out-group, with the human and chimp lineages sharing some brief period of common ancestry after the gorilla line split off.

Well, one might say, so what? What does that picture reveal beyond ancestry? One answer lies in chimpanzee and gorilla locomotion: Both are knuckle-walkers, with the middle knuckles providing support for the front half of the animal. According to the human tree (see Figure 4.1), chimpanzees and gorillas share no lineages with each other that they don't share with us. So knuckle-walking evolved in the lineage ancestral to all three descendant lines, and all three share some period of knuckle-walking in their ancestry.

That's evolutionary logic, but is there more direct evidence? Watch a lecturer at a lectern or table and notice the knuckle-walking position of the hands and wrist. Why that strange position that otherwise occurs only in the extant African apes? Then look at your own knuckles—especially the middle ones. Note that they are strangely hairless (typically, but not always). Finally, study the three- or four-point stance that football linemen often take—again, middle knuckles down. The three observations are not definitive proof but surely have to be taken seriously.

The argument gains some strength when one tries to resolve the adaptive changes that ultimately resulted in human-style locomotion. First, as already noted, we were brachiators from perhaps 15 millions years ago to . . . when? Well, the fact is that we're still pretty good at it, but the ability is exhibited relatively infrequently—on the so-called monkey bars (which are really ape bars) and in gymnastics. Because a largish ape does not spend all of its time in the trees, the selective process will notice the usefulness of the animal's having some terrestrial abilities as well. Palms-down, the way any monkey would do it, is incompatible with the wrist of a brachiator, where the lack of a direct articulation between the ulna (the bone on the outside of the forearm, opposite the thumb) and some of the wrist bones tends to push the forearm through the wrist. Knuckle-walking was the compromise. When one considers the adaptation unique to the human line, bipedalism (walking erect on two feet), it becomes clear that knuckle-walking was the ideal intermediate stage.

Finally, in a paper published in *Nature* in 2000, two anatomist/ anthropologists showed that the knuckle-walking adaptations seen in the wrists of chimpanzees and gorillas were retained in early hominids (australopithecines). Again, early molecule-based scenarios are being confirmed by new information from the realms of neoanatomy and paleontology. To again give Morris Goodman his due, he was the first person (1961) to develop data that had to be interpreted as essentially a trichotomy (three-way split) among the three African ape lineages (human, chimp, gorilla). In 1967 Washburn saw, when others did not, that the three-way split implied a knuckle-walking phase in our ancestry.

## WHAT DO MOLECULAR CLOCKS
## RUN ON AND HOW DO THEY RUN?

In the next chapter we apply the molecular clock to the questions of the origins of our species and of races within it. We show that it works there as well, though, not surprisingly, new problems arise, and their satisfactory solutions depend on viable answers to the two questions in the heading of this section. The clock worked when applied to the very contentious matter of human origins, true enough, and one didn't have to think too deeply into why—that it worked was enough, and it seemed pretty clear that it would work effectively over a very wide time span. Nonetheless, succumbing to the black-box quality of our approach (we got good, reliable numbers—for both genetic distance and time—but didn't know where they came from) was unsatisfactory. We could tell ourselves that it didn't make any difference, and actually believe that for a while, but we always came back to "how and why?" it worked. So here's what matters look like today compared to then.

In the mid–1960s we were working at what was going to be the tail end of a major successful revolution in thought among organismal biologists, and one among many of its accomplishments was getting people away from looking for so-called nonadaptive characters to help in sorting out relationships. This argument had two parts: First, looking for such characters (note: nonadaptive does not mean maladaptive) was an inherently chancy proposition, because there were no criteria for distinguishing among "nonadaptive" characters and any other kind; second, we should have learned a lesson when so many characters once thought to be nonadaptive were shown to be adaptive when more sophisticated tools were applied to the problem.

When Allan and I discussed these matters among ourselves at great length, it slowly became clear to us that, yes, there was an interesting conundrum here, but we'd best stand clear of it. How? By insisting that whether the clock worked or not was a matter that could be tested in the lab, and once its presence was so demonstrated, it could be put to use. The nature of the changes involved (whether adaptive or neutral) was, however, irrelevant to the matter of using the clock with some degree of confidence. I should also note here that Allan had much more riding on our being right (or, at least, not demonstrably wrong) than I did—he would be dealing with the matter of tenure, whereas I was pursuing only a dissertation.

In any case, whenever the question came up, we would insist on separating the matter of whether it worked from why and how it worked. Our problem was that we had learned, practically as a mantra, that the only way one could get the fixation of neutral mutations (no one was going to take the idea of clocks fed by adaptive mutations at all seriously—there was no way that adaptive changes could accumulate in a regular fashion) was in small populations by genetic drift (chance), and that obviously wasn't going to work as an explanation over so many millions of years over so many lineages.

The electrophoresis people were showing that molecular variation was ubiquitous when one looked within species, and that they really had an embarrassment of riches, as anyone could seemingly find more variation than he knew what to do with just by looking. Remember that most of these workers were looking for meaning (that is, why was this or that variant there), not the use of the data for relationship matters.

The classic case here, of course, was the sickle-cell polymorphism present among humans in many lowland tropical environments, where the normal homozygote (two normal alleles) was at serious risk from malaria in the first few years of life, the heterozygote (one normal, one sickle-cell) was protected from *falciparum* malaria without any detrimental side effects, and the sickle-cell homozygote was basically dead.

The larger truth here—that in fact most variation and change at the level of DNA and proteins have no functional consequences— did not, and really could not, begin to be taken seriously until we began to get some idea as to the nature and extent of that variation and change, involving two quite distinct lines of evidence, in the 1960s. In the first, beginning with, as noted earlier, the work of

Emile Zuckerkandl and Linus Pauling in 1961, continuing with
that of Emil Smith and Emmanuel Margoliash in 1963 and of Allan Wilson and me in the period 1965–1967 (following the logic of
Zuckerkandl, Pauling, Smith, and Margoliash; and, to some extent, Goodman's data), the evidence showed that the serum albumins of the various higher primates (including ours) were pretty
much equally different from those of prosimians like galagos and
tarsiers, leading us to propose that the various primate albumin lineages were accumulating change (that is, amino acid substitutions)
as a function of time—in other words, that there was an albumin
clock.

In the other realm, involving protein comparisons within
species, the early workers suffered from an embarrassment of
riches. Variation was ubiquitous, and it seemed anyone could find
far more than he could know what to do with just by looking. The
idea then became to explain the variation by appealing to natural
selection; that, in effect, we were simply observing multitudes of
sickle-cell cases, with multitudes of malaria analogues maintaining
the polymorphisms observed. This explanation became the pre-
ferred one for several years in the late 1960s and 1970s, undoubt-
edly because, in part, it gave the believers something to look
for—unlimited variation in the proteins of the organisms and potential selective variables in the environment made it possible to
go a long way on faith in the essential lack of positive results. The
idea that most of the variation was simply mutations random-
walking their way along an adaptive landscape that for them was
flat was just too frustrating to have to accept.

Lewontin caught it perfectly in his *The Genetic Basis of Evolutionary Change* (p. 116) (for paradise, read electrophoresis):

Geneticists like variation and find genetic uniformity rather dull.
The excitement of seeing a new genetic segregation in a new
organism is real and seductive. . . . A. D. Hershey is reported to

have described heaven as "finding an experiment that works and doing it over and over and over." Population geneticists too have found paradise.

Amen, provided we note "seductive."

The problem was that it proved to be extremely difficult to in fact find even a few of those multitudes; that is, to demonstrate a convincing, causal connection between some protein polymorphism and some environmental variable. Those few of us in the molecular-clock school at the time (late 1960s—early 1970s) did not find this failure surprising, as the only way we could see to rationalize our observations was to accept an argument made in print by Motoo Kimura in 1967 and by Jack King and Tom Jukes in 1968. My own introduction to that argument was one of those perfect moments that scientists live for and yet so rarely get to enjoy—a true epiphany. (One more will appear in a few pages.)

Allan Wilson and I were by then (late 1967) convinced that the molecular clock was the rule, not the exception, for proteins; that is, a given protein would tend to accumulate substitutions at pretty much the same rate in all the lineages in which it was found. But we lacked a satisfying explanation for that phenomenon—or, more fairly, we lacked a satisfying explanation for the only available explanation; specifically, that the six or so differences between our albumin and that of a chimpanzee had no functional consequences; that you could put our albumin into a chimp and vice versa with no ill effects. The problem was that we thought we could only explain it as drift (that is, chance variation), and we—along with practically everyone else at the time—"knew" that drift was a significant phenomenon only in small populations.

The standard example was of an Eskimo band in which only one individual carried a blood group B allele. He met with a kayaking accident—no more B in that population. The fact that he had the B allele obviously had nothing to do with his demise, so selection wasn't involved; nonetheless the allele was now gone—purely by chance. But if we now went to a village of 1,000 individuals, we might have ten with the B allele, and it would be much less likely that all ten would be lost; and it would take much longer to lose them if they were. So the lesson was that although the idea of explaining molecular clocks and the multitudes of protein polymorphisms that we and many others were observing was the result of mutations that made no difference as they took a random walk from appearance to either chance extinction (the norm) or ultimate fixation (for the fortunate few) was an appealing one, we couldn't get past the notion that "drift is only significant in small populations."

Jack King (then a geneticist at Berkeley) then came to the lab to give a seminar. He argued as follows (these are not his actual words, but are my attempt to convey the sense of the meeting some thirty-five years later):

Look at the hemoglobins of ourselves, chimps, and gorillas. The only difference is in the gorilla, which has lysine in position 104 of the β-chain, whereas we and chimps have arginine. Given that the relationships involved closely approximate a trichotomy, the simplest explanation is that somewhere along the gorilla lineage, after ours and that of chimps had split off, the arginine at position 104 mutated to lysine in one gorilla, and eventually all gorillas came to have lysine instead of arginine—not because it was "better" for gorillas to have a lysine there, but simply that it made no difference. Along the way, of course, an observer sampling gorilla hemoglobins would have seen variation in his gels and reported this new polymorphism. So today almost all gorilla hemoglobins have lysine at position 104. At some time in the past, only one of them (the recipient of the new mutation) did. And this will necessarily be true for any amino acid at any position in any protein in any species—no matter what its frequency today, it started as one mutation in one zygote.

Now let's denote the rate (per year, say) at which new, neutral mutations occur with the Greek letter $\mu$ (mu, for mutation). The number of those occurring in any particular population will then be the mutation rate multiplied by the number of genes that can mutate; that is, two per individual (we have two copies of each chromosome except for the Y in males):

$$\mu \times 2N$$

So far, so good. Now for the critical part. What is the likelihood that one of those new, neutral mutations will be a "successful" one that ultimately reaches something close to fixation in some descendant population? Well, there is, to begin with, one of it, and $2N - 1$ of those destined to go to extinction. So the probability of going to fixation is simply

$$1 \text{ in } 2N \text{ or}$$
$$1/2N$$

The overall number of neutral substitutions over time, then, is the number that appear times the probability of fixation:

$$(\mu \times 2N) \times (1/2N) \text{ or, simply and remarkably:}$$
$$\mu$$

In other words, for neutral mutations, the rate of substitution is equal to the rate of occurrence in the sense that if you have one new neutral mutation per million genes per year, the rate of substitution will be one per million years.

The bugaboo of population size disappears. One comes to understand that, yes, drift is more likely in small populations, but larger ones have more neutral alleles drifting around.

Oh, said I to myself. What a beautiful demonstration. How simple and perfect. That's why the clock works. That's why there is so much functionally meaningless genetic variation in natural populations. How profound.

Sometime later, Richard Lewontin, among others, dealt with the question of variation in natural populations more directly by showing something that those few of us in the molecular-clock school had argued for some time—that it was inherently impossible for very much of the observed protein variation within populations to represent balanced polymorphisms of one sort or another.

The truth here, then, is that in fact most variation and change at the level of DNA and proteins has no functional consequences. So it becomes easy to argue that not only is the amount of between-population genetic variation very small by the standards of what we observe in other species (true), but also that most variation that does exist has no functional, adaptive significance (also true). What, then, controls the amount of interpopulational variation? Simply the length of time the populations have been effectively separated from one another. So the very small genetic differences present today among human populations tell us that it wasn't all that long ago that they were, in effect, one.

# Homo sapiens
# and Its Races

*In this chapter we describe how the molecular methods were then ap-*
*plied to resolving the riddle of the origin of races. Only within the past*
*three years have three separate molecular dating methods—autosomal*
*DNA, mitochondrial DNA (which is inherited only through the mater-*
*nal line), and Y-chromosome DNA (which is inherited only along the*
*paternal line)—converged to produce a consistent picture that now*
*proves the monogenist viewpoint correct. Our species first arose in*
*Africa only about 50,000 years ago. None of the living races can be*
*traced back to before this date.*

Having the perspective of almost forty years serves to emphasize
how easy the battle was: an obviously wrong scenario, being in
the right place at the right time, one bright idea, a clear-cut answer, and the rest was history. It was also a history that did not
impinge uncomfortably on our views of ourselves. That we were
most similar in anatomy to chimps and gorillas was not all that
much of a surprise, and the work of Jane Goodall in particular

was providing the behavioral connection. Also, five million years was still a comfortably long time, and the connections did not impinge on everyday lives.

I (Sarich) thought of Thomas Henry Huxley's assessment of 1863:

> [E]very bone of a Gorilla bears marks by which it might be distinguished from the corresponding bone of a man; and that, in the present creation, at any rate, no intermediate link bridges over the gap between Homo and Troglodytes.. . .
>
> It would be not less wrong than absurd to deny the existence of this chasm; but it is at least equally wrong and absurd to exaggerate its magnitude, and, resting on the admitted fact of its existence, to refuse to enquire whether it is wide or narrow.

I had this comment on Huxley: "This study has had as one of its foci an inquiry into the breadth of that chasm. To give an answer 105 years later, it may be said that the chasm is indeed narrow, but very deep."

But that wasn't the only chasm. We have long seen, and still continue to see, when we observe one another, if not exactly chasms, then at least some very definite groupings separated by what seem to be substantial gaps. And we have long provided explanations for what we saw, going back to well before 1859. Why? Basically, because we had to. Concern with ancestry is a human universal. Every human society has had a system of kinship that links every individual within it with every other member, and the individual's position in the system is that person's major feature. Ancestry and relationship have come to mean everything to a social, fluent species like ours. Thus, it is not surprising that when some groups of humans made the acquaintance of others who were recognizably different from themselves at the group level, they would inquire as to the nature of a kinship system that might encompass all of them.

The answer varied from group to group, but for the purposes here, it is appropriate to start with that given by a monotheistic people: the story in Genesis (*bereishit* in the original) plus later commentaries—the Garden of Eden, the Flood, Noah's Ark, the Tower of Babel, and so on—where our species was created once, with subsequent racial differentiation taking place "naturally" (monogenesis). This answer was fine until it was noticed, as described in Chapter 3, that people of 4,000 and more years ago were also seen as forming separate groups, and those groups looked very much as they did today. That didn't seem to leave nearly enough time for them to have become as different as they were within the 6,000 or so years the Scriptures seemed to allow. At first, a few Renaissance thinkers dared to challenge the orthodox interpretation. Then, by the middle of the nineteenth century, a small group of polygenists, particularly those of the American School of Anthropology, argued that the major races had to have been created separately.

Recent debates concerning the origin of our species and of races within it are eerily reminiscent of concerns expressed before Darwin's *Origin of Species* was published in 1859. Monogenesis since has become the "Garden-of-Eden" or "out-of-Africa" model of human evolution, and polygenesis the "multiregional-evolution" or "regional-continuity" model. Both models, then and now, have what appear to be the same competing—and incompatible—scenarios. In the first, there is a single creation/speciation event in which the new species is somehow genetically advantaged over the other human populations around at the time. It then expands out of its homeland and, because of those genetic advantages, rapidly takes over much of the Old World. In the religious (Creation) rendition of the first scenario, there were no other people.

In the evolutionary rendition (the Garden-of-Eden model), there were other people, but they have no living heirs. Their genes are not present in recent or extant populations or in ancestors of them.

There are also two renditions of the second scenario. In the religious rendition, the major races are created separately in more or less the same form they appear today. In the evolutionary rendition, they evolve into anatomically modern *Homo sapiens* in parallel from nonmodern forms. The evolutionary rendition of the second scenario allows for enough peripheral gene flow between the races to maintain a single large gene pool (at least with respect to those features that make people "human") but not enough to blur the regionality. Thus, whatever quibbling there might be about the formal taxonomic assignments of the various forms involved, the racial lineages are deep, extending into populations that no one would confuse with recent humans.

Thus, just as in the dispute over hominid origins (described in Chapter 4), here there are two quite distinct scenarios, a good deal of squabbling (and worse) about them, and an ever-growing panoply of molecular probes with which to try to decide the issues. And these exist not only in the real world. For example, in Kathryn Lasky Knight's mystery novel *Mortal Words*, the protagonist investigates a creationist organization vaguely reminiscent of the Institute for Creation Research in El Cajon, California, which claimed to have some human skulls showing that the races had been created separately. Frustrated because she has been unable to examine them, the investigator declares:

> They do claim to be doing some further testing. That's why they said the skulls weren't available to look at.
>
> But why haven't we heard about the initial discovery? And if they're doing testing, I sure as hell haven't heard anything about

it. I talk to the Berkeley folks almost weekly. The molecular guys there work hand in glove with the paleoanthropologists now. They got all the hardware to run any kind of test. State-of-the-art stuff. I would have heard about this from them. Good Christ, Vincent Sarich figured out ten years ago how to biochemically determine when humans separated from apes. This would be small potatoes for him to figure out this racial thing. He would have been the first person they would have gone to.

Well, it was a nice thought, but it hasn't been small potatoes for anyone, never mind especially me, Vincent Sarich. Why not? After all, the hominid-origins problem had yielded easily once Allan Wilson and I figured out what genetic differences to count and how to count them, with the apparent lesson being that all one had to do with the matter of racial relationships in time and space was to find something appropriate to count and then to count in an appropriate manner.

The problem with that naive deduction is that races aren't species—they are not, among other things, reproductively isolated from one another. Thus, the contemporary proponents of the multiregional/regional-continuity scenario have, following Franz Weidenreich, always included a degree of gene flow among these regions in their picture. This gene flow (plus culture flow) could then account for the fact that we (or, at least, a number of us) tended to see more in the way of continuity, and relatively little in the way of discontinuities, in the fossil and archaeological records.

It also provided a way out of the more irksome aspects of the out-of-Africa/Garden-of-Eden scenario, aspects no less irksome now that this scenario seems to be the more likely one. It requires one to accept that all recent and living humans derive from a single population that evolved genetic adaptations that in turn selectively advantaged them over all other populations around at the time, *and* that there was no gene flow from "us" to the "others." Accepting one of these propositions is difficult enough; accepting both seems to require accepting, literally, two miracles—almost as if there really had been a creation event and the Garden of Eden a real place in real time. Consider first the lack of gene flow. Can one really imagine males of our species being that selective in their choice of mating partners? We can't. But that forces one to accept that among the "evolved genetic adaptations" is reproductive isolation—that there might have been plenty of sex, but it didn't produce any babies. That's miracle number one. And what about the other "evolved genetic adaptations"? If we succeeded because we were somehow genetically advantaged, the question becomes "advantaged at what?" What was it that our ancestors could do that the "others" couldn't do?

One popular and obvious suggestion has been "language as we know it." But that answer forces one to accept that the single human feature that without question requires a highly developed brain evolved with no accompanying increase in brain size. In fact, the largest brains in the human fossil record belong to some of the Neanderthals.

Going on in this vein, however, would mean very fallible humans addressing the most vital of issues concerning their origin, and allowing "ought" to lead to "is"—in other words, to allow how one thought things "ought to be" to cloud one's judgments as to how they actually were. The fact that things may seem to make no sense is often a matter of who is looking, and with which part of the brain they are looking. After forty years or so of thinking about these matters, and trying to do something about resolving them, I see all too many instances where the "wish was father to the fact"—and that the same has been true for most, if not all, of the major players in the field. Dispassionate science has not been a conspicuous presence.

## RACES AREN'T SPECIES

No, as we've noted, they're not, and this has made it difficult to decide objectively among the competing scenarios. Once possible gene flow is factored into the equations, and that is essential when dealing with races, then a measured genetic distance among populations could refer to any number of times of original separation, depending on how much gene flow has taken place among them since those origins. This makes the time dimension of the within-human trees (and, of course, they aren't true trees because of gene flow) potentially very squishy. Thus, the area is by definition messy, but that has not prevented useful work at the genetic level from being carried out.

There has been work with blood groups, which since their discovery in 1901 have been known to vary among individuals (indeed, they were discovered precisely because they did so vary), and which were shown in 1919 to vary in frequency among populations. For example, the frequency of B-type blood decreases as you go west in Europe. Thus, blood group variation gives us something that can be counted objectively. Further, a large number of human populations have been sampled for such variation at a number of blood group loci.

A simple case is the MN system. It has two alleles, M and N, and three genotypes, MM, MN, NN. Their corresponding phenotypes are MM (which reacts only with anti-M), MN (reacts with both anti-M and anti-N), and NN (reacts only with anti-N).

This example could then be expanded to all known blood group loci and counted as follows:

- Both individuals are MM, MN, or NN—difference = 0
- One individual is MN and the other is MM or NN—difference = 1
- One individual is MM and the other is NN—difference = 2

This system would give a within-human count of respectable numbers of differences separating individuals and groups, and people used it. The results were an approximation of sorts, but that is true of most measurements, and they were perfectly adequate to address, even answer, some long-standing anthropological puzzles. For example, there are two groups of people with the combination of dark skin and frizzy hair—sub-Saharan Africans and Melanesians. The latter have often been called "Oceanic Negroes," implying a special relationship with Africans. The blood group data, however, showed that they are about as different from Africans as they could be.

In another realm, the data could be used to assess degrees of admixture. For example, what is the proportion of European-derived genes in "black" (as socially defined) Americans? The answer in 1969 was about 25 percent. The answer in 2001, with an enormously larger, mostly DNA-sequence database, was about 25 percent. In short, genetic differences can be counted in a useful and reliable manner.

## THE TIME DIMENSION

Aside from the gene-flow issues just mentioned, there was a much more difficult proposition. In the late 1960s and early 1970s, a number of us had tackled the basic question squarely: How do we measure within-human differences and human-ape differences *on the same scale*, so that we can calibrate the former in terms of the latter? (This is the second major utility of that 5-million-year figure.) Could we use the same protein (serum albumin) as was used to do the human-ape comparisons? Albumin (about 7 percent of total serum protein) is a linear chain of 584 amino acids, of which, we estimated, only 6 to 8 differed among humans, chimpanzees, and gorillas. That was a small number considering the 10 million years (5 million along each lineage) separating each line from the other two—an average of less than one change along each lineage every million years. And albumin was one of the more rapidly evolving proteins known at the time. We had two options:

- Find proteins that evolved more rapidly than albumin with which to measure the much smaller time spans (tens to hundreds of thousands of years) involved in within-human differentiation (but there didn't seem to be any, and mtDNA was still well in the future); or
- Look at many more proteins (as DNA sequencing was still a dream).

The latter we could do, using a technique called electrophoresis. In that procedure an electric field is used to move the proteins through an appropriate medium, thus separating them on the basis of their charges and shapes. Fortunately, a substantial number of proteins could be compared by electrophoresis. The estimates at the time were that this would allow us to see about one-third of the amino acid substitutions that had actually occurred, so one albuminlike protein might accumulate one mutation visible to the electrophoreser every 4 million years (my) or so.

8 per 10 my = 0.8 per my
1/3 visible = 0.8 visible per 3 my = 1 visible per about 4 my

We had a good supply of such proteins in blood sera (20–25, depending on the species involved and the quality of the sample), so that we could expect to see, on the average, one difference for every 150,000–200,000 years (4 my divided by 20–25) of separation between two lineages. That was the theory.

When I actually came to run human, chimpanzee, and gorilla sera in the same gel, the large majority of bands (20 or more of the 25 or so that could be discerned) had different mobilities in any of the three comparisons—chimp-human, chimp-gorilla, or gorilla-human. To convert these raw data into actual distances, one had to allow for the fact that a given protein might accumulate more than one change along a particular lineage, but the mobilities could only be scored as same or different. The 20–24 differences observed thus implied about 40–70 actual changes $[(-\ln 0.2–0.05)(100)(25) = 40]$ (where ln means natural logarithm). Thus, our original prediction using theory was very close to my experimental results. Calculating 40 changes over 10 million years of separation works out to one change along one lineage or the other roughly every 125,000 to 225,000 years.

Compared with what science can do today, my methodology was crude, but it was better than anyone else had come up with at the time. We were able for the first time to show that pygmy chimpanzees were cleanly distinguishable from common chimpanzees, that the Sumatran orangutans and the Bornean orangutans were at least as different from one another as were the two chimp species, and, at a less esoteric level, that dogs and wolves (which are not yet distinguishable genetically from each another) were distinct from coyotes.

And people?

Only a few gels rapidly convinced me that there was no significant intergroup variation at this level in our species. Although a given comparison between two individuals might show a difference or two, proceeding to interpopulational comparisons didn't increase the number of differences significantly. The minimal interpopulational (racial) differences we could observe today were entirely consistent with times of separation of no more than 100,000 years among human populations. Thus, races as we know them were young. The data simply didn't indicate any great antiquity for racial origins. But, as we already noted, this finding didn't help with respect to using such data for choosing among the competing scenarios. Regional continuity plus appropriate levels of gene flow could give the same degrees of racial genetic differentiation as did the Garden-of-Eden model.

This is the first place where the inquiry became personally frustrating. I had been doing well enough in this human evolution business: I knew what the questions were; I had the answers (in the form of my gels) staring me, quite literally, in the face day after day; and yet I did not see what I might or should have seen. The fact that no one else did either (many people studied those gels) is no comfort, as I had the data, and they didn't. What I might or should have seen is that the two scenarios made very different predictions with respect to the overall genetic diversity to be expected among modern humans.

If, for example, we contemplated a human presence in much of the Old World a million years ago (and recent discoveries in the Republic of Georgia and in Java show this to have been a conservative figure), and four "regions," then we would be talking about 4 million years of opportunity for mutations to have accumulated. One electrophoretically detectable substitution per 4 million years per serum protein locus would mean that most loci would show a relatively high frequency difference in one or the other of the four regions, and thus I ought to have been able to see that that presence, in the regional-continuity perspective, should have produced, in extant populations, far more alleles, at each of a substantial number of serum protein loci, than were evident in my gels. In other words, never mind the levels of intergroup diversity on which I and most others were fixated; there simply wasn't sufficient diversity in the species as a whole to account for a million years of existence. And this shouldn't have been a tough call: It wouldn't have taken great mathematical skill to do the obvious calculations—like those described a few paragraphs back. Gene flow would have reduced the amount of intergroup diversity; it should not have significantly affected overall diversity. Yet I didn't do those simple calculations, nor did anyone else. There was a mental glitch somewhere, and it took a very different system and better minds to overcome it.

## MITOCHONDRIAL DNA

Thus, there was still the search for a Holy Grail—a system that measured within-human differences on the same scale as it measured human-ape differences, did so more convincingly than electrophoretic comparisons of the serum proteins did, and, most important, addressed the Garden-of-Eden/regional-continuity conundrum more clearly and effectively.

And then it suddenly appeared—almost as if by magic—from Wes Brown's Cal Tech doctoral dissertation on the evolution of animal mitochondrial DNAs and his subsequent postdoctoral research at the University of California at San Francisco that included, for the first time, within-human comparisons with that molecule. Wes estimated that individual humans differed from one another by about 0.36 percent (or at about 50 of the roughly 16,500 base pairs in their mtDNA), whereas chimps differed from humans at about 10 percent of the positions. These were crude early estimates based on limited data, but showed, to the prepared mind, enormous potential. Wes saw that potential, but was wary of wading into the morass of human individual and racial genetic variation; Allan Wilson also saw it, but more optimistically, and invited Wes to bring his mtDNA technology and insights to Berkeley. Wes did so, and the rest, as we could again say, is history.

Of course, it wasn't quite that easy, and the history was messy at times, but it is relatively clear that the mtDNA work in Allan's lab will come to be seen as the single most important effort in the decipherment of the origin of our species and of racial variation within it.

To see this requires understanding what is special about mtDNA. First, it is small and cleanly isolable from the mitochondria, which themselves had a fairly easy source in placentas. It should be noted that this work started before the PCR (polymerase chain reaction) revolution made the isolation of any piece of DNA in any quantity desired a routine procedure, so source and concentration were of primary importance. Another useful property of mtDNA is that it is denser than nuclear DNA, and therefore it could be separated out, in those technologically primitive days, by thirty-six hours in the ultracentrifuge, a straightforward though tedious procedure. It was known at the time that mtDNA was inherited clonally by daughter from mother (males have mtDNA but do not pass it on to their offspring); the fact that mtDNA derives from only one parent is its critical advantage. This meant that mtDNA types were not involved in the messy businesses of gene mixture and gene recombination—so that we could follow one lineage at a time from its origin (which could be many millions of years ago) to the time we got to study it in the lab. Next, Wes had shown that mtDNA evolved (changed sequence) much more rapidly than did nuclear DNA (the material in our forty-six chromosomes). Human and chimp nuclear DNAs, we estimated at the time, differed by about 1 to 1.5 percent, the mtDNAs by 10–15 percent. In short, we needed to examine much less DNA to find enough of those critical differences that would allow us to conclude something about our prehistory.

Within the year, Allan, Wes, and Matt George (a graduate student in the lab) had put together a jointly authored article for *PNAS* (*Proceedings of the National Academy of Sciences*) entitled "Rapid Evolution of Animal Mitochondrial DNA." In it they answered all the basic questions and even provided numbers that, though derived from crude technology, parallel remarkably the best ones we have today, more than two decades later. For example, in the abstract we find:

> By plotting the degree of divergence in mitochondrial DNA against time of divergence, the rate of base substitution could be calculated from the initial slope of the curve. The value obtained, 0.02 substitutions per base pair per million years, was compared with the value for single-copy nuclear DNA. The rate of evolution of the mitochondrial genome appears to exceed that of the single-copy fraction of the nuclear genome by a factor of about 10.

and later in the text this:

> In a comparison of 68 cleavage sites in mtDNA from 21 racially diverse humans, the average value for $p$ was 0.002 (unpublished data). $p$ = mean difference between 2 humans.

That was in 1979. In 2003, with complete sequences available, these are the results (where bp = base pairs):

"0.02 substitutions/bp/my" is now 0.017
"by a factor of about 10" is now about 13
$p$ for 21 racially diverse humans = 0.002

The time involved for developing those within-human differences in 1979 was thus (0.002/0.02 subst/bp/my) or about 100,000 years, a number right on target with the best answer we have today—about 100,000 years.

In hindsight, matters got both clearer and more confused as the mtDNA database increased exponentially during the 1980s.

## THE CANN EFFORT

The big step was taken by an anthropology graduate student, Rebecca Cann, working in Allan's lab and picking up the human work where Wes Brown had left it to take a faculty position at the University of Michigan. In the next couple of years (today it would be a couple of days or, at most, weeks), Becky collected some 130 additional placentas, purified their mtDNAs, and using the same techniques, compared about 10 percent (1,500 bp [base pairs]) of their sequences. Finally, she constructed a tree of relationships among the 140 individual DNA samples—the now-classic U-shape from her dissertation.

That tree shows one clear, critically important pattern. The deepest (oldest) lineages are African; that is, the largest differences observed are among Africans and between them and non-Africans—and all of the latter derive from a single African lineage. That is the genesis of the out-of-Africa scenario in its recent form, and the latest data, published in *Nature* in December 2000, fully and unequivocally vindicate her. There the authors report having worked out the complete (roughly 16,550 bp) sequences of 53 recent human mtDNA samples, and they present trees that show, using ten times the resolving power Becky had available to her, precisely the same pattern of relationships she found—the deepest lineages lead to living Africans, and all extant non-Africans derive from another African line.

This is a good time to pause to consider what is and isn't meant by the above conclusion. It means that the mtDNA at the base of the tree had an ultimate origin in one woman, whom, inevitably, we called "Eve." Her most direct descendants are living Africans—thus "African Eve"—and everyone else derives from a lineage that also leads to Africans—thus "out-of-Africa." That the study works out this way topologically is a statistical necessity, as every time a woman has no daughters, her mtDNA lineage becomes extinct, and if the study goes far enough back in time, every mtDNA lineage will necessarily derive from a single, statistically fortunate mtDNA found in a single woman who lived, somewhere, a long time in the past. How long ago? And where? Well . . . .

Here's where Becky's work went off-track for a while. She spent a number of pages in her dissertation struggling with each of those matters. The basic problem in each case was that there was an enormous amount of what is technically termed "homoplasy" (parallelisms and convergences) in her trees. That is, the same mutation would appear in parallel or convergently along different lineages. For example, imagine she observed a C-T variation at position 3391; most humans had a C there, the rest a T. So somewhere, at some time, there had been a mutation from C to T (if the ancestral form was C) or from T to C (if it was T). Ideally, the mutation would have occurred just once, with the result that all the people with, say, T could be seen as belonging to one lineage, and all those with C to another. If this procedure was followed for all the variants, the directionality question (was it T→C or C→T?) would be answered directly; that is, the answer would be the direction that minimized the number of changes required in the tree to explain the observations, and assuming a molecular clock, the root of the tree would be placed between the two groups most different from one another.

That's the theory—practice was another matter entirely. Becky observed 89 phylogenetically informative (occurring in at least two individuals) variants but required 368 mutations on her tree to account for them. For the example above, neither the individuals with a T at 3391, nor those with a C, would hang together as a group when other variants at different positions were brought into the analysis. Nor was this a minor effect; for 368 mutations to account for 89 variants means that each mutation occurred, on the average, three times, that is, on three different lineages, in the tree. The problem is that there were then many trees that could account for the observed variation (they weren't necessarily the same three lineages in each tree). This led to two more problems. First, if there was this much homoplasy simply among humans, then variation among chimps was essentially random as far as the human variation was concerned, and this made the use of a chimp distance to calibrate the human tree dicey indeed. At this point, the alert reader might ask: "Ummm . . . didn't you just show precisely that calculation from the 1979 article to point out how some very bright people got it right back then?" Yes, we did. Lucky or very smart? Mostly lucky—incidentally, most of the more rapidly evolving control-region sequences were omitted.

The problem for Becky was that, in a very real way, she knew too much and too little at the same time. The basic problem lay in the fact that rates of change vary enormously among segments of the mtDNA molecule; in particular, the 1,000 or so positions in the "control region" (D-loop) are accumulating mutations at about ten times the rate of the other 15,500. But even that is just an average across the whole control region; detailed study showed a decidedly nonrandom pattern of change. Certain mutations were much more likely than others, and certain positions were much more likely than others to experience a mutation, resulting in the apparently paradoxical result that human-chimp percent sequence difference across the control region was no greater than the figure for the rest of the molecule (in fact, it was less). The human-chimp difference is 17 percent for all noncontrol-region DNA and only 12 percent for the control region—in other words, the high control-region rate is significant only for short-term comparisons.

But Becky couldn't know the problem at the time; indeed, it wasn't until 1991 that the appropriate chimp data appeared (as described later). So the within-human variation had not been ac-cumulating at the same effective rate as that between chimps and humans, and Becky's inability to correct for this phenomenon (she had the human but not the chimp data, and couldn't have been expected to see that she needed the latter) meant that her date for Eve was more ancient than the true one. We couldn't know how much more ancient, but should have appreciated that her date of about 250,000 years for the base of the human tree was more likely to be wrong high than wrong low. And if that were the case, then the other problem resulting from the high homoplasy levels—whether it was really "out-of-Africa"—became much less of an is-sue because we had no lineages old enough to be consistent with the predictions of the regional-continuity scenario.

This is the particular strength of mtDNA. If we are to take the regional-continuity scenario seriously, then we would expect to see old (approaching at least 1 million years) lineages in different portions of the world. But instead it seems there are no old line-ages—period! In other words, the shape of the tree seemed clear. The next and final step was to get the date straight.

## THE STONEKING EFFORT

The first step on the tortuous path that finally led to "figuring out this racial thing" was taken by Mark Stoneking, then a Berkeley graduate student in the Genetics Department, who had taken on the project after Becky left for a faculty position at the University of Hawaii. Mark addressed himself to the matter of calibrating a human mtDNA clock internally. He reasoned as follows: Imagine a small group of humans successfully colonizing an area previously devoid of human habitation, inevitably leading to a marked and rapid increase in their numbers and in the numbers of various of the mtDNA types they had brought with them. These will then begin accumulating mutations of their own, producing new types specific to the area and more similar to one another than to related types elsewhere. Thus we will be able to count the number of in situ changes along each mtDNA lineage, and, given some information from the archaeological and/or fossil records as to how long ago the colonization began, calculate a rate of change for mtDNA types in the area and, by extension, in the species as a whole. The logic was ingenious and ultimately successful.

Mark began with (and continues to work among) Papua New Guinea (PNG) populations, where the archaeological record then available indicated that people arrived there some 30,000–40,000 years ago. If modern New Guineans are descended from those first colonists, their mtDNA also should be descended from the types present among those colonists, having differentiated from one another in New Guinea. And they were. It looked as though four quite distinct mtDNA types had given rise to most of the sequences present in today's population. The oldest within New Guinea differences in each of the four groups averaged about 0.7 percent, as against 3 percent for the world as a whole. Thus if it took 30,000–40,000 years to achieve a 0.7 percent difference, 3 percent would require about 130,000–170,000 years. Given the uncertainties inherent in the whole enterprise, the fact that this date was reasonably consistent with Cann's, and that the difference from hers was in the direction of making the multiregional model (with its requirement for ancient mtDNA lineages) even more unlikely, were factors that legitimately increased confidence in the overall time scale. This finding convinced Allan Wilson to publish the results in a major journal; the now-classic *Nature* article of January 1, 1987, titled "Mitochondrial DNA and Human Evolution" carried the by-line R. L. Cann, M. Stoneking, and A. C. Wilson. This article, in effect, unveiled Eve to the world. That it didn't appear until five years after Becky's 1982 dissertation is probably indicative of Allan's inability in this instance to dot as many i's and cross as many t's as he was accustomed to doing.

Then came the sad but critical year of 1991. It was sad because of Allan's tragically early death from leukemia but critical because of the appearance of three confirmatory articles that seemed to dot many of those i's and cross many of the t's. Two of the articles dealt with the time dimension and were coauthored by two postdoctoral students in Allan's lab—Tom Kocher, working on the chimpanzee-based calibration, and Anna DiRienzo, on the internal calibration.

Anna's work involved the control region of some 100 mtDNA types from, in the main, Sardinia and the Levant. Her tree showed a major proliferation of new lineages at a time equivalent to a sequence difference of about 0.6–0.7 percent (just like Papua New Guinea). In other words, there was a rapid increase in the size of the human population in the circum-Mediterranean area at that time. What human population? And when? The most obvious events would be the entry into the area of anatomically modern humans (for example, the Cro-Magnons) and their displacement of the Neanderthals—somewhere around 30,000–35,000 years ago; this time frame is consistent with what Stoneking found for PNG and with a time for the mtDNA Eve of around 120,000–140,000 years ago.

Tom Kocher had determined the sequences for the control regions of the fourteen humans most distinct from one another on the basis of Cann's earlier RFLP (restriction fragment length polymorphism) comparisons, plus two chimpanzees. Then he studied an 896 base-pairs sequence from a coding region that had been the object of an extensive study some ten years previously among the large apes. For both areas the average within-human differences were about one-thirtieth of those separating humans and chimpanzees, and the date for mtDNA Eve was thus about 150,000 years ago.

By 1991, therefore, the externally calibrated time scale and the internally calibrated time scale had come into reasonable agreement, and it remained clear that there were no existing old mtDNA lineages consistent with the expectations of the multiregional scenario. (It should be noted here that there has been a tendency to conflate two quite distinct "Eves"—one for all human sequences, the other for the out-of-Africa group—the latter being the later Eve.)

The third critical article of 1991, posthumously coauthored by Allan with Linda Vigilant and Mark Stoneking of the Berkeley lab and Henry Harpending and Kirsten Hawkes of the University of Utah, appeared in the September 27, 1991, issue of *Science* and offered a highly advanced (technically) version of the classic Cann, Stoneking, and Wilson 1987 *Nature* study. Here about 610 base pairs of the control regions of 189 human mtDNA types (121 of them native Africans) were sequenced.

The story again gets personal for me (Sarich). For all the impressive internal consistency that had increasingly characterized the human mtDNA data from the late 1970s to the early 1990s, I remained uncomfortable with the scenario that came to be drawn from them. In particular, I had great difficulty finding supporting evidence in the archaeological and fossil records for the implied speciation event. In other words, we humans were being told that we were the eventual outcome of a classical speciation, an event in which some small, localized population in Africa evolved a new, gene-based capability that enabled them to expand out of that homeland and "replace" all other human populations in the world. My problem, however, was that I could not provide a principled alternative interpretation of the data and was left muttering, mostly to myself, for a good ten years, "There's something wrong here." I also was aware that my reaction was disturbingly reminiscent of remarks voiced by many with respect to the hominid-origins battle of the late 1960s. There was a black-box quality to what Allan and I had done then, which allowed critics to say, "There's something wrong with their data, and/or the logic that led them to that date of 5 million years ago. I don't understand the work, and I'm not going to waste my time becoming enough of a geneticist/biochemist/immunologist to be able to critique it on its own terms, but the results don't make any sense, and that's enough for me."

Maybe I wasn't quite that bad, but there is also no doubt that I spent an unconscionable amount of time trying to see how the molecular time scale could be expanded to better fit the multiregional scenario (which I had personally favored and taught in my courses over the past twenty-five years), totally ignoring the possibility that it might require significant contraction. Still, even the most stubborn mule is sometimes fortunate enough to run into a two-by-four that gets his attention, and my enlightenment began in 1992.

## GETTING THE MITOCHONDRIAL
## TIME SCALE STRAIGHT

Steve Mack, another genetics graduate student, had extended the Cann-Stoneking-DiRienzo effort to a study of American Indians, and I persuaded him to give me a one-on-one seminar concerning his results one day early in 1992. The picture he presented was the by-now-familiar one, with the individuals in his sample generally falling into one or another of four mtDNA groups that were pretty much Amerindian-specific, and the differences at the bases of the groups again at 0.6–0.7 percent. The problem rapidly became obvious: What event involving American Indians could be posited for the time corresponding to that sequence difference—that is, 30,000–40,000 years ago? Well, that obviously was going to be a difficult task, given that the earliest evidence of a major human presence in the Americas, the Clovis culture, dates back no more than about 13,000 years.

So Steve and I agreed unanimously that there were two potential rational interpretations of his data: (1) Perhaps there was a human presence in the Americas 30,000–40,000 years ago but archaeologists simply hadn't found it yet, or (2) the calibration was simply wrong. Given the choices, we would opt for the second every time. In other words, as far as we were concerned, the *absence of evidence* of 30,000–40,000-year-old humans in the Americas was indeed *evidence of absence*, and our job was to figure out how to square the 0.7 percent difference figure in New Guinea, the circum-Mediterranean area, and the Americas with major population expansions dating around 10,000 years ago. To ask that question was to answer it. The problem had been getting around to asking it, and no one had contemplated the possibility of interpreting the mtDNA data within so recent a time frame— for, as explained later, what appeared to be an excellent reason.

For the Americas it was straightforward: an empty continent to expand into beginning around 13,000 years ago. The other two areas also were simple: the coming of agriculture—well known in the Middle East, though not so well known in New Guinea but very likely existing in the highlands—around 10,000 years ago, with the inevitable consequence of human population suddenly increasing ten- to a hundredfold and leaving evidence of those increases in the patterns of diversity among contemporary mtDNAs. So that first step was not a major problem, but its implications were. Suddenly our dates had been cut by a factor of three or four, and the out-of-Africa or, at least, out-of-somewhere event was taking place at most some 40,000 to 50,000 years ago.

Time for a deep breath.

That was 1992. Beginning the next year, I put these conclusions on several e-mail discussion lists. But I never wrote them up into a draft for serious publication, for all this development seemed to have brought me back to where I started some thirty to forty years ago, encumbered with all the baggage that scenario carried—an eminently unappealing and unsatisfactory state of affairs. Such an intellectual environment then selected for that something's-wrong-here meme, and there was no lack of data and controversy in the literature to sustain it, however "unscientific" that attitude might have been at times. The fact was that the mtDNA system, for all its apparent and often realized potential, was not nearly as "clean" as I might have liked, and this had been clear almost from the beginning.

## ANOTHER CLONAL
## SYSTEM—THE Y-CHROMOSOME

From Berkeley to Stanford, a mere fifty miles to get the mtDNA problems sorted out—by studying another molecule.

Women inherit twenty-three pairs of chromosomes (including two Xs, the sex chromosomes); men the same twenty-two pairs plus an X and a Y, which carries the sex-determining genes. The Y chromosome is by far the smaller of the two, and 95 percent of it is not involved in recombination. The Y is passed from father to son along a single lineage, just as the mtDNA is passed from mother to daughter, and with the same potential for resolving questions of branching order and times of divergence. By "potential" I mean that the critical information is there as a DNA sequence, but it is not nearly as easy to get at as is mtDNA. On the other hand, there is a great deal more of it—on the order of 30 million base pairs, compared with 16,500 for the mtDNA. Finally, there is practically no homoplasy (parallelisms and convergences) present in the Y-chromosome results, and therefore none of the ambiguities that bedeviled researchers trying to derive trees from the mtDNA data.

The problem for several years was the fact that the Y-chromosome DNA evolves at a rate similar to that for the rest of the nuclear DNA (1.25 percent per 10 my per lineage); thus two humans whose Y-chromosome lineages were 100,000 years old would have only one substitution for every 4,000 base pairs. In other words, you would, on average, be examining 4,000 base pairs to find a single variant. Clearly, a screening procedure was needed to identify manageable pieces of DNA containing a variant, and that was provided by two of the Stanford group, Peter Underhill and Peter Oefner. Just how much they found was indicated in an article they published in 2001 in which they reported on 218 variants, of which 13 have been found by all other groups, and 205 by theirs.

In June of the previous year, the same group at Stanford had published the first reliable Y-chromosome dates in an article of major importance that, most appropriately, was published in the first year of the new millennium. In "Population Genetic Implications from Sequence Variation in Four Y-Chromosome Genes," the thirteen coauthors described finding 1,067 substitutions separating humans and chimpanzees at the 78,399 positions sampled. At the same time, they looked at 53 humans from all over the world and found, first, the standard three-deep lineages that are African and then an out-of-Africa limb branching out from one of those three that now contains most Africans and all non-Africans. The modern humans belonging to this out-of-Africa unit differed from one another by about 6.5 substitutions.

In crude terms, the time of most recent common ancestry is the human-human difference divided by the human-chimp difference (6.5/1,067) times the human-chimp divergence time (5 million years)—note how useful it is to have that date—which equals about 30,000 years ago. The terms are "crude" because a difference of 6.5 is small, and it is unknown to what extent current variation in the species reflects a sudden expansion in numbers beginning with its origin. But the precise date is not that important, just as it wasn't for the human-chimp study thirty-five years ago. Nonetheless, the quantitative similarity to that earlier situation is striking. First, the estimated albumin difference was close to 5 substitutions and certainly not more than 10. Second, limits could be put on the possible dates involved. The best estimate for the earlier australopithecines (which would be the latest possible human-chimp divergence time) was about 3 mya; the oldest would have to be substantially less than 10 mya (otherwise the time scale for earlier divergences among primates would become terribly distorted).

By the same token, the Y-chromosome date for the beginnings of racial differentiation in *Homo sapiens* cannot reasonably precede the exodus out of Africa, nor can it be more recent than, for example, perhaps twice the time of the Amerindians in the New World, or about 25,000 years ago. At this point, people who know this field are likely to raise the case of native Australians, who scientists believe have been there for at least 40,000 and perhaps as much as 60,000 years. It is also known, for certain, that recent Australians are not an out-group to all other human populations. Thus, if they have been separated from the latter for 40,000–60,000 years, the time of most recent common ancestry for the latter must be much greater. What is going on here? The likely answer is that those 40,000- to 60,000-year-old Australians have nothing to do with Australians with whom other people are familiar. First, the degree of known linguistic diversity in Australia need not have taken more than about 10,000 years to evolve. Second, there is no cultural (archaeological) continuity between sites more than 10,000 years of age and those less old. Third, those less than 6,000 years old seem to form a single cultural complex (including dingoes) that is intrusive. Last, the amount of morphological diversity among recent Australians (discussed later) is very small and does not increase much when Tasmanians and other Melanesians are included in the comparisons. Thus, we would not look for great age for determining antiquity of branching among the three groups.

## THE *HOMO SAPIENS* PHYLOGENY

The two definitive articles on *Homo sapiens* molecular phylogenies appeared, again appropriately enough, in November and December 2000. In the first, the Stanford group presented the Y-chromosome tree of 1,062 "globally representative" humans sampled at 167 sites that gave a tree of 117 haplotypes (a haplotype is a specific nucleotide sequence). The second, authored by a group at the Max Planck Institute for Evolutionary Anthropology in Leipzig, headed by Svante Pääbo, presented trees derived from the complete sequences of 53 human and 1 chimpanzee mtDNAs. An indication of why the mtDNA data previously available had proved so resistant to producing definitive trees from control-region data was evident from a comparison of the control region to the rest, which showed that the difference between chimp and human control regions was 12 percent, as against 17 percent for all the rest (this result was mentioned earlier). This in spite of the fact that the main reason for using the control region was the "fact" that it evolved more rapidly than the rest. Here is another object lesson for those who investigate Mother Nature: Apparently she set up a system that rapidly recycled mutations at a relatively small number of control-region sites, such that the underlying tree is blurred—sometimes hidden—by the homoplastic noise. The way out, obviously, has been to look at systems with minimal homoplasy—the noncontrol region to trace female lineages; the Y chromosomes for male lineages.

## THE SHAPES OF THE TREES

For purposes of this discussion, the trees presented in the two papers published in 2000 are congruent, showing common mtDNA and Y-chromosome trees with three lineages deriving from a common ancestor in each. Two of those could each be termed "old African"; that is, they contain only Africans, whereas most

Africans and all non-Africans for each molecule belong to a third. It is the third lineage that was present in the Homo population that evolved some adaptation to give it an ultimate advantage over all other Homo groups around at the time, colonizing Africa and the rest of the habitable world and making extinct any other existing populations. The question then becomes "what ultimate advantage?"

And the dates?

The calculation is still crude, but in the range of 40,000–50,000 years ago for the later out-of-Africa Eve.


## EPIPHANY 2

A few pages back, at the beginning of the discussion of Jack King's 1968 seminar on neutral changes (see pages 123–125), we promised to recount a second epiphany and we discuss it briefly here. The occasion was a lecture on his most recent Y-chromosome data by Peter Underhill in January 2001. We were in attendance. I (Sarich) had asked Peter as to that bugaboo of molecular efforts—homoplasy and he answered succinctly that, for all practical purposes, there wasn't any. A given variant would, more than 99 percent of the time, occur only once in the tree. Tree-drawing then became a trivial paper-and-pencil exercise, there being no question about which variant went where. After that glimpse of the Holy Grail, we sat and listened as Peter delivered as elegant a lecture as we had ever heard. It was really epiphany 2—a beautiful data set and an unequivocal tree. No more fuzzy trees or fuzzy scenarios. It took me (Sarich) back to when my Fall 1964 seminar paper opened my eyes to the molecular clock implications for human origins. And it also made this book possible. It killed, in one fell swoop, the possibility of any old Homo sapiens lineages. It was out-of-Africa and something to be lived with.

## CHAPTER SIX

# The Two "Miracles"
# That Made Humankind

*In this chapter we examine two major problems that the new synthesis of human evolution has yet to resolve. If racial differentiation is very recent, having taken place only as ancestral humans migrated out of Africa, and none of the earlier fossil human species, the best known being the Neanderthals, have any living descendants, (1) what was the advantage that allowed our ancestors to replace all of these other species; and (2) since there is no evidence of their DNA in modern populations, why were those species not capable of interbreeding with our ancestors?*

*Neither we nor anyone we know has the answers. We tentatively propose that the augmentation of preexisting gestural language by spoken language provided a quantum leap in communicative ability. The reason for genetic isolation is unknown.*

It should be eminently clear by now that I (Sarich) believe people won't get very far by continuing to argue with Mother Nature. Whatever problems they may have with certain realities, it is best to recognize that if a problem doesn't have an acceptable solution, they better embrace that fact and regard it no longer as a problem but simply something to be lived with and adapted to as well as they can. Our origin then becomes a classic speciation event— some new genetic adaptation giving the small population in which it developed some major advantage over all other humans around at the time, and that the latter were unable (presumably, because of a genetic deficit) to copy. At the same time, our ances- tors developed some sort of gene-based reproductive isolation, such that even if interspecific sex did occur—and we, knowing human males all too well, feel that it must have—the matings must have been sterile. Note that the reproductive isolation of our ancestors makes them a separate species, necessarily taking the name *Homo sapiens* and denying it to all those other contempora- neous humans. My discussion of this with a good friend—a lin- guist with a marked interest in human evolution—led her to comment that I was looking for two miracles, and I think that's a very good way to view it—two adaptive "something specials."

Language, yes, but what about it? Does that refer to all derived language abilities evolving in a not-so-mythic African Garden of Eden some 50,000 years ago? That seems utterly untenable for any number of reasons, not the least of which is that we would then be left with an even greater puzzle to deal with—the steady increase in brain size from 600 or so cubic centimeters (cc) in early *Homo* days some 2 million years ago to more than 1,500 cc in the latest Neanderthals. Brain tissue is by far the most expen- sive tissue in the body, which makes it certain that we didn't gain those extra ccs incidentally. If not incidentally, then there is only one adaptation imaginable that could use up all that brain tis- sue—language.

But then what was the deficit in all those other (well, until now we could have called them *Homo sapiens*) soon-to-become extinct *Homo* lineages? What were they missing that our ancestors did so much with but without significantly affecting the size of their brains?

Very tentatively and diffidently, we suggest you think about the following situation: You're on the phone, which is, let's say, in your left hand. What is your right hand doing? Resting calmly in your lap? Doubtful. Typically, it is energetically gesturing. To whom? That person at the other end of the line whom you can't see, and who can't see you.

Similarly, lecturers generally accompany their words with gestures, and indeed many, perhaps most, are incapable of delivering a lecture unaccompanied by gestures. The only way to avoid gesturing is to read the presentation, but reading itself is clearly a very recent artifice, and certainly not something humans in any sense evolved to do. A lecture is something very different from and much more natural than a written-out talk. However, academics often find this point of view somewhat alien, even when a matter as important as a job presentation is involved. Time after time a job candidate has come to give a seminar and then reads for some fifty minutes. If that's the best the applicant can do, why not simply bring enough copies for everyone in the audience to read and discuss? Typically, such a presentation is a précis of the candidate's doctoral dissertation that has consumed the applicant for years, and it is amazing how someone who will be lecturing more than 100 hours a year in his classes (if he is hired) can't manage an hour on something he presumably knows better than anyone in the audience (probably, the world).

Many academics have spent so much time with the printed word that they have come to take for granted that it is the norm or, perhaps, the ideal. That sort of thinking leads nowhere with respect to the origin and evolution of language. No matter how difficult it might be, we need to accept, at least for the sake of consideration and discussion, the idea that the origin of gestural language came first starting about 2 million years ago, and that the growth of our brains over most of the next 2 million years was tracking the increasing sophistication of gestural languages.

This raises the possibility that the very late addition of speech was the first of the "miracles" giving rise to *Homo sapiens* somewhere in Africa about 50,000 years ago. (The second, as noted earlier, was the essentially contemporaneous development of reproductive isolation.) Why the advantage? We don't know, but the fact that people can "say" anything with their hands and face that they can say orally does not mean that they "say" it as effectively under all conditions. After all, they would still need to see the signer face-to-face and in the light, and those are fairly serious limitations compared with spoken language.

Given this, we have had in recent years any number of studies that have addressed the situation within a language-acquisition framework. The authors of the explicitly titled "Why People Gesture When They Speak" lay out two nonmutually exclusive interpretations of their results: (1) Speakers gesture simply because they see others gesture and learn from this model to move their hands as they speak, and (2) speakers gesture because they understand that gestures can convey useful information to the listener. The experimental protocol was simple and ingenious, and the article fills but a single page in *Nature*.

In the first experiment 12 sighted and 12 blind young people, matched for age (range 9–18, means 11:11 and 12:10) and sex (4 M, 8 F), were videotaped while responding spontaneously to a series of reasoning tasks known to elicit gesturing in sighted children. They found that all 12 of the blind subjects "gestured as they spoke, at a rate not reliably different from the sighted group . . . and conveyed the same information using the same range of gesture forms."

In the second, 4 additional younger (5:0–8:6) subjects blind from birth were tested in the same reasoning task, where they were told that the experimenter herself was blind. It didn't make any difference. All the blind subjects gestured, and did so at rates not reliably different from those seen in sighted-with-sighted or sighted-with-blind pairings.

Following is the concluding paragraph of the article: "Our findings underscore the robustness of gesture in talk. Gesture does not depend on either a model or an observer, and thus appears to be integral to the speaking process itself. These findings leave open the possibility that gestures that accompany speech may reflect, or even facilitate, the thinking that underlies speaking."

What about deaf children? Their performance gives the strongest support to the "gesture is primitive" notion. If they are raised in a signing environment, their acquisition of language follows the same trajectory as that of hearing children in a spoken environment. Typically, their first signs show up at around their first birthday, just as do words in a speaking child. Around the second birthday, they begin to have two-word and two-sign periods, and soon after they exhibit a reliable word or sign ordering (that is, the beginning of syntax). At about thirty months, morphology becomes evident (for example, the plural marker "s" in English, or the appropriate sign), and they embark on a few months of very rapid language acquisition.

If parents are aware and interested, deaf children will get responses to their first signs (babbling), and parents and children will go on to develop their own language. So will a group of deaf children in, for example, a community where several of them are grouped together.

For all practical purposes, then, it would appear that our brains had evolved the neural circuitry necessary to language long before the adaptation to spoken language had begun. The odds on this being the answer? As we wrote a few pages back, we are tentative and diffident. We would not be surprised to be proved right, nor to be proved wrong. We await the ingenious, well-crafted experiments to resolve the matter.

## CHAPTER SEVEN

# Race and
# Physical Differences

*In this chapter we refute the three most cogent, coherent, and influential arguments against the reality of race. First, geneticist Richard Lewontin has shown that only 15 percent of the variation within our species is between races. We point out that this 15 percent figure, while correct, must be placed in context in order to give a true measure of interracial differences. Next, the late paleontologist Stephen Jay Gould argued that there has not been enough time for evolution to produce significant racial differences. We explain that elapsed time does not determine the amount of change in traits that have survival value. Anatomical differences among human races can exceed those found between chimpanzee species. Finally, evolutionary biologist Jared Diamond has argued that the characteristics chosen to distinguish between races are arbitrary. Choose a different set of characteristics and you will come up with a different set of races. We demonstrate that the comparison of randomly chosen DNA variants produces the same races as the commonsense view, the art and literature of ancient, non-European civilizations, and anthropology.*

## THE NATURE OF GENETIC
## VARIATION IN OUR SPECIES

So we finally have what seem to be reliable trees, with both times and branching order, for recent *Homo sapiens* populations and various primate species. We have made the claim that this is the necessary beginning to the development of the evolutionary sce-narios for the organisms involved. With that beginning, what comes next? For many, when the subject is race, nothing biologi-cal is next. These include people who, by any serious criteria, have the requisite talents to be able to comment on the signifi-cance of human racial variation, if there were any. They have spoken, and their answer is "significance: minimal" with respect to understanding our species. For them this book is inherently ir-relevant. We obviously disagree. Here is why.

Our species is in fact readily divisible into a large number of . . . well, of what? An answer developed out of a request I (Sarich) sent out on a couple of e-mail networks (italics represent e-mail communications):

*One thing that intrigues me about this subject is the tendency of the "no race" people to avoid defining what it is that they claim doesn't ex-ist. In other words, what characteristics would human races have if they did exist? Would anyone care to try to address that one? Or pro-vide a reference to a recent effort that does?*

The only significant response I received from a "no-race" advo-cate was the following:

*Then the human species would be divisible into a reasonable number of reasonably discrete groups on the basis of reasonably objective criteria, with some reasonably evolutionary explanation attached to the division (that is, short-medium-tall would not be a useful racial classification, though small and objective).*

My comment was:

*Okay, so what are we fighting about anyway?*

or

*So let's be reasonable.*

The fact is that, for reasonable people, our species is divisible into a number (I see no way of making a judgment as to why it should be a "reasonably small number" and what number would be "reasonably small" here—that's for Nature to tell us) of reasonably discrete groups (yes) on the basis of reasonably objective criteria (yes) with some reasonably evolutionary explanation attached to the division (yes).

This is where we should start. Few people would deny that most of us do see groupings of humans above the level of the individual and below that of the species. These, as previously mentioned, are races in the common sense, the *Oxford English Dictionary* point of view. Yet the trend, especially among individuals who should be the experts here (e.g., sociologists and anthropologists), has been distinctly toward the "no-race" camp—a camp that by now has a large cadre of some very prestigious, reliable, and voluble defenders. So, in an effort to be "reasonable" here, what is it that the no-race people, treated as serious and reasonable intellects, say on their behalf?

## A BATTLE IS JOINED

We start with one sort of objection, which was perhaps best illustrated by Jared Diamond, a deservedly well-received author of many articles and books (e.g., *The Third Chimpanzee; Guns, Germs, and Steel*) on the human condition, on pages 90–99 of the November 1994 issue of *Discover*. The article was entitled "Race Without Color" and was subtitled in the contents as "Want to

change your race? Or someone else's? Change some arbitrary criteria and you can group Nigerians with Norwegians, Chinese
with Cherokee."

What are these arbitrary criteria that we can change to produce these magical results? Just how can we group Nigerians with
Norwegians, other than simply as two *Homo sapiens* populations?

Quoting the text that appears in a box entitled "Race by Resistance" that appears beside the Diamond article, we read:

> Traditionally we divide ourselves into races by the twin criteria of
> geographical location and visible physical characteristics. But we
> could make an equally reasonable and arbitrary division by the
> presence or absence of a gene, such as the sickle-cell gene, that
> confers resistance to malaria. By this reckoning, we'd place
> Yemenites, Greeks, New Guineans, Thai, and Dinkas in one
> "race," Norwegians and several black African peoples in another.

Note his phrase "an equally reasonable and (equally) arbitrary division." So Diamond is arguing that there are no objective reasons for choosing any one division over any other. And he notes
toward the end of the article:

> We could have classified races based on any number of geographi-
> cally variable traits. The resulting classifications would not be at
> all concordant. Depending on whether we classified ourselves by
> antimalarial genes, lactase, fingerprints, or skin color, we could
> place Swedes in the same race as (respectively) either Xhosas, Fu-
> lani, the Ainu of Japan or Italians.

Most of us, upon reading these passages, would immediately sense
that something was very wrong with it, even though one might
have difficulty in specifying just what. How can Xhosas (a South

African group) go with Swedes (and, of course, Norwegians) rather than with their fellow sub-Saharan African Fulani from Nigeria? Because, Diamond tells us, they both lack the sickle-cell allele, whereas the Fulani have it.

Our response is straightforward—this is a meaningless association because the character involved (the lack of the sickle-cell allele) is an ancestral human condition. Associating Swedes and Xhosas thus says only that they are both human, not a particularly profound statement. Exactly the same logic applies to the lactase situation; that is, not producing lactase as an adult says only that you are like most humans and virtually all other mammals. So associating Swedes and Fulani just makes them human and mammals—which is true, but again of no use in our grouping enterprise.

There is a further critical flaw here. The proportion of individuals carrying the sickle-cell allele can never go above about 40 percent in any population, nor does the proportion of lactase-competent adults in any population ever approach 100 percent. Thus, on the basis of the sickle-cell allele, there are two groups (possible races by Diamond's criteria) of Fulani, one without the allele, the other with it. So those Fulani with the allele would group not with other Fulani, but with Italians with the allele. Those without it, along with the Italians without it (in both cases the majority) and all the Swedes, would form another unit—in effect, primitive *Homo sapiens*.

Perhaps not, you might argue. Diamond is talking of frequencies of traits in populations, and the frequencies of lactase-competent adults are more similar in Swedes and Fulani than in Swedes and Italians or Fulani and Xhosa (one should note here that lactase-competence has clearly evolved independently in Europeans and Africans). And, yes, he is. But the discordance issue he raises applies within groups as well as between them. He is dismissive of the reality of the Fulani-Xhosa black African racial unit because there are characters discordant with it. Well then, one asks in response, what about the Fulani unit itself? After all, exactly the same argument could be made to cast the reality of the category "Fulani" into doubt.

Diamond's no-race position is thus clearly logically untenable and need concern us no further.

## 85 PERCENT–15 PERCENT: CAN THAT BE RIGHT?

A more informative approach, probably the best-known in this realm, is that of Richard Lewontin, dating back to 1972. He looked at the data from 17 genetic loci (about half blood group) in numerous human populations and apportioned the variability observed into its within- and between-population components: about 85:15—that is, 85 percent of the genetic variability was seen among individuals within populations, and only an additional 15 percent was added by comparing individuals in different populations. Lewontin's assessment was correct for its time, and remains true for the much, much larger body of data that has accumulated since 1972.

Lewontin then drew a famous object lesson:

> It is clear that our perception of relatively large differences between human races and subgroups, as compared to the variation within these groups, is indeed a biased perception, and that, based on randomly chosen genetic differences, human races and populations are remarkably similar to each other, with the largest part by far of human variation being accounted for by the differences between individuals.
>
> Human racial classification is of no social value and is positively destructive of social and human relations. Since such racial classification is now seen to be of virtually no genetic or taxo-

nomic significance either, no justification can be offered for its continuance.

He put the same message in a different form in his 1982 book *Human Diversity:* "If, God forbid, the holocaust occurs and only the Xhosa people of the southern tip of Africa survived, the human species would still retain 80 percent of its variation."

We noted earlier that the variation occupying Lewontin here is, in the main, selectively neutral, and, therefore, a measure of time—the lower the amount of between-group variability, the less the amount of time separating the two populations. That is straightforward. But the 85:15 somehow still feels wrong—and it is in two ways. First, it is simply an average across the genetic loci on hand, saying nothing about the variation at individual loci. Eighty percent of the variation in the Rh or Duffy blood group loci? Or at the HLA loci? Again, not even close. And looking at bodies. Eighty percent of the variation in skin color? In hair form? In stature? In body build? Hardly, and no calculations are necessary to know it. Nor does it mean anything with respect to our abilities to look at individual Xhosa and decide that they are all far more similar to one another than any one is to any Scot, any Laotian, any Tahitian, any Mayan, any Somali, any _____(fill in the blank as desired—there are plenty of names left).

What of the body? Beneath the skin, no-race adherents claim, we're really all the same. Perhaps the most familiar and influential statement pertinent here is found in a Stephen J. Gould November 1984 *Natural History* essay entitled "Human Equality Is a Contingent Fact of History" (p. 32):

Human groups do vary strikingly in a few highly visible characters (skin color, hair form)—and this may fool us into thinking that overall differences must be great. But we now know that our usual metaphor of superficiality—skin deep—is literally accurate. . . .

Other plausible scenarios might also have led to marked inequality. *Homo sapiens* is a young species, its division into races even more
recent. This historical context has not supplied enough time for the
evolution of substantial differences. But many species are millions of
years old, and their geographic divisions are often marked and deep.
*H. sapiens* might have evolved along such a time scale and produced
races of great age and large accumulated differences—but we didn't.
Human equality is a contingent fact of history.

Lewontin and Gould tell it all: Racial variation is quantitatively insignificant (for genes) and, quite literally, a superficial
(for bodies) aspect of the biology of our species.

Of course, if we believed this, there would be no book to
write—except, perhaps, one telling the sorry history of human involvement with race and racial matters, but that one has already
been done many times over (and much of the effort is well worth
reading)—but in our view, both Gould and Lewontin are dead
wrong in the implications they draw from the data and observations they cite.

Why? We're going back a relatively long time in some new and
rapidly advancing fields; surely if there were something basically
wrong with the above messages, somebody (and given the statures
of Gould and Lewontin, it would have been numerous somebod-
ies) would have corrected them. Yet the world had to wait until
2002 for someone to explain the basic problems with Lewontin's
famous 15 percent. It was Henry Harpending replying to a question from Frank Salter.

Lewontin had noted that 85 percent of the genetic variability
was among individuals within populations, and only an additional 15 percent was added when individuals in different populations were compared. However, this analysis omits a third level
of variability—the within-individual one. The point is that we
are diploid organisms, getting one set of chromosomes from one

parent and a second from the other. To the extent that your mother and father are not especially closely related, then, those two sets of chromosomes will come close to being a random sample of the chromosomes in your population. And the sets present in some randomly chosen member of yours will also be about as different from your two sets as they are from one another. So how much of the variability will be distributed where?

First is the 15 percent that is interpopulational. The other 85 percent will then split half and half (42.5 percent) between the intra- and interindividual within-population comparisons. The increase in variability in between-population comparisons is thus 15 percent against the 42.5 percent that is between-individual within-population. Thus, $15/42.5 = 32.5$ percent, a much more impressive and, more important, more legitimate value than 15 percent. It's interesting that Henry Harpending noted in an e-mail to us that no one has ever published this calculation.

One might argue here that the genetic distances involved are so small that it makes no difference what level is being discussed—100 percent of nothing is still nothing. The appropriate and effective rejoinder, as previously noted (and will note again), is "dogs, dogs, and more dogs." There the amounts of both anatomical and behavioral variation added by going to between-breed comparisons are obviously far greater than for similar human between-race comparisons (though certainly no one doubts they are gene-based, while the degree of genetic variation is minimal, apparently much as in us).

Now to Gould. The basic reason Gould gives for his no-race position is this: "*Homo sapiens* is a young species, its division into races even more recent. This historical context has not supplied enough time for the evolution of substantial differences." (This from the man famous for his theory [with Niles Eldridge] of punctuated equilibria.)

And the take-home lesson: "Human equality is a contingent fact of history."

No, we say. If there's one thing the evolutionary process cannot produce, it is equality. We will give the reason for this in a few pages.

This is a numbers issue, but because there is a distinct paucity of relevant ones in the literature, we must produce our own. Basically, we want to compare the amounts of morphological change along various lineages of interest here to see, for example, whether in fact going beyond skin deep markedly reduces the amount of variability present. My (Sarich's) involvement in this realm began in 1994 with the publication of and controversy around *The Bell Curve*. In a debate, I made the flat statement that "racial morphological distances within our species are, on the average, about equal to the distances among species within other genera of mammals. I am not aware of another mammalian species whose constituent races are as strongly marked as they are in ours." And then I always had to add, "except, of course, domesticated dogs." But I left it there for several years until I was able to get some ape measurements from Colin Groves of the Australian National University in Canberra. Our data set was then cranial/facial measurements on 29 human populations, 2,500 individuals, 28 measurements, from W. W. Howells at Harvard; 17 measurements on 347 chimpanzees (Groves); and 25 measurements on 590 gorillas (Groves). Chimps are generally divided into two species (the pygmy chimpanzee, or bonobo, *Pan paniscus*; and the common chimp, or *P. troglodytes*), which has three subspecies (races if one wishes): *troglodytes*, *verus*, and *schweinfurthii*. There is less agreement on gorillas, but there are two distinct groups, probably species, *Gorilla gorilla* in the west and four closely related groups in the east.

The metric I have used is the percentage difference per size-corrected measurement (expressed as standard deviation units), and the numbers given are the percent increases in distance going from within-group to between-group comparisons of individuals. Thus, the increase in average distance in going from the paired comparisons of two males to similar comparisons for male and female pairings in some human populations is about 1–2.5 percent: for example, for Zulu, 1.15 percent; Australia, 1.87 percent; and Santa Cruz Island (California), 2.16 percent.

For pygmy chimps, the corresponding increase for male-female versus male-male comparisons is 4.7 percent; for common chimps it is 10.4 percent. These figures are consistent with the general sense that the degree of sexual dimorphism increases as we go from humans to pygmy chimps to common chimps.

Comparing distances among the three common chimp subspecies or races (for males) gives about 6 percent between *verus* and either *schweinfurthii* or *troglodytes*, and 1.6 percent (which is essentially noise level) between the latter two. From bonobo to *verus* is about 20 percent; to *troglodytes*, 14.6 percent; and to *schweinfurthii*, 8.8 percent. These three bonobo morphological distances are correlated with the corresponding geographical distances, and one has to wonder to what extent the smaller *paniscus-schweinfurthii* number is due to parallel evolution and how much to gene flow between the two sometime after the basic chimp-bonobo split occurred. Neither I nor anyone else as yet presumes to have the answer to that one.

For gorillas the basic split is between the western form (G. *gorilla*) and four eastern populations (three races of G. *graueri* and G. *berengi*, the "mountain gorilla"); those percentages are 17.3, 19.8, 22.9, and 24.7, respectively. Between *graueri* race 1 and the other three eastern forms, the percentages are 7.9, 12.8, and 12.3. Between *graueri* race 2 and the others, the differences are 4 percent and 11.1 percent. Between *graueri* race 3 and *berengi*, the difference is 8.4 percent.

Those are the ape numbers I've calculated to date. What about humans? These data come from comparing three African samples: the Dogon of Mali, the Teita (Kenyan Bantu speakers), and the South African Bushman. The percentages are Dogon to Teita, 9.9;

Dogon to Bushman, 13.4; and Teita to Bushman, 14.9. Thus the Dogon or Teita to Bushman "racial" distance is very much like the 14.6 percent separating two chimpanzee species (using the *P. t. troglodytes* to bonobo number). Similar percentages (16.3 and 15.5, respectively) are obtained when comparing a sample from Hokkaido (Japanese, not Ainu) and two Amerindian groups (the Arikara from South Dakota and a sample from Santa Cruz Island). Other comparisons that help put these distances in perspective are South Australia to Tolai (a New Britain group), 10 percent; Dogon to Norse, 19.4 percent; and South Australia to Norse, 26 percent.

The largest distance among chimpanzees or gorillas (the 24.7 percent between *G. gorilla* and *G. berengi*) is slightly less than that separating Howells's Norse and the South Australian samples (26 percent), but even this doesn't begin to exhaust the range of human variation. The largest differences in Howells's sample are found when comparing Africans with either Asians or Asian-derived (Amerindian) populations. Thus Teita to Tierra del Fuegans is 32.4 percent; Zulu to Tierra del Fuegans or Santa Cruz yields about 36 percent. The largest difference for any of the human data sets is 46 percent, which comes from comparing Teita with Buriat (who live in the Lake Baikal area and speak a Mongolian language).

I will also note here that putting these results on a bell curve would mean that each increase of 15 percent in distance is worth about one standard deviation, and that the absolute within-group variation does not vary significantly among the three genera (humans, chimps, and gorillas) involved. To my knowledge, these are the first such comparisons to be made (and the first time any such data have been published). The results seem well worth the effort.

Who would have predicted that the racial morphological distances in our species could be much greater than any seen among chimpanzees or gorillas, or, on the average, some tenfold greater than those between the sexes? I think it fair to say no one. I have posed the question to a number of audiences and individuals, lay and professional, and the modal estimate has tended to be about twofold—that is, about twice the distances between human sexes.

So now we have some useful numbers that help to solve the matter of whether the degree of variation in morphological features is high, low, or just middling. The answer cannot be known without having a standard of comparison available. Here the chimp and gorilla can be the standards. The two chimpanzee species differ from each other by about 15 percent on the morphological distance scale, and a comparable pair of human populations are Japanese and Arikara. But not until the data are put on a time scale does the significance of this experiment become clear.

Molecular data suggest that the two chimpanzee lineages separated around 1.5 million years ago; the comparable human figure is on the order of 15,000 years. In other words, the two chimp lineages are 100-fold older, yet show the same amount of variation. That is a remarkable result, the implications of which take a while to sink in. The implications follow this logic: Human races are very strongly marked morphologically; human races are very young; so much variation developing in so short a period of time implies, indeed almost certainly requires, functionality; there is no good reason to think that behavior should somehow be exempt from this pattern of functional variability.

What about performance? When push comes to shove, just how much can trained performance vary among individuals and groups in our species? For this I am inevitably drawn to the track, where humans compete on the basis of how well they can use one of our primary adaptations—bipedalism.

Analysis begins with a restatement of the ruling orthodoxy here: Yes, racial variation does exist in our species, but it is quantitatively and functionally inconsequential; furthermore, there is every reason to believe that it couldn't be otherwise.

Why is there "every reason to believe" that racial variation couldn't be anything other than quantitatively and functionally inconsequential? Why should social scientists feel comfortable penning statements such as "Bipedalism (or intellectual ability) is such a critical aspect of the human adaptation that one would not expect to see great differences in bipedal (or cognitive) performances at either the individual-to-individual level, or between populations?" Ideological desires aside, they would argue that the fuel for natural selection is heritable, functionally significant variation (obviously true), and that therefore adaptation will use up some portion of that variation, decreasing the amount left for us to observe.

Further, the more important the feature (bipedalism, a large brain, language ability), the more the genetic variation underlying it would be consumed, and the less variation would be seen in it today. If this argument holds at the individual level, and if individual variation is much greater than group variation (which it is), then gene-based group variation with respect to those features critical to human adaptation simply cannot be worth worrying about when trying to explain such variation as is observed in, say, quality of bipedalism (measured as running performance) or level of mental ability (IQ tests). All of this sounds reasonable, and the basic theory underlying it has indeed been for decades a standard part of the thinking of evolutionary biologists and a fixture in evolutionary biology textbooks.

## THE RACE IS TO THE SWIFTEST; THE SWIFTEST ARE THE KALENJIN

That's theory. What about data? What do the numbers at running venues reveal? Well, as many of you are already well aware, there are major differences in performance by race, and real data should make the case for race differences in sports performance obvious to all.

The venue was the World Cross-Country Championships in Turin, Italy, in 1997. The competition included 275 runners from sixty countries. They took part in a test of human bipedal ability (12 kilometers, lots of up-and-down) similar to what our ancestors faced in the (imagined) Environment of Evolutionary Adaptation (EEA).

The results? For the twelfth consecutive year (eighteenth as of 2003), the team title went to Kenya. Kenyans took two of the three medals and five of the first ten places, finishing 1st, 3rd, 4th, 6th, 7th, 17th, 19th, 24th, 28th, and 47th (no country then being allowed more than ten entrants, now only six). The winning time was 35 minutes, 11 seconds. The ten Kenyans averaged 36:04, which if obtained by a single runner would have placed him 12th overall. These results don't begin to tell the whole story on the magnitude of group differences, as most of the Kenyan runners come from one tribe, the Kalenjin, who number only 3 million and make up about 10 percent of Kenya's population.

Over those twelve years of Kenyan domination, if the Kalenjin runners had been a team of their own, they would have won the team title eight times and taken eighteen of the thirty-six medals. In other words, the Kalenjin have been "overrepresented" among the medalists by a factor of about 1,700 (3 million Kalenjin versus 5 billion of the rest of us). The Kalenjin won half the possible medals; the rest of the world together got the other eighteen.

Recall the received dogma that "bipedalism is such a critical aspect of the human adaptation that one would not expect to see great differences from either the individual to individual, or between populations." Can anyone disagree that a factor of 1,700 can legitimately be seen as a "great difference"?

The next step is to compute the difference in running ability between the average Kalenjin and the average for the rest of the world. The most useful metric here is the standard deviation, where for a normal (bell curve–type) distribution, the area that falls within one standard deviation (SD) on each side of the mean includes 68.26 percent of the sample; two SDs, 95.6 percent; three, 99.3 percent; and so on.

How many standard deviations is the Kalenjin mean beyond the mean of the rest of the world? How is a ratio of 1,700 obtained? Assume that the cross-country medalists are ultimately selected from 20 million males of the appropriate age worldwide. That means that the winner is about 5.3 SD above the world mean; that is, at +5.3 SD on the bell curve we are looking at the best individual among 20 million competitors. But only about 12,000 of those 20 million (1 in 1,700) are Kalenjin, and the best among 12,000 is only 3.8 SDs above the Kalenjin mean. The Kalenjin mean thus would be about 1.5 SD (5.3 SDs minus 3.8 SDs = 1.5 SDs) beyond that of the rest of the world. That is an enormous difference for any measure of human performance. Put that figure in the more familiar IQ context and the Kalenjin have an RQ (R for running) of about 122 compared with a world mean of 100 (I am indebted to Steve Sailer, president of the Human Biodiversity Institute, for this way of putting it). Another way of looking at it is to remember that the 1.5 SD advantage the Kalenjin have over the average human population suggests that there is likely some population that is 1.5 SD below the mean, and separated from the Kalenjin by 3 SD, as are Buriat from Teita in the example just above.

How much is 1 SD of RQ worth in cross-country finishing time? If the best runners are 5.3 SD beyond the world mean (a probability of 1 in 20 million on the bell curve), then 1 SD slower equals 4.3 SD above the world mean, which is about 150-fold more frequent. As the finishing times in the 1997 race were 1st place = 35:11 and 150th = 38:44, one SD was worth about 3.5 minutes. So a properly conditioned male with average genetic potential and of an appropriate age would require 35:11 plus 3.5 minutes per SD times 5.3 SDs, or about 55 minutes to complete the course—a full 20 minutes behind the winner.

As for women, their times are, on the average, about 11 percent slower than men's across the whole range of race distances, and here that would be about a 1.1 SD difference (11 percent of 35:11 is 3:52). But the Kalenjin men are 1.5 SD better than the world mean, which means that the Kalenjin women, even after allowing for their slowness when compared with Kalenjin men, should still be better (by perhaps 0.4 SD), on the average, than the rest of the world. In other words, and to provide a testable example, all this would suggest that the best, say, ten Kalenjin women, could, as a team, outrun (over a cross-country course) the best ten men from many, if not most, other human populations of a similar size (that is, about 3 million people). Any takers on this one?

The cultural bias against Kenyan women running competitively seems to be moderating, and there may be a good test of this proposition sooner than later. The potential result may have been presaged in the Peachtree 10-kilometer run held in Atlanta, Georgia, in summer 2003: The Kenyan men took seven of the first ten places; the Kenyan women took seven of the first ten places.

For a marathon distance of 26 miles, 385 yards (42.2 kilometers), the average, well-conditioned, human male would take some 4.5 hours to cover it, as against a world best of around 2.1 hours (calculations omitted). In other words, Everyman would not have reached even the halfway point by the time the best runner had crossed the finish line.

We know of no other analyses of this sort, so confirming the results must await a relevant critique and/or completion of the critical experiments.

## WHY DOESN'T NATURAL SELECTION CONSUME GENETIC VARIATION?

Any number of characters surely have been under intense selection for very long times without reducing variation. We've just seen the situation with respect to bipedalism; another example is brain size. The tripling in size of the human brain over the past 2 million years is one of the most rapid evolutionary changes that can be documented in the fossil record. Given the costs involved (delayed maturation, birthing problems, energy costs to run the brain, the travails involved in training it), it is certain that the selective processes involved must have been indeed intense, and yet brain size within the species remains one of the most, not least, variable features. It is easy to find pairs of perfectly normal humans whose brain volumes differ by enough to sustain a chimpanzee (400 cubic centimeters [cc]), and there are populations that differ in their mean brain sizes by close to 300 cc (more than 2 SD).

There are innumerable other well-known examples from agriculture and animal husbandry. One study has been under way at the University of Illinois–Champaign-Urbana for more than a century. The scientists there have been selecting for oil content (both high and low) in maize (corn) kernels, with the results seen in Figure 7.1. Note that in the line selected for higher content it has increased almost fivefold (20 SDs) and at a fairly steady rate, indicating that the underlying genetic variability has not been running out. Today's average is close to three times the highest values one might have seen in the 1880s when the experiment started with a grand total of twelve ears.

We should note here that it has taken natural selection some 20,000 centuries to increase human brain size the 20 SDs that intense human-guided selection with maize has managed for oil content in one century. That kind of comparison gives a much better sense of the possible, and strongly reinforces the point about not depleting heritable variation under intense selection— especially considering that over the course of 20,000 centuries, a fair amount of new variation will be added by new mutations.

By definition, short-term human examples are much harder to come by. We don't deliberately breed humans for particular char-

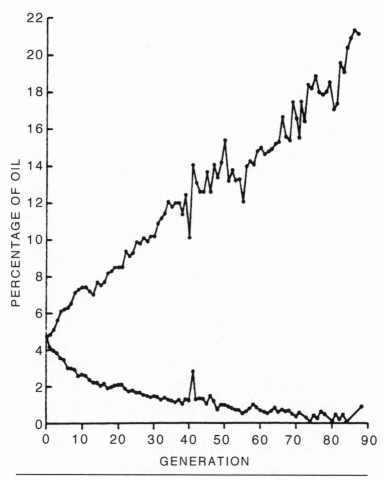

FIGURE 7.1    Selection for high and low oil content in corn kernels

acteristics, we don't (more fairly, we shouldn't) cull those who don't have them, and generation times are long, making even the results of natural experiments difficult to discern. Nonetheless, one natural experiment has produced very obvious results in a relatively short period. In his recent book *The Lapita Peoples*, my Berkeley colleague, Patrick V. Kirch, has summarized the linguistic, archaeological, morphological, and genetic evidence, showing that today's Polynesians derive from a population, or populations, living off the eastern end of New Guinea. Over the past 4,000 years, they have spread out to cover a vast triangle of islands from New Zealand in the south to Hawaii in the north and to Easter Island in the east. This expansion meant crossing thousands of miles of ocean that could be chillingly cold at night, and doing so in large outriggers for which upper-body strength would have been at a premium, thus apparently selecting primarily for larger body size (Bergmann's rule) and, by extension, proportionately even larger upper bodies (there is positive allometry between overall body size and upper-body size in apes and ourselves). That big-bodied people live in the tropics at first glance seems odd, but they are there. Jon Entine has noted that more than fifty Polynesians have been in the National Football League, making them by far its most "overrepresented minority." (Extended visits in Auckland have left me [Sarich] noting to myself that "scrawny Polynesian" would appear to be a null set.)

Thus the data, be they from corn or people, don't mesh with the idea that strong selection on important features reduces the amount of heritable variation in them. But why doesn't it? What's wrong with what seems so eminently logical? Things might work that way if only one or a small number of genes were involved in producing a complex character like the brain or the various structures involved in bipedalism. But that isn't the case. The argument that selection was involved at only one or a small number of genetic loci can be disposed of with a simple thought experiment. Imagine that this were the case. Then the idea would be correct, and variation would rapidly be consumed.

And then? Well, yes, that's the problem, isn't it? No more variation, no more natural selection, no more adaptive change, rapid extinction. More formally, this sort of process would rapidly lose out to one in which the variation used to produce the adaptation was in fact spread out among as many genes as possible, such that new mutations could readily reconstitute such variation as was lost to selection. And the more important the adaptation, the more likely it would evolve that way—that is, by involving as many loci as possible in the selective process. That's why we see all that functional variation out there in precisely those features that have been so important in our evolution.

## OUT OF AFRICA

It is time to revisit African dominance in road and track. Well, let me say this: (1) It's genes, genes, and more genes; (2) nobody knows why Africans should be so dominant. How do we know that statement (1) is correct? Because the results over the past few decades are consistent with a genetic model, and inconsistent with the "it's all society and culture" model. If the latter model held, then as opportunities for individuals of African descent began opening up, first on the track and then in various professional sports and finally, and especially, in Africa itself, there would have been an increase in African participation and competitiveness, to the point that their numbers would be strongly correlated with their numbers in the arena from which the participants were being drawn. The NBA would be about 10 percent black; we'd see a Kalenjin only every few years at the cross-country championships; the sun would rise in the east and west on alternate days. If, on the other hand, the genetic model applies, the results would be exactly what they have been—particular genetic populations in very different social and cultural settings producing very similar results.

At least some factors that could very likely be contributing to African dominance are clear. First, remember that our lineage arose in Africa some 4–5 million years ago and has spent most of its time since then exclusively in Africa. Bipedalism began in Africa, stone tool making began in Africa, we first spoke in Africa, humanness began in Africa, much of the increase in brain size occurred in Africa, and so on. Our basic adaptations are African. Given that, it would seem that we would have had to make adaptive compromises, such as to cold weather, when populating other areas of the world, thus taking the edge off our "African-ness." Body-fat levels seem to be at a minimum among African populations; the levels do not increase with age in them, and Africans in training can apparently achieve lower body-fat levels more readily than is the case for Europeans and Asians. These factors are an adequate springboard to explaining such African dominance as exists in the sporting world.

## THE FINAL TABOO

It is here that things get messier. Many, probably most, people have this fear that allowing some part of a genetic explanation in one area leads to the possibility of genetic explanations (explanation is really influence) in all areas, and one of these—the touchiest of all—is going to be brain power. The idea that being smart and being a good athlete poses mutually exclusive traits has strong appeal, and its presence is often, unthinkingly, taken for granted. The stereotype, then, is not so much "blacks as physical brutes and whites as thinking beings" but the more general one going back perhaps to Platonic types of "thinking beings" being designed by nature to rule over "physical brutes." At a personal level, I should, were I the type to do so, resent that stereotype, being, for sure, a "physical brute" but also, by any reasonable standards (such as thirty years as a professor at Berkeley), a "thinking being." I can see no necessary, or even likely, negative correlation between the physical and the mental. On the contrary, the data show an obvious, strong, positive correlation among class, physical condition, and participation in regular exercise in the United States. At the "runner" end, for example, our fitness/running booms were not driven by mindless "physical brutes." At the "sprinter" end, professional football teams have, in recent years, been known to use the results of IQ tests as one indicator of potential in rookies. And a monumental study of intellectually gifted California schoolchildren begun by Lewis Terman in the 1920s that followed them through their lives showed clearly that they were also more gifted physically than the average. In any case, it is long past time to get this "brains or brawn" business out of our systems. Doing so would let us look at the "why Africans?" matter far more intelligently, if for no other reason than that it would bring the power of many more previously timid individual brains to bear on it.

Jon Entine has broken the taboo in his 1999 volume of that name. In a calm, measured, and reasoned discussion spread over some 375 pages, he documents what just about all the sports authorities he quotes in his book have acknowledged, mostly in private, for decades but rarely dared to say out loud. As noted above, Africans are better than the rest of us at some of those things that most make us human, and they are better because their separate African histories have given them, in effect, better genes for recently developed tests of some basic human adaptations. The rest of us (or, more fairly, our ancestors) have had to compromise some of those African specializations in adapting to more temperate climates and more varied environments. Contemporary Africans, through their ancestors, are advantaged in not having had to make such adaptations, and their bodies, along with their resulting performances, show it.

There is an important lesson in this example demonstrating that genetic variation is the norm, and that competition is a discovery procedure. We can't begin to know what is possible until we encourage and allow as much of that variation as possible to express itself. *Taboo* illustrates how much all of us have gained because of African genetic variation having free rein. That lesson should not be ignored in the name of racial equality. Individuals are not equal, nor are races. They cannot be. That can sometimes be a problem; far more often, it is an opportunity. But there will be neither an opportunity made available nor results to take advantage of if we cannot accept that we can't make it come out "even."

So be it.

## CAN DOG BREEDS TELL US
## ANYTHING ABOUT HUMAN RACES?

This discussion now turns from matters of race on the outside to the matter of physical differences on the inside, with a major issue being the extent to which race should be a factor in medical practice. The relevance of race in this arena, along with every other feature of race, has become controversial in the past few years. Because these are often life-or-death matters, the truth may come more rapidly—at any rate, one can hope.

We begin with a discussion of breed differences in man's best friend—and our favorite example—the domestic dog. The discussions between the two of us that eventually became this book began when Vince was addressing the question of whether the fact that all humans (and races) are so alike genetically proves that race is meaningless, except for the most superficial traits. He noted that the morphological differences between human races can be greater than those between species of chimpanzees, whereas the genetic differences among the chimp species are much greater than the genetic differences among human races. The two simply don't track against each other.

I (Miele) then raised the question of dog breeds. I've liked dogs since I was a kid and am now on my third (the first two bullterriers and now a Great Dane). I've also been to a number of dog shows and even took my first bull terrier to an AKC championship. In addition, I've read widely both in the popular literature on dogs as well as in scientific journals that cover canine behavior genetics. I pointed out to Vince that there were huge differences between dog breeds, both in morphology and in behavior. How different were they genetically? Had the same methodology been applied to sorting out dog breeds as was described for humans in Chapter 5? With such large morphological and behavioral differences, shouldn't there be large DNA differences between the breeds? (It is now well known that the morphological and behavioral characteristics that distinguish breeds from one another are genetically based.) Vince's surprising answer was that (at that time) not only were there no known DNA differences between the breeds, but these methods couldn't even distinguish between domestic dogs and wolves. Although it was possible to identify individuals with the same microsatellite approach that has been in use for the past two decades, only this year (2003) have researchers been able to distinguish between a few dog breeds by DNA differences.

Then in December 2002, Dr. Ted Gagné, who's been treating my dogs for over twenty years, heard Professor Arthur Jensen and me being interviewed on a radio program about my previous book, *Race, Intelligence, and Genetics: Conversations with Arthur R. Jensen.* Ted and I had a number of conversations about the interview and the book, and I told him about the controversy over the question of racial differences in medicine, where the evidence was increasingly showing that drugs can work differently in different races. (It must be kept in mind in discussions of racial differences that we are talking primarily about *average* differences between groups; very few are *absolute.*) I asked Ted if there were any differences between dog breeds in their reactions to various medications. He mentioned one—the potentially lethal effect of giving ivermectin (the active ingredient in the standard heartworm medication) to collies and collie mixes and kindly lent me his copy of *Veterinary Drug Handbook*—comparable to the *Physicians Desk Reference* used by medical doctors). I have very briefly summarized some of what I found. (Any mistakes or misinterpretations are mine alone, not Dr. Gagné's.)

One might think at first that my question in the heading of this section is naive, even verging on silly. Nevertheless, the study of dogs provides carry-over usefulness for humans in both the physical/genetic and behavioral/genetic realms. The differences between pit bulls, Pekinese, poodles (which come in standard, miniature, and toy sizes), and most of the other more than 200 recognized breeds have been produced in the past few hundred years by intense and artificial selection exercised by breeders. Whatever differences there are between human races have been produced by (1) natural selection, (2) genetic drift (a lottery-type process in which survival of the trait is a matter of luck), and (3) maybe sexual selection, though there has been no convincing evidence of it yet in humans. (Sexual selection is survival of the fairest but not the fittest, based on selecting mates for some trait that has zero, or even negative, survival value. The peacock's tail is the classic example. It makes him more attractive to females but more conspicuous to predators.)

Appeal to authority is far from the strongest form of argument. But in this case, there are two very strong authorities to whom to appeal. First is Charles Darwin, who developed his theory of evolution by natural selection based in part on his observations of the effects of artificial selection exercised by breeders (hence the converse term, "natural" selection) and offered numerous examples in *Origin of Species* as support for his theory. Selection is just that—selection. It's a matter of which genes survive into future generations and which ones don't, regardless of whether it is environment, the breeder, or the opposite sex that does the selecting. The artificial selection exercised by breeders is analogous to the microscope, the telescope, or time-lapse photography, allowing us to see objects and events too small, too distant, or too slow for us to have noticed otherwise.

Then we cite the codiscoverer, with Francis Crick, of the double helix structure of DNA and author of the best-selling book by the same name (*The Double Helix*), James D. Watson. Watson and Crick (along with Maurice Wilkins) were awarded the 1962 Nobel Prize in physiology or medicine.

In February 2001, Watson participated in a colloquium sponsored by the California Academy of Sciences in San Francisco. The moderator was Matt Ridley, author of *Genome* and *Nature via Nurture*. Ridley asked Watson whether we should unravel the chimpanzee genome in order to match it against our own and to zero in on the differences between us and our genetically nearest living relatives.

Watson replied, "I wouldn't waste any American money on the chimp." The dog genome, he went on, would be a better target, because dogs vary so widely in appearance and behavior that unraveling their DNA is bound to reveal something about the interplay between genes and observable traits.

## CANINE PHARMACOGENETICS

Pharmacogenetics is, as the name suggests, the study of genetic differences in the tolerance and effectiveness of pharmaceuticals—in this case, between dog breeds. Following are two examples from the *Veterinary Drug Handbook*.

As mentioned, ivermectin is the active ingredient in the most commonly prescribed medicine for prevention of heartworms, which can be deadly. Used in the proper milligram-of-medication per kilogram-of-body-weight dosage, it is quite safe, killing the microfilaria (the preadult heartworm stage) without having any adverse effect on the dog—except for collies, collielike breeds, and collie mixes. For them, a dose that wouldn't faze other breeds can produce a serious reaction or death. Veterinarians have to inform owners of collie-type dogs of the risk and advise them of alternatives.

The potentially serious effects of ivermectin on the collie-type breeds have two possible causes: Their blood-brain barrier allows more of the drug to reach the brain than is the case in other breeds, and a greater amount of ivermectin accumulates in their central nervous system. The latter is more likely, because it would be the result of some mutation producing an enzyme deficit, and such mutations are not uncommon. The mutation would then have been spread by the deliberate breeding of collies with other collies, not other breeds. In the case of mixed-breed dogs, the mutation could have been inherited from their collie parent.

Until veterinarians began prescribing ivermectin to protect dogs from potentially deadly heartworms, however, the mutation that took place in collies would have had no harmful effect. It is quite possible that when human races were evolving, analogous mutations that caused an intolerance to drugs could have occurred but would not become a problem until the drugs were developed millennia later. When population numbers were quite low, such mutations could have become fixed within races and subraces. Isolated populations like those on small islands would be particularly at risk for such a sequence of events.

Another canine example that is relevant because of the readily observable racial differences in body build is the potentially lethal effect of the ultrashort-acting thiobarbiturate Thiopental in greyhounds, whippets, other coursers, and similar breeds. In these slightly built coursing and racing dogs, much more of their total body weight is muscle and much less of it is fat than in other dogs. Fat is able to take up more barbiturate than muscle can. With so much less fat to hold the barbiturate, greyhound-type dogs take much longer to metabolize the drug floating around their system.

Consider two breeds—bulldogs and greyhounds—whose differences somewhat resemble those of the thin peoples of East Africa, who as described earlier in this chapter outperform the rest of our species in distance running, and Eskimos of the circumpolar regions. The breed standard calls for bulldogs to be 14 to 15 inches in height and to weigh between 40 and 50 pounds. The greyhound breed standard for the show ring is 27 to 30 inches in height and 60 to 70 pounds in weight. The greyhounds that race around the track rather than strut around the show ring can range from 40 to 80 pounds, however. If Thiopental were administered as an anesthetic to a greyhound at the same dosage (the milligram-of-medication per kilogram-of-body-weight standard dosage) as to a bulldog, the racing dog would take much longer to revive, if it indeed did. Instead of Thiopental, *Veterinary Drug Handbook* recommends the use of Methohexital as an anesthetic for greyhounds and other coursers.

Dog owners have given no thought to the subject of breed differences in body chemistry such as those described above. Naturally, the owners are delighted that their beloved pets or valuable working dogs get the best possible treatment and don't die on the operating table. In fact, they might have a claim for malpractice if their veterinarian didn't consult *Veterinary Drug Handbook* with tragic results.

## RACE AND MEDICINE

One would think that we humans would be as intelligent and as humane in dealing with our own health as with that of our pets. Now that similar genetic principles are being applied to the differences between human races, however, it has generated a great deal of academic snarling and backbiting.

Vince and I are by no means alone in believing that race is real. Writing in the online journal *Genome Biology*, Dr. Neil Risch of Stanford University challenged the social-constructionist views expressed in an editorial in the *New England Journal of Medicine* that repeated the "'race' is biologically meaningless" mantra and a more alarmist one in *Nature Genetics* warning of the "confusion and potential harmful effects of using 'race' as a variable in medical research." Note that the offensive four-letter R-word appeared in quotation marks to indicate the two editorialists did not believe it had any biological reality. This usage is not unique to them. It is becoming the standard.

Nonetheless, the same *New England Journal of Medicine* that carried the no-race editorial also reported an investigation of differences in the effectiveness of two types of hypertension medication in black and in white patients. Black patients, on average, did not derive as much benefit as whites from one class of ACE-inhibitors (ACE is the acronym for angiotensin-converting enzyme), generally considered the standard treatment for heart failure.

The current explanation for the difference involves the role of nitric oxide, a gas that is normally produced by the cells that line blood vessels. Nitric oxide dampens contraction of the muscle cells, relaxing the vessels and lowering blood pressure. Blacks are more likely than whites to have nitric-oxide insufficiency. Why, no one currently knows. But because ACE-inhibitor drugs probably lower blood pressure by interacting with nitric oxide, individuals with less of the gas, regardless of race, will not respond as well. A sense of the problem is gained from the results of a study in which black and white patients were randomized for treatment with either an ACE inhibitor or a placebo. Both blacks and whites taking the placebo fared no worse than black patients taking an ACE inhibitor with regard to blood pressure control and hospitalization for worsening heart failure.

Jay N. Cohn, a professor of medicine at the University of Minnesota School of Medicine, has patented a drug called BiDil, a combination diuretic and vessel dilator that he believes can replenish nitric oxide. The Food and Drug Administration has authorized the testing of BiDil, the Association of Black Cardiologists is recruiting patients, and the Congressional Black Caucus supports the project. And with good cause—blacks have twice the rate of heart failure as whites, and those afflicted are twice as likely to die.

Another drug response with racial variation was seen with the first useful antituberculosis drug, isoniazid, which was introduced soon after World War II. It was soon found that the drug was not very effective in Eskimos, because they had a variant enzyme that metabolized isoniazid so rapidly that it never had a chance to show its effectiveness against the disease.

Dr. David Goldstein, a population geneticist at University College in London, opposes the use of race, as such, in medicine. Instead he argues for analyzing patients' DNA. This is very similar to the DNAPrint methodology (discussed in Chapter 1), and Goldstein argues that it produces a more accurate measure of the correlation between each individual's genes and how the person will respond to drugs. It also avoids the R-word, which many feel opens the door for R-ism.

Dr. Risch has turned the tables on Goldstein, however, by arguing that taking account of race is the best way to determine which differences are genetic and which are not. For example, African Americans have a higher rate of hypertension than do whites. This could be a genetic difference (part of Rushton's matrix of race and life-history traits). It could also be the result of the socioeconomic differences between them. And, of course, it could be some mixture of the two. If researchers look only at the relation between specific genes and medical conditions, they will not be able to identify the true cause.

And then there is populational, but not racial, chemical variation. A classic example is lactose intolerance, the standard or default condition for all mammals except those in a few human groups. Lactose is a specific mammalian sugar, whose only function is to help feed the young human until weaning. Lactose production ceases at weaning, and the presence of lactose thereafter can produce digestive upsets. However, the few human groups that have developed herding have also tended later to develop lactose tolerance among adults (presumably by turning off those genes that turn off lactose synthesis). It is relatively easy to knock out a function, which is why there were a number of centers of the development of herding cultures with lactose-tolerant populations (though nowhere is there 100 percent tolerance).

In sum, we feel that the no-race or there-shouldn't-be-races positions will lose out first in the medical realm because so much is at stake. In matters of life and death, it is difficult to deny reality when someone shows where and how race applies. If we can come to grips with the reality of race differences and body chemistry, perhaps we can look at differences in behavior as well.

## CHAPTER EIGHT

# Race and Behavior

*In this chapter we break the ultimate taboo—race differences in behavior. First we describe a classic study of behavioral differences among puppies of four dog breeds. Next we describe the difficulties the same author experienced when he tried to publish an almost identical study, but this one of behavioral differences between neonates of human races.*

*Even among those who agree that race is a meaningful biological concept and has behavioral consequences, there are disagreements regarding uncertainties and questions still to be resolved. Specifically, we examine these issues: race, brain size, and intelligence; income inequality and intelligence; and the mean sub-Saharan African IQ of 70.*

Even when we are dealing with morphological measurements such as height, head shape, cranial capacity, facial features, and weight (which provides an informative contrast with height), the nature-nurture issue is always open to debate. When behavioral measurements and psychological tests are at issue, unraveling that Gordian knot becomes even more difficult. This is especially so when it comes to race differences in something like IQ, which our society rewards so highly.

There is a significant genetic component in intelligence. Its size is assessed by behavior geneticists using a statistic called heritability, which is the portion of the inter-individual variation caused by genetic variation. It is generally agreed that the heritability of intelligence within the white populations of Europe, the United States, and Australia is between 0.50 and 0.87 (that is, between 50 and 87 percent of the individual differences in intelligence in those groups is attributable to genetic differences), depending on the specific model used. The 0.5 is perhaps too low, and 0.87 too high, but both are highly significant. This is also true for Japanese in Japan, and limited data suggest that it is true as well for the African-American population.

The high heritability of a trait within two groups, however, is not proof that the average difference between the groups also has a significant genetic component. The classic example here goes back to Charles H. Cooley's 1897 analogy that corn seeds given a normal environment produce plants of full height but in a deprived environment produce plants of stunted height. The conclusion was that even if the genes are the same, environmental differences produce different outcomes.

The results of Cooley's now-famous experiment were nothing new. Jesus expressed them much more poetically, and in a way that was meant for common folk to understand, 2,000 years earlier in the Parable of the Sower and the Seeds (Mark 4:3–8):

Behold the sower went out to sow. And as he sowed, it happened one indeed fell by the roadside; and the birds of heaven ate it. And another fell on the rocky place where it did not have much earth. And it sprang up at once, due to not having deepness of earth. And the sun rising it was scorched. And through not having root, it was dried out.

And another fell among the thorns, and the thorns grew up and choked it, and it did not yield fruit. And another fell into the good ground and yielded fruit, going-up and increasing; and one bore thirty, and one sixty, and one a hundred-fold.

Pointing to the results of Cooley's experiment, if not the Parable of the Sower, social scientists increasingly argued that cultural deprivation, not heredity, was the cause of black-white IQ differences, since the differences in socioeconomic factors and the history of slavery and Jim Crow were obvious for anyone with eyes to see.

When we consider the possible role of a genetic factor in the average difference between racial groups, the Gordian knot becomes even more tightly bound and the analytical swords with which we can cut it become less sharp. Not only can human groups differ in easily measurable variables such as income, but we also have to take into account attitudes, perceptions, and past history. This is the case when examining the different rates of medical conditions such as high blood pressure and prostate cancer. Controversy over the existence of a genetic factor reaches the boiling point when we start to speak about racial differences in IQ because that two-letter measure is so predictive of, and associated with, so many aspects of success in our society, not just income. (Another two-letter measure, BP [blood pressure], is highly predictive as well. People who visit a doctor know first to expect the nurse to take their temperature and blood pressure, even if an injured arm occasioned the visit.)

Why is IQ so important and so controversial? The top actors, athletes, musicians, and supermodels are among the most highly paid individuals in our society, but very few people who compete for these high-recognition jobs get anywhere near the peak. Most barely get by, and many give up and quit. Across the range of occupations, cognitive ability as measured by IQ is by far the best determinant and predictor of wealth and status in modern technological society.

The most extensively documented research on race differences in behavior concerns the fifteen-point difference between the average IQs of white Americans and African Americans, whites being higher, but Asians have a slightly higher average IQ than do whites. The existence of that average group difference is no longer a matter of dispute. It has been shown to be consistent over chronological time, age groups (children, teenagers, adults), and even when the groups are equated for socioeconomic conditions. What is in dispute is the cause or causes of the difference.

Evolutionary genetic explanations went virtually unquestioned until the twentieth century. In the aftermath of World War II and the Holocaust, and with the linkage of the civil rights movement in the United States to decolonization in the Third World in the Cold War struggle, genetic interpretations of race differences in behavior were understandably highly scrutinized and generally scorned. Research funded by the Great Society programs of the 1960s initially offered great promise that compensatory education and social welfare programs could eliminate both race and class differences in intelligence. The genetic argument returned to the mainstream of behavioral science only in 1969 with the publication of Arthur Jensen's famous article, "How Much Can We Boost IQ and School Achievement?" in the highly respected *Harvard Educational Review*.

During the ongoing controversy surrounding *The Bell Curve*, in 1994 the American Psychological Association appointed a special task force to look into the nexus of intelligence, race, and genetics and evaluate the book's conclusions. Based on review of twin and other kinship studies, the task force for the most part agreed with

Jensen's (1969) *Harvard Educational Review* article and *The Bell Curve*, that within the white population the heritability of IQ is "around .75" (p. 85). As to the cause of the mean black-white group difference, however, the task force concluded: "There is certainly no support for a genetic interpretation" (p. 97).

## THE EVOLUTIONARY PERSPECTIVE
## AND THE BURDEN OF PROOF

Consider these two statements:

In his decades-long debate with Carleton Coon, Ashley Montagu cited an earlier paper he had coauthored with Theodosius Dobzhansky, which said:

> [T]he mental capacities of the different populations of mankind were probably much-of-a-muchness because in the evolution of every human population much the same mental traits had been at a premium.

Next, the PBS documentary *Race: The Power of an Illusion* asked viewers to

> try a paradigm shift. Every time the mind gropes toward the seemingly evident—that, say, black people are better at sports, or Asians at math and music—deconstruct it. Look for the social reasons, the economic reasons, the cultural reasons why these stereotypes only seem to hold true. But don't bother looking for some smoking gun in our DNA; the scientists interviewed tonight don't believe it exists.

We take issue with the arguments (1) of Gould that race differences in IQ cannot exist because racial differentiation didn't occur

over a sufficiently long time to produce them; (2) of Lewontin
that race differences in IQ do not exist because there isn't enough
difference between "races" rather than within a given "race" to allow for such differences; and (3) of Alan Goodman that even if
such differences can exist and do, we should not study them because it will tend to justify racism. We believe these statements
contradict, rather than follow from, the evolutionary perspective.

Contrary to these scholars, and they are distinguished ones at
that, we argue that from the evolutionary perspective, the default
position is that some genetic influence in average group differences is the expected case, not the exception. We begin our argument for the default position by revisiting our canine companions.

## THE CANINE COMPARISON

The classic study was carried out by Daniel G. Freedman for his
doctoral dissertation. Freedman spent every day and evening
rearing four dog breeds—beagles, wire-haired fox terriers, Shetland sheepdogs, and basenjis—from age two to twelve weeks.
Here's what he noticed.

> It became clear, as the ears and eyes opened, that the breeds al-
> ready differed in behavior. Little beagles were irrepressibly friendly
> from the moment they could detect me, whereas Shetland sheep-
> dogs were most sensitive to a loud voice or the slightest punish-
> ment; wire-haired terriers were so tough and aggressive, even as
> clumsy three-week-olds, that I had to wear gloves in playing with
> them; and, finally, basenjis, barkless dogs originating in central
> Africa, were aloof and independent.

All domestic dogs are descended from wolves; no foxes or jackals
got into the mix. For all their differences in appearance—and

behavior—there is only one measurement on which wolves and dogs do not overlap, and that is absolute tooth size. Even with these large differences in body and behavior, we are only beginning to be able to differentiate between breeds—or even between wolves and dogs—on the basis of their DNA. Wolves and dogs also share much the same ethogram—the basic set of behaviors. One difference is that for all their howling, wolves do not bark and cannot be taught to. Interestingly, neither do basenjis. Read on to see why.

Many of today's breed differences are cosmetic, but originally breeds were selected to excel in certain elements of the basic wolf-dog ethogram (that is, their behavioral repetoire) and to reduce or eliminate others. All of these differences, including the barklessness of the basenji, make perfect sense in terms of what we know about the traits for which the different breeds were, or were not, selected.

Beagles are scent hounds. They run in packs and use their sense of smell (which is better than that of most other breeds) to track foxes and other small game. They have been selected not only for increased olfactory tracking ability but also for diminished aggression. Beagles are a band of brothers (often literally), and each has a job to do. They were usually kenneled together and would howl to other members of the pack when finding a scent or needing help. Fox hunting is sometimes called "riding to hounds" because that is what one does, mounted on horseback and following the pack as its members pick up the fox's scent.

Fox terriers (there are two varieties, wire-haired and smooth-haired, but this is largely a cosmetic difference), like beagles, were bred to participate in the sport of fox hunting, though that activity is increasingly viewed as what Oscar Wilde termed "the unspeakable chasing the uneatable." But their job is far different from that of the beagles. The fox terrier literally gets a free ride in the hunter's saddlebag, at least, that is, until the fox, as hunters say, "goes to earth." This means no fun for the hunters because it ends the chase and their chance to bag the fox. It's a game to the fox, or so it would seem. But now the fox terrier must earn his seemingly free ride and free lunches. The hunter grabs the terrier by his short tail and hurls him to the ground, where his job is to enter the den and convince the fox to resume the game by "making him an offer he can't refuse." No beagle in its right mind would want any part of this. Terriers, on the other hand, are born scrappers and thrive on such opportunities. There is a reason behind the expression "a pack of hounds" but not "a pack of terriers"—rather than a peaceful assembly, it quickly becomes the canine analogue to a gladiatorial. Even the smallest terriers, like the Jack Russell (made famous by the TV program *Frasier*), think nothing about taking on a rottweiler or a pit bull, hence the saying "It's not the size of the dog in the fight, but the size of the fight in the dog." Among terriers (unless separately crated) "two's company, three's battle royal." Many people have purchased Jack Russells thinking they will have a companion like the TV dog, only to find they've brought a canine Mike Tyson into their house. With its new popularity, breeders have started to select for less aggressiveness in the Jack Russells, for better or worse.

Dedicated fanciers of any breed will insist that the worst thing that can happen for them is for a breed to become popular overnight because of some movie or television show. The heightened demand often is met by unscrupulous "puppy mills," and even a dog from a reputable breeder can end up with an owner or family totally unsuited for it.

The third breed in Freedman's study was the Shetland sheepdog, often affectionately termed "Shelties," or incorrectly, and to the annoyance of their owners, "miniature collies." They are indeed sheep-herding, not sheep-protecting, dogs. The Sheltie motto is "herd 'em, don't hurt 'em." The breed has been selected for, on the one hand, being highly responsive to commands from humans and, on the other hand, inhibiting the part of the wolf-dog ethogram that says "Look at all that nice mutton, here for the taking." Shelties are excellent dogs for obedience training and competition. When I (Miele) took my Great Dane, Payce, to beginner obedience school, I like to think he was the second-best pupil. The Sheltie in the class was better.

One of the most basic behaviors taught in obedience school is for the dog to walk alongside the handler and stop and sit as soon as the handler halts so that its front paws are parallel with the handler's toes. Payce had no trouble learning to sit. At 127 pounds and over six feet tall when he is up on his hind legs, however, it wasn't that easy to put on the brakes and stop on a dime. In any case, the Sheltie in our class almost always stopped and sat dead even with her handler. Then one time she didn't and ended up about six inches out in front. She looked around and quickly backed up until her front paws were even with her handler's toes, hoping he wouldn't notice (very much as both Vince and I had when we were in basic training, hoping the drill instructors wouldn't see us). The obedience-school instructor pointed to this episode as an example of just how much dogs can learn. Both humans and dogs have been selected for intelligence and conscientiousness.

The fourth and final breed in the Freedman study was the basenji. These dogs are more recently domesticated than most of the better-known breeds. Like wolves, basenjis have never added barking to their behavioral repertoire. (Barking may be an exaggeration of the pup calling to its mother, and selection has enhanced the behavior as a means of communicating with humans.) With their tails carried up in a corkscrew, basenjis belong to a group that is generally called pariah dogs, which includes semidomesticated breeds around the world. When humans cease selective breeding, the distinctive breeds disappear, and the surviving dogs take on a pariahlike appearance.

Basenjis do not lack canine IQ, but they are at the opposite pole from the Shelties in conscientiousness. They dislike taking orders and are born canine scofflaws.

In another classic study, experimenters put out dog chow for pups and told them "No!" Then they exited the room to observe the pups through a one-way mirror to see if they would go for food. If they did, the experimenter went into the room and scolded them "No!" while also swatting them on their backside, painlessly, with a newspaper. Shelties are so inhibited that they wouldn't touch the food. Some of them even had to be hand-nursed back into feeding again. The basenjis, in contrast, started to gobble chow the minute the experimenter turned his back, before he even left the room.

Another study compared the same four breeds in getting through a series of increasingly difficult mazes. The major breed differences were not in the ability to master the mazes (a rough measure of canine IQ) but in what they would do when they were placed in a maze they couldn't master. The beagles would howl, hoping perhaps that another member of their pack would howl back and lead them to the goal. The inhibited Shelties would simply lie down on the ground and wait. Pugnacious terriers would try to tear down the walls of the maze, but the basenjis saw no reason they had to play by a human's rules and tried to jump over the walls of the maze.

Shelties can easily be made neurotic (as in the food example), beagles are natural extroverts, fox terriers are given to aggression, and basenjis just don't care about the (human) rules.

We can already see opposing counsel, hackles raised, rising to object that these results are irrelevant and immaterial. Dogs are dogs, and people are people. Further, dog breeds have been produced by artificial selection of the breeders, not by natural selection. Few of these breeds could survive in the wild, and because of excessive inbreeding, many are subject to genetic diseases. If left to mix in the wild, dogs quickly return to the morphology of pariahs like the basenji.

In answer to these objections, we first point out that selection is selection and that observing the artificial selection practiced by breeders of domestic species played a key part in Darwin's thinking that led him to the concept of natural selection. The argument of opposing counsel is in many ways analogous to that of the biblical creationists—for example, Ken Ham and Duane Gish (senior author Sarich has debated Gish several times)—along the lines that "all selection ever produces is another type of dog, cat, cow, etc. It never produces a new species."

We next enter into the transcript the following quotation from Professor Freedman, who conducted some of the most important of these studies:

> I had worked with different breeds of dogs and I had been struck by how predictable was the behavior of each breed. A breed of dog is a construct zoologically and genetically equivalent to a race of man. To look at us, my wife and I [Freedman is Jewish; his then wife, Chinese] were clearly of two different breeds. Were some of our behavioral differences determined by breed?

## BREEDS AND RACES—WHAT A
## DIFFERENCE A WORD MAKES

Freedman and his wife set about designing experiments to test that hypothesis; they are interesting both for their scientific results and for the different receptions they received in even the most prestigious scientific journals. The Freedmans decided to observe the behavior of newborns and infants of different races. The tests they used were the Cambridge Behavioral and Neurological Assessment

Scale. Unlike the typical reflex tests performed by pediatricians, these tests, called "the Brazelton" after their developer, measure social and emotional behavior.

How easily did the baby quiet? Was it able to turn to the examiner's face and voice? Did it prefer face over voice or voice over face? How did interest in the voice compare with interest in a ball or a rattle? Was the baby very active or did it just lie quietly? Did it fit comfortably in the examiner's arms or did it fight being held? Did it generally resist or accept our testing? Was it floppy or stiff? And then there were all the reflexes: were they crisp or just barely elicited?

White and Chinese neonates were different even though hospital conditions and prenatal care were the same.

Caucasian babies started to cry more easily, and once they started, they were more difficult to console. Chinese babies adapted to almost any position in which they were placed: for example, when placed face down in their cribs, they tended to keep their faces buried in the sheets rather than immediately turning to one side, as did the Caucasians. In a similar maneuver (called the "defense reaction" by neurologists), we briefly pressed the baby's nose with a cloth, forcing him to breathe with his mouth. Most Caucasian and black babies fight this maneuver by immediately turning away or swiping at the cloth with the hands, and this is reported in Western pediatric textbooks as the normal, expected response. However, not so the average Chinese baby in our study. He simply lay on his back, breathing from the mouth, "accepting" the cloth without a fight. I must say that this finding is the most impressive on film, and audiences have been awed by other intergroup differences.

Other, more subtle differences are equally important. For example, both Chinese and Caucasian infants would start to cry at about the same point in the examination, especially when they were undressed, but the Chinese babies would stop crying immediately, as if a light switch had been flipped, whereas the crying of Caucasian babies only gradually subsided.

When the Freedmans tested Navajo neonates, they were like the Chinese, which might have been expected, given our knowledge of probable Navajo origins. From traditional anthropology to linguistics to DNA, Amerindians, especially the Na-Dene tribes like the Navajo, are most closely related to Asians, and not Europeans or Africans. This was impressed upon me (Sarich) one afternoon when I was flipping channels and found myself watching a girls high school basketball game. I wondered, "Where in Asia were we?" Then something appeared that clued me in. I was with Navajos, but the resemblance to northern Asians was striking.

Freedman submitted the paper on racial differences in neonate behavior to *Science*. The most prestigious scientific journal in the United States, it had published his study of behavioral differences in pups of different dog breeds without any problem or controversy. The paper on race differences, however, was rejected by a split vote of the reviewers. Freedman then submitted it to *Nature* (the British analogue to *Science*), where it yet again drew a split decision by the judges. Fortunately, the editor broke the deadlock by casting his deciding vote in favor of publication.

Freedman's studies are important not only because they allow a very similar experimental design to be used with humans and dogs, but also because, unlike for IQ, our society does not automatically consider being more or less active as being better or worse. It should be noted, however, that in J. P. Rushton's life-history theory of race differences, the earlier motor development of African children fits into a matrix of sixty life-history variables that provide measures of maturation, personality, reproduction, and social organization as well traits, including the rate of dizygotic (two-egg) twinning; maturity at birth as measured by pulmonary function, amniotic fluid, and bone development; continued maturity as measured by average bone growth, greater muscular strength, and a more accurate reach for objects; age of sitting, crawling, walking, and putting on their own clothes; faster rate of dental development; earlier age of sexual maturity, first sexual experience, and first pregnancy; rate of myopia, in addition to average IQ, brain size, and reaction time. In Rushton's system, on average, Africans and their descendants fall at one end, East Asians and their descendants at the other, with whites intermediate but nearer Asians.

Freedman's testimony is also important because he has quite openly expressed his "discomfort" with the research of Rushton and Jensen on intelligence, race, and genetics: "not with the assemblages of data but with the emotionally distant nature of the scientific presentations. In this arena, especially, cold science will not do, for only with love and warmth will the proper things be looked at, the proper things said, and a sympathetic picture of the study participants emerge."

Freedman's words are reminiscent of the last two paragraphs of Nathan Glazer's commentary on *The Bell Curve*:

> The authors project a possible utopia in which individuals accept their places in an intellectual pecking order that affects their income, their quality of life, their happiness. It may be true that we do not commonly envy the intellectual capacities of others we allow Albert Einstein and Bobby Fischer their eminence—though I think even at this level the authors underplay the role of envy and rancor in human affairs. But how can a group accept an inferior place in society, even if good reasons for it are put forth? It cannot.

Richard Wollheim and Isaiah Berlin have written: "If I have a cake, and there are ten persons among whom I wish to divide it, then if I give exactly one-tenth to each, this will not . . . call for justification; whereas if I depart from this principle of equal division I am expected to produce a special reason." Herrnstein and Murray have a very good special reason: smarter people get more and properly deserve more, and if there are more of them in one group than another, so be it. Our society, our polity, our elites, according to Herrnstein and Murray, live with an untruth: that there is no good reason for this inequality, and therefore our society is at fault and we must try harder. I ask myself whether the untruth is not better for American society than the truth.

In fairness to Freedman, when Rushton was threatened with loss of his position, Freedman testified to the value of Rushton's work as well as his right of academic freedom. For this we commend him.

## THE REALITY OF HUMAN RACES

We begin this trip out of political correctness and into reality by noting that there is a substantial amount of agreement in the field on a working definition of the term "race" (when the author bothers to define the term, of course), as in our discussion of race and law earlier. Races are populations, or groups of populations, within a species, that are separated geographically from other such populations or groups of populations and distinguishable from them on the basis of heritable features.

How far can this definition take the discussion? Everyone can agree that at one level we are all members of a single species—*Homo sapiens*—and that at another each of us is a unique individual. Races then exist within that range to the extent that we can look at individuals and place them, with some appreciable degree of success, into the areas from which they or their recent ancestors derive. The process involved is readily illustrated in a thought experiment in which one imagines a random assortment of fifty humans and fifty chimpanzees. No one, chimp or human, would have any difficulty in reconstituting the original fifty-member sets by simple inspection, and so no doubt could have *Australopithecus*. The same would be true within our species with, say, fifty humans from Japan, fifty from Malawi, and fifty from Norway. Again, by simple inspection, we would achieve the same 100 percent sorting accuracy. Granted, in the second experiment, fewer sorting characteristics would be available, but not nearly so few as to produce any doubt as to the placement of any individual. Extending this look-see experiment to the whole of the human species would produce a substantial number of such geographical groupings, and the addition of direct genetic evidence—from blood groups to DNA sequences—would provide further resolving power. Again, everyone can agree on the results, but in this area such findings tend to be the last point for which such a claim can be made. Herein lies a real problem that goes well beyond ideology and political correctness.

## The Nature of Categories

We might exemplify the problem in the realm of color. Speakers of languages that have a term for what English speakers gloss as "red" (and who also have a comparable number of basic color terms) will also show a remarkable degree of agreement as to the range of the spectrum to which the term applies, and as to which hues are better reds than others. When we view a rainbow, we tend to see not continuity but a small number of specific colors that we have no trouble naming. This example tells us that whatever may be happening with respect to cognitive processing of the visible light spectrum, we have no operational difficulties in at least this realm with the notion that *categories do not have to be discrete*. Red does, with respect to the spectrum itself, shade imperceptibly into orange and orange into yellow, but we have no difficulties in agreeing as to where red becomes orange, and orange, yellow. This capability is presumably based on the fact that we have only a finite number of different color receptor molecules (three, to be specific), but that is not the important point. That has already been highlighted: *Human cognition can deal with categories that are not discrete*. The flip side of that is, presumably, that categories can be real without necessarily being enumerable—and that is the critical point for this discussion.

In other words, we can easily forget that categories do not have to be discrete. If this were not so, why should the notion of "fuzzy sets" have been deemed so revolutionarily productive?

Races are, if you wish, fuzzy sets.

Thus, it is certainly true that the phrase "substantial number of such geographical groupings" (that is, races) has tended to lead to questions of "How many races are there?" and "How should we classify them?"—but we do not have to accept either of these as a valid question. The first is in fact a classic example of a wrong question—that is, one that implies a counterproductive answer. "How many" requires a precise integer as an answer—3, 7, 15, whatever. But the nature of the category "race" is such as to make a precise answer impossible, depending as it necessarily does on the degree of sorting accuracy required in a context where the categories involved are not, nor can they be, discrete. Races, after all, are not species—all humans being fully interfertile. Therefore races necessarily grade into one another, but they clearly do not do so evenly. Even today, for example, to drive along the road in Egypt from Aswan north to Luxor (100 miles or so) is to cross a portion of ancient boundary between (to use old, familiar, and still useful terms) Caucasians and Negroes. These two large groupings have been separated for millennia by that necessity for race formation, a geographical filter, here in the form of the Sahara Desert. That is, the human population densities north and south of the Sahara have long been, and still are, orders of magnitude greater than in the Sahara proper, causing the northern and southern units to have evolved in substantial genetic independence from one another. And that is also all that is needed for race formation—geographical separation plus time.

## How Many, and Should We Care?

The answer to the question "How many races are there?" then becomes "It depends on the sorting accuracy, with respect to individual humans, required." If it's close to 100 percent, then the areas involved could become smaller and more distant from one another, with at least twenty races easily recognized; or larger and less separated, in which case there would be the few "major" races that everyone has tended to see. If, however, the criterion were nearer the 75 percent that has often sufficed for the recognition of races in other species, then obviously the number would be very large. To illustrate this for those most familiar with recent Europeans, a thought experiment would involve first going to a globe and noting just how small a place non-Russian Europe really is, and then asking what degree of sorting accuracy we could achieve with a sample of 100 living humans: fifty, say, from Athens, and fifty from Copenhagen. Most of us could still manage something close to 100 percent. This exercise shows that the number of 75 percent cases for populations defined by, say, language plus geography must be very large—though no one, to the best of our knowledge, has ever provided any semblance of a numerical estimate for "very large" in this context. Nor, we might add, is there any good reason to attempt to provide such an estimate. Counting and classifying should not be the goals here. They can add nothing to our understanding. The productive questions pertain to how races came to be and the extent to which racial variation has significant consequences with respect to function in the modern world.

To summarize, if we employ a straightforward definition of race—for example, a population within a species that can be readily distinguished from other such populations on genetic grounds alone (that is, using only heritable features)—then there can be no doubt of the existence of a substantial number of human races.

And the simple answer to the objection that races are not discrete, blending into one another as they do, is this: They're supposed to blend into one another, and categories need not be discrete. It is not for us to impose our cognitive difficulties upon Nature; rather we need to adjust them to Nature.

### Races in Time

All that is needed for racial differentiation is geographic separation and time. But that is also all that is often needed for speciation as well, and so an obvious question is why humans remain a single species. The answer, and it's not the one I (Sarich) gave in 1995, from a paper published at the time, is that we have been through a very recent speciation event, such that the other contemporaneous species, and races of them, rapidly became extinct without issue. Races of our species then developed into a rather empty world and basically raciated by distance. Thus, for example, if we study fossils found in areas of Caucasian occupation today and dating from 35,000 to 15,000 years ago, they do not look especially Caucasian but rather appear to be a random sample of contemporary non-Africans. This suggests that Caucasian features evolved within the past 15,000 to 20,000 years. As yet, there aren't the fossils to perform this test anywhere else in the world.

## Why Does Time Matter Here?

Two quite opposed views have predominated for almost two centuries now, but only one remains viable today—the one that posits an African Garden of Eden. Most people in the field have tended to see its former alternative (multiregionalism) as implying much more significant racial differences—the reason being that they would have had so much longer to develop. This has also been a major factor contributing to its relative lack of support.

But, as the late Glynn Isaac, at that time a Berkeley professor of anthropology, pointed out to me (Sarich) in a Berkeley seminar many years ago, it is the Garden-of-Eden model, not the regional-continuity model, that makes racial differences more significant functionally. It does so because the amount of time involved in the raciation process is much smaller, but the degree of racial differentiation is the same and, for human morphology, large. The shorter the period of time required to produce a given amount of morphological difference, the more selectively/adaptively/functionally important those differences become. The Garden-of-Eden model in its earlier formulations envisioned perhaps 40,000 years for raciation within anatomically modern *Homo sapiens*; for a time in the late 1980s and 1990s, driven by the mtDNA work, dates of 100,000–150,000 years were common; the most recent molecular evidence (mtDNA and Y-chromosome) fits comfortably with the 40,000-year date. But that might not be all of it. During the past 10,000 years, human cultures have differentiated to a much greater extent with respect to achievement than was the case previously. Thus not only might the time involved in raciation have been brief, but also the selective demands on human cognitive capacities might have differed regionally to a substantially greater extent than could have been the case previously.

## ARE PEOPLE WITH
## BIGGER BRAINS SMARTER?

This is an aspect of the race issue that ultimately divided Darwin and Wallace. Darwin appeared to have been entirely comfortable with the notion that the human mind (= soul, = human nature) evolved through natural selection just as had the human body. Wallace, on the other hand, to the end of his much longer life, insisted that although the human body had evolved, the mind must have been created. A century later came the influential *Mismeasure of Man* by Gould, which also, in effect, denies that human brains evolved. Gould spends the first two chapters (100 or so pages) explaining that brain size and intellectual performance have nothing to do with each other without once noting that human brains have not always been the size they are today. Nor is that awkward fact mentioned anywhere else in the book. One could never learn from it that brain size in our evolutionary lineage increased from around 400cc to 1,300–1,400cc over the past 4 million years. Why this omission? I think the answer is quite straightforward. That part of Gould's psyche concerned with basic evolutionary biology knew that those large brains of ours could not have evolved unless having large brains increased fitness through what those large brains made possible—that is, through minds that could do more. In other words, individuals with larger brains must have been in some way, on the average, in the long run, slightly better off than those with smaller brains for a long time. How advantaged? Dare one say it?—by being smarter, of course. What else?

But Gould's behavioral-creationist side, which clung to the notion that deep down we are really all the same, couldn't allow
him to admit this, because then he would have found it impossible to honestly sustain his argument (pp. 30–112) that brain size,
as far as we know, does not matter. To conclude otherwise, he
would have had to recognize that if the variation did once matter
(and it must have), and if the variation is still there (it is), then it
almost certainly still matters—and if one is going to argue that
it does not matter, then one must explain why it does not. I do
not think one can do this while maintaining one's intellectual
honesty and integrity, and, presumably, neither did Gould. Thus,
he simply ignored the demands of the evolutionary perspective by
denying, implicitly, that our brains had evolved.

The evolutionary perspective demands that there be a relationship—in the form of a positive correlation—between brain
size and intelligence. That proposition, I would argue, is not
something that need derive from contemporary data (although,
as discussed later, those data do give it strong support). It is what
would be expected given our particular evolutionary history; that
is, *it is the evolutionary null hypothesis* and, thus, something to be
disproved. Indeed, it seems to me that a demonstration of no correlation between brain size and cognitive performance would be
about the best possible refutation of the fact of human evolution
(I did write this, though no creationist has as yet noticed). It took
me a long time to figure out the general point here: Darwin's descent with modification by means of natural selection has been,
and continues to be, the reality. It is what we start with, not
something we must prove for each new issue that arises. In other
words, there was no particularly good reason to have to do the
cognitive performances as they relate to brain-size studies. They
have simply confirmed what we expected given human evolutionary history and the nature of the selective process. But cre-

ationists in general, and behavioral creationists like Gould in particular, are very good at pushing our scientist buttons, and we fall
so easily into the trap they have set for us. Show us the data, they
ask—and we try to respond, forgetting that the realities of evolution, evolutionary processes, and evolutionary lineages are data—
and usually rather good data.

In other words, then, natural selection must have genetically
based phenotypic variation to work on. Throughout the period of
change in brain size, a substantial amount of genetic variation
must have been present for brain size; likely, the greater the advantage of larger brains, the greater the underlying genetic variation for brain size. I had long been frustrated by the canalization
(that is, continual reduction in one direction) argument with respect to human intelligence, my teaching experiences telling me
that cognitive performance was one of our most, not least, variable features, yet at the same time being unable to refute the logic
of the canalization argument. This quandary lasted until, sometime around 1983, I remembered Fisher's Fundamental Theorem
of Natural Selection: "The rate of increase in the fitness of any
organism at any time is equal to its genetic variance in fitness at
that time"—which says it all. An earlier statement of the general
argument was made by the late Bernard Davis in 1976:

> Let me further emphasize that, even if no one had ever devised a
> test for measuring IQ, we could still be confident, on grounds of
> evolutionary theory, that our species contains wide genetic vari-
> ance in intelligence. The reason is that natural selection cannot
> proceed unless it has genetic diversity, within a species, to act on;
> and when our species is compared with its nearest primate rela-
> tives, it is obvious that our main selection pressure has been for an
> increase in intelligence. Indeed, this change proceeded at an un-
> precedented rate (on an evolutionary time scale): in the past

three million years the brain size of the hominid line increased threefold. . . . Such rapid selection for increased intelligence could not have occurred unless the selection pressure had a large substrate of genetic variation to act on.

## Brain Size and Cognitive Performance: Initial Statement

I think it fair to say that any suggestion on one's part that people with bigger brains are in fact on the average smarter by virtue of those bigger brains leads the listener to doubt your intelligence, if not your sanity. The general idea in society is that this inherently sexist and racist notion died an ignoble death sometime in the nineteenth century. Its recent resurrection can be seen as beginning with a 1974 *American Journal of Physical Anthropology* article by Leigh Van Valen, a paleontologist at the University of Chicago. In it Van Valen reviewed the literature and concluded that the published correlations between brain size and intelligence (as measured by standardized tests) were unrealistically low, because they did not allow for the fact that external measurements of head size were an imperfect indicator of brain size. Correcting for this attenuation indicated that the actual value was probably about 0.3. (I also note here that Gould's *Mismeasure of Man* does not even mention Van Valen's work—even in the second edition.) Since 1987 there have been numerous studies on this subject in which the brain size of living individuals was measured directly and accurately using magnetic resonance imaging, and these suggest that Van Valen's estimate was, if anything, conservative—their consensus being in the area of 0.4 or a bit more. Although, as argued previously, a positive relationship was to be expected on the basis of simple evolutionary considerations, the actual correlations found are higher than just about anyone would have predicted prior to Van Valen's pioneering effort.

A correlation of 0.4 means that two individuals differing by one standard deviation (about 130–140cc) in brain size would, on the average, differ by 6 points (that is, 0.4 × SD; the IQ SD = 15) in measured IQ. The same holds for populations, and existing human populations can differ in their means by as much as 2 SD in brain size; thus this variable could by itself lead to nearly a 1 SD difference in mean intellectual performance among them. With respect to the difference between American whites and blacks, the one good brain-size study that has been done indicates a difference between them of about 0.8 SD; this could correspond to an IQ difference of about 5 points, or about one-third of the actual differential found.

It should be noted that these data can also be seen as indicating that IQ tests are in fact measuring something that has been significant in human evolution, given that performance on them correlates so nicely with something that we can know for certain has been significant; that something is brain size. As to the common accusation of circularity seemingly implicit in the oft-quoted statement that intelligence is what the tests test, Daniel Seligman noted in A *Question of Intelligence* that

> [Herrnstein] said it was not at all intended as a put-down of IQ tests, certainly not as a complaint about circularity. It represented, rather, the perspective of a psychologist who believed (a) that "intelligence" needed to be anchored to some unambiguous operational definition and (b) that the cluster of abilities measured by IQ tests constituted a reasonable anchor. Fast analogy: You could define length . . . as "a distance or dimension expressed in units of linear measure." You could also define it as the thing that tape measures measure.

## Individuals and Groups

I have to this point tended to go from group to individual and back again without addressing the fact that any number of commentators on *The Bell Curve* have argued that (1) individual variation within groups is generally greater than variation between groups and (2) the existence of functionally significant genetic differences among individuals (with which most of them apparently feel comfortable) does not necessarily imply such among populations (with which they, along with most people, definitely aren't). But the obvious truth of these two assertions in no sense justifies the object lesson we are supposed to draw from them—that group variation therefore is not something that need particularly concern us. First, the fact is that group differences can be much greater than individual differences within them; in, for example, hair form for Kenya and Japan; or body shape for the Nuer and Inuit. And even where the first assertion is correct, as it is for most human characteristics, the differences between groups can, as already noted, be quite consequential. There is a much weaker case to be made for the relevance of the second assertion. Although a qualification such as "does not necessarily" makes it technically correct, the statement as a whole implies that we should expect a connection between individual and group variation to be the exception and not the rule.

The evolutionary perspective begs to disagree. Consider again the example of brain size. Within sex and population, the coefficient of variation (standard deviation/mean times 100) is about 10 percent, a value typical for mass or volume characters. Two randomly chosen same-sex individuals within a population would then differ in brain size by about 12 percent, or about 150cc. But so, as already noted, can two populations. And this should not be surprising. Remember that our brain has increased in size some

1,000cc in the past 3 million years. This is often termed "an ex-plosive rate of growth," yet it works out to only a fourth of a drop per generation. Given what we know of individual variation and heritability for the character, growth could have proceeded much more rapidly. That it didn't implies that the huge advantages conferred by having more brain to work with must have been off-set by (almost) equally large disadvantages. In other words, the adaptation here is best seen as a very slowly moving compromise involving small differences between large forces. We should then have no expectation that those advantages and disadvantages would have balanced out in the same way in different populations at differing times and in differing ecological and cultural circum-stances—and a look around confirms that they haven't.

This same argument will apply to most aspects of individual variation. Given the number of characteristics in which func-tional variation is present, the ways in which they will balance out in two populations evolving more or less independently of one another are almost guaranteed to be different in the two. The balancing will take place at the level of individual phenotypes, and thus there will generally be a direct, inescapable connection between individual and group variation whenever evolutionary change is taking place—that is, always.

## A Mea Culpa

I (Sarich) have written this as an object lesson to myself and a warning to others. From an evolutionary perspective, there must be a positive correlation or relationship between head/brain size as such and cognitive performance or ability as such, as noted in the past few pages. Proving it directly is another matter entirely. In the past, the largest problem was getting a good estimator of brain size, since, obviously, it couldn't be measured directly.

There is, of course, a strong relationship between external measurements of the cranium and brain size, but it falls far short of perfect.

When coauthor Frank Miele was researching the long-running debate between Ashley Montagu and Carleton Coon, he came upon a dispassionate review of the data by D. G. Paterson. Interestingly, both Coon and Montagu cited the review to support their positions. Though written in 1930, it could have been written just yesterday (except that the word "inferior" would have to be replaced; Paterson meant it in only an objective, quantitative sense):

> Comparative studies have shown, that, from a phylogenetic point of view, increase in head size and cultural evolution have, in general, gone hand in hand. The association, however, does not warrant immediate acceptance of the proposition that, within any given cultural group, variations in head size are necessarily paralleled by variations in intelligence.
>
> A critical review of available evidence tends to dissipate claims put forth in behalf of an intimate relation between head size and intelligence. Although inadequate statistical methods characterize most of the research studies and although no satisfactorily standardized method of measuring head size is adopted in them, *it can be said with considerable assurance that whatever positive correlation exists must be of a low order. Our confidence in the validity of this conclusion is increased by the fact that its acceptance frees us from the necessity of accounting for mental equality between the sexes in the face of tremendous sex differences in head size* [emphasis ours]. It also frees us from the necessity of explaining away the possibility that a mentally inferior racial group should exhibit a superior head size. These two instances make the position of those who stress an intimate relationship between intellect and head size embarrassing if not quite untenable. It appears that variation in head size is a

function of race, sex, and family stock. It does not vary between individuals in correspondence with intellect.

Not only is head size shown to be of minor importance as a physical correlate or sign of intellect, but the same may be said of head shape. Head shape also varies as a racial characteristic irrespective of the intellectual qualities exhibited by several racial groups. Within a given racial strain, head shape appears to be indifferently related to intellect.

The highlighted text is the most telling, in particular the comments about women. In every human group men have brains that are, on the average, about 10 percent larger than women's, and little of this can be attributed to body-size differences. It might have been wise to explain why sex does not seem to make much of a difference before proceeding to within-sex and within-population theorizing.

Here again, disagreement exists. Frank referred to the various hypotheses that have been offered to explain this male-female conundrum. I'm well aware of them but consider them speculations. There is still no hard evidence, in my opinion, to support any of them.

In any case, it seemed to me that this matter could be settled by a new technology, magnetic resonance imaging (MRI), which allowed one to get quite precise measurements of brain size overall as well as portions (gray matter) *in vivo*. The first brain size/IQ study using MRI appeared in 1987, and numerous studies have followed with results rather consistent with one another—a within-sex correlation between brain size and cognitive performance of 0.4 or a bit higher—which seemed to me and others to settle the facts of the matter, if not the interpretation of those facts.

It took Arthur Jensen to ask the critical question, and a graduate student of mine (Tom Schoenemann) to set up the research.

Specifically, Jensen asked how much the 0.4 correlation was affected by going from between-family to within-family comparisons of adults (the environmental effects will be minimized in
within-family comparisons). Tom expressed interest in the project as a dissertation topic. Then things got confusing, and the
confusion remains.

Tom recruited thirty-six pairs of sisters, measured their brains
and portions thereof, and gave them a number of different cogni-
tive-function tests. The between-family comparisons produced
results consistent with the literature; that is, the correlation was
around 0.4 (0.4 is respectably high for this sort of work). This
gave Tom confidence that everyone seemed to be doing things in
the same way. That made the within-family results especially disturbing—the correlation was zero. That is, there was no tendency
at all for the larger-brained sister to show a higher IQ (or, more
fairly, a higher "g").

The implication is that there is some third factor that operates
differentially for between-family versus within-family comparisons, but it would have to be a very strong effect, and the obvious
candidates (for example, socioeconomic status) do not begin to
produce it. For example, the correlation between socioeconomic
status and brain size was an insignificant 0.05.

The purpose here is not only to report results but also to draw
object lessons. One is that it is easy to have a large effect over
evolutionary time without being able to see it at all in real-time
tests. For example, Tom pointed out that a correlation of as little
as 0.05 could still easily produce what we see in evolutionary time
with a selective differential of a mere 0.1 IQ point. In other
words, it would be entirely possible—indeed, to be expected—
that processes acting over evolutionary time can easily produce
results impossible to replicate in laboratory time. All scientists in
this field know this; we are forever explaining to our students and
the public that we don't see new species forming in front of our

eyes because the rates of change involved are a thousandfold too slow to be seen as even moving, never mind getting anywhere.

The point is that my earlier story was right as far as what had happened in evolutionary time, and why, but there was no reason to expect that we should be able to see such large effects in real-time. We should have recognized that it wasn't in the cards that the two crude metrics of brain size as such and IQ as such should correlate at levels of 0.4 and more. It was, again, one of these seductive results that turned off critical faculties. When I reflect on the episode with 20/20 hindsight, it is obvious that the lack of male-female differences should have warned us, just as it did Paterson. Then I wouldn't blunder into a statement like "It seems to me that a demonstration of no correlation between brain size and cognitive performance would be about the best possible refutation of the fact of human evolution."

Although we don't know how to prove it directly, and suspect that it isn't provable directly, the fossil record tells us that brain size has increased threefold over the past 2–3 million years; as already noted, this growth must have occurred because bigger brains were advantaged over smaller ones. This is trivially true. The next step—that bigger ones are today somehow better ("better" here obviously has no moral component)—poses unnecessary difficulties, as we have demonstrated. But there remain these large size differences between males and females that we have not yet explained, and they are complemented by racial ones and by claims that a significant portion of racial IQ differences can be explained in terms of racial brain-size differences. This is unlikely.

## INCOME INEQUALITY AND IQ

It seems to us that the messages from *The Bell Curve* become increasingly timely as time goes on. Another message appeared in 1998 (data from 1993) as a short monograph entitled *Income*

*Inequality and IQ.* In his study, Murray made within-family comparisons of IQ and income among young (ages 28–36) adult siblings. They were divided into five groups: very bright IQ mean 125; bright 114; normal 99; dull 86; very dull 75; and then compared against certain variables. Perhaps the most telling result came from what Murray called his "utopian sample" (basically, growing up in intact families). Median earnings (in dollars) for the five IQ categories were 38,000; 27,000; 23,000, 16,000; 11,000. For the sample as a whole, they were 36,000; 27,000; 21,000; 13,000; 7,500. For siblings, the figures were 33,500; 26,000; 22,000; 17,000; 12,250. Thus each IQ point was worth several hundred dollars of income. But more important is that Murray's utopian sample did very little better than the sample as a whole. In his words: "We are not comparing apples and oranges here—not suburban white children with inner-city black children, not the sons of lawyers with the sons of ditchdiggers—but siblings, children of the same parents, who spent their childhoods under the same roof. They differed in their scores on a pencil-and-paper mental test."

Here it might be useful to look at a less controversial subject, stature. We are all comfortable with the idea that adult stature is the result of a genetic background working through various environments, and with the fact that those environments have had quite substantial effect. A recent sample of Dutch males, for instance, produced a mean stature of 6'0", against perhaps 5'7" a hundred years ago. Will the mean be 6'6" in another hundred years? Not likely. It would appear that we have "improved" the environment, as far as its effect on stature is concerned, as much as possible, as indicated by the fact that the rate of increase is sloping to zero. Murray's results suggest that much the same is happening with respect to cognitive improvement in this society for much of its population.

That is a controversial viewpoint, but we haven't seen a substantive critique of Murray's work, nor even of *The Bell Curve*. The basic conclusions are holding up, though not, unfortunately, as far as public policy is concerned.

## THE DEBATE ON SUB-SAHARAN AFRICAN IQ

Perhaps the most enigmatic and controversial results in the IQ realm pertain to sub-Saharan Africans and their descendants around the world. The most puzzling single finding is the apparent mean IQ of the former of about 70. One can perhaps accept this as a well-documented fact, but it is difficult to sustain any far-reaching implications of it. Consider what an IQ of 70 means in the United States. It was the boundary for what once was called educable mentally retarded (EMR). It is about 15 percent of the African-American population, which is a stunning number in view of arguments that an IQ of 70 should prevent an alleged criminal from being treated as an adult in court. For one-sixth of the population to be fundamentally incompetent makes no sense. Arthur Jensen, who worked with the EMR in his early days at Berkeley, has pointed out that a measured IQ of 70 has very different implications for American blacks and whites. Whites with 70 IQ are obviously substantially handicapped over and above their IQ scores. It is difficult to imagine their being able to form a social system among themselves. They are a blip on the IQ bell curve, suggesting a semilethal single-locus detrimental mutation as the cause.

Black kids with an IQ of 70 are another matter entirely. Except for having a low IQ, they are eminently normal, happy, functional, and so on, and there is little doubt that they could do just fine with regard to formation and maintenance of a social unit as a test for functionality. In other words, it would appear to be an apples-and-oranges situation.

The same is of course true for Africans in Africa. Interacting with them belies any thought that one is dealing with IQ 70 people. Illustrative of this is an anecdote in a note from Henry Harpending, who was doing fieldwork among the Bushmen in Botswana some thirty-five years ago. He was responding to a recent e-mail request from me (Miele):

*Frank Miele of* Skeptic *magazine here.*

*I was wondering if I could cite for publication your example of the Bushman repairing the Jeep with a broken bendix spring or whatever it was (my auto mechanical skills are near zero)?*

Harpending replied:

*Sure, of course, you are welcome to it and to quote me.*

*Working in the northwest Kalahari. We had a 3/4 ton 4-wheel drive pickup. We were returning to camp from a trip on a heavy sand track, i.e., sand that required full-time four-wheel drive. We stopped to make coffee, then when we tried to start off again we discovered the starter simply spun with no effect. There is a thingie in a starter called a "bendix drive" that is like a ratchet so that once the engine starts it can turn the starter motor with no harm. It had gone bad.*

*We had no hope of push-starting the truck in the sand, and after some thought I was getting water containers together for a long walk out. Then a young fellow who worked for me came up with the idea of jacking up a rear wheel, winding a rope around it, and starting it like a lawn mower with 3 guys pulling on the rope. It worked like a charm, and in fact we had to start that truck that way for months until we obtained a new drive.*

*He was a kid who was wearing a loincloth when I hired him as a general helper and gofer. After a year he had picked up a lot of English and a lot of truck mechanics. Later he obtained a driver's license (no small thing in backwoods Botswana) and a good government job, but he lost it after several years because of inability to cope with alcohol.*

*Best, Henry*

I e-mailed back:

*The Tale of the Bushman and the Bendix Spring is hardly consistent with the average IQ of 70 for sub-Saharan Africa, which is pretty consistent for paper-and-pencil tests.*

*I guess this is just part of being a skeptic [working for* Skeptic *magazine], but is there any chance that at some earlier time he had seen a professional crew of mechanics using that procedure (for the bendix, or something else) and simply remembered it and gave it a try?*

*Just thought I needed to ask. Thanks again—FMiele*

Harpending responded:

*No, I don't think so, I grilled him pretty carefully about it. There were hardly ever any vehicles in that part of the country at that time (1960s).*

*All of us have the impression that Bushmen are really quick and clever and are quite different from their neighbors. There are similar stories about Eskimo. Bushmen don't look at all like their black African neighbors either.*

*I expect that there will soon be real data available from the Namibian school system about the relative performance of Bushmen, Hottentot, and Bantu kids. Or, more likely, they will suppress it.*

So I offered a hypothesis:

*Could this be related to lessened selection for intelligence (or at least cleverness) with the coming of agriculture, versus hunting-gathering?*

Harpending replied:

*Sure, absolutely. The problem is how to test this. Did anyone ever say that the Shoshone of the Great Basin were clever? I never read any such thing, but they were hunter-gatherers surrounded by farmers. And remember that "agriculture" is not really a good variable. In history, or across societies, there is a continuum between (a) gardening on the one hand and (b) labor-intensive agriculture on the other. Along this transition there is a change from bride-price to dowry, from males being cads to males being dads, from males being fierce to males being drab workers, and so on. Gardening societies are at most invariably associated with females doing the work and men being rather worthless [or] else heavily involved in local warfare.*

*Almost any hypothesis about all this can be falsified with one sentence. For example: (1) Hunter-gathering selects for cleverness. But then why do Australian Aborigines do so badly in school and on tests? (2) Dense labor-intensive agriculture selects for cleverness, explaining the high IQ scores in the Far East and in south India. But then why is there not a high-IQ pocket in the Nile Valley? And so on. I don't have any viable theory about it all.*

That's where Henry and I ended the dialogue, with the question of the true African IQ getting only more complicated rather than resolved.

The mean IQ score of 70 for the region is not a fluke. Further research has confirmed not only the reliability of the data (they are repeatable) but also their validity (that is, they predict other variables such as school performance just as well as they do for other groups). And they do measure the general factor of intelligence (Spearman's *g*). In short, the test results from sub-Saharan Africa are consistent with those for other races, around the world:

> Studies in southern Africa have also found the mean Black-White IQ difference is mainly on *g*. Lynn and Owen (1994) were the first to explicitly test Spearman's hypothesis [that Black-White differences are greatest on *g*] in sub-Saharan Africa, administering the Junior Aptitude Test to 1,056 White, 1,063 Indian, and 1,093 Black 16-year-old high school students in South Africa. They found a two standard deviation difference between the Africans and Whites (yielding an average African IQ of about 70) and a one standard deviation difference between the Whites and Indians (yielding an average Indian IQ of 85). They then tested Spearman's hypothesis and found the African-White differences correlated .62 (p < 0.05) with the *g*-factor extracted from the African sample, but only .23 with *g* extracted from the White sample. They did not find any White-Indian differences on *g*.

Jensen (1998b, p. 388) noted some problems with Lynn and Owen's (1994) South African study, but their results on Black-White differences have been well corroborated since then and extended to include East Indians and Coloreds. Thus, Rushton (2001) re-analyzed data on ten sub-tests of the WISC-R published on 154 high-school students in South Africa by Skuy et al. (2001) and found African-White differences were mainly on *g*. Rushton and Jensen (in press) compared data on the WISC-R from 204 African 12- to 14-year-olds from Zimbabwe published by Zindi (1994) with the U.S. normative sample for Whites and found 77% of the between-group race variance was attributable to a single source, namely *g*.

Spearman's hypothesis has been confirmed in South Africa using test item analyses as well. Rushton and Skuy (2000) studied 309 university students at the University of the Witwatersrand and found that the more an individual item from the Raven's Standard Progressive Matrices measured *g* (estimated by its item-total correlation), the more it correlated with the standardized African-White difference on that item. Rushton (in press) analyzed the item data from 4,000 high-school students in South Africa on Raven's Standard Progressive Matrices published by Owen (1992) and found the four-way African-Colored–East Indian–White differences were all on *g*. In two studies of engineering students, Rushton et al. (2002, in press) found the more the items from both the Standard and the Advanced Progressive Matrices loaded on *g*, the better they predicted the magnitude of African-East Indian-White differences. The *g* loadings showed cross-cultural generality; those calculated on the East Indian students predicted the magnitude of the African-White differences.

I (Miele) got back on e-mail and asked Richard Lynn and Phil Rushton their reasons for arguing that the low value for sub-Saharan IQ is valid. Rushton noted that an IQ of 70 translates to a mental age of 11.2, so an IQ of 75 (median for African IQ reported in *The Bell Curve*) is mental age of 12, assuming the average IQ of 100 is set at 16 years. The African American IQ then yields a mental age of 13 to 14 years old, as compared to the white average of 16, an East Asian American average of 17, and a Jewish American of 18. Viewed in this way, these data do not seem out of line.

Following up on this line of thought, Lynn noted that since the average white 12-year-old can do all manner of things, including driving cars and even fixing them, estimates of African IQ should *not* be taken to mean half the population is mentally retarded. Given the nature of the bell curve for intelligence and the difference in group means, there are proportionately fewer whites with IQs below 75, but most of these are the result of chromosomal or single-gene problems and are recognizable as such by their appearance as much as by their behavior.

The problems of black "ghettoes," he explained, may be exacerbated by the absence of a significant number of higher IQ "buffers." Once a problem starts, it's like that old example with the Ping Pong balls loaded on mousetraps as an illustration of a chain reaction.

Lynn stated that there is probably some critical mass of low IQ. Once it is reached, it becomes impossible to maintain a modern, technological, self-regulated society. The only alternative to chaos or decline to a lower level of technology and economy may be the imposition of (sometimes draconian) outside force.

Lynn also provided me with the real-world value of IQ tests as predictors of job performance and school grades as being the same for African students. He referred me to the book he coauthored with Tatu Vanhanen, *IQ and the Wealth of Nations*, in which they demonstrated a strong correlation between average national IQ and measures of income.

Rushton pointed out that these IQ estimates also "fit" with brain size and other elements in his race-behavior matrix and with the record of human evolutionary history. Even if cultural factors were involved in lowering the average African IQ (and so therefore it should be adjusted upward to some degree), the general trend of race differences in IQ and related measures of performance would remain the same.

We believe that one of the "thought blocks" that has prevented a coherent look at the question of race differences in *average* intelligence is the persistence of the typological viewpoint. It is simply wrong to think of all members of a race as being the same on almost any important measurement of performance, not just IQ. It is much more correct to think of each race as having similar bell-curved distributions, in which the means differ.

A look at the demographic data for any group makes one thing quite clear. The overwhelming number of human matings are not random. Individuals tend to mate with those who are like themselves, a process called assortative mating. Within each race, especially in a society such as ours where IQ is so closely tied to success, mating in any race overwhelmingly occurs within subgroups (that is, higher IQ/higher income; medium IQ/medium income; and lower IQ/lower income). Should the relative reproductive rates of those subgroups change, the average IQ for the entire racial group would change.

There are examples that this process probably has taken place. Furthermore, it need not have consumed very much time. Probably the most obvious case for Americans is the adventure of European Jews. Arriving usually in poverty, with backgrounds of repression and discriminated against here, they nonetheless became our most marked immigrant success story, with average family incomes at least 50 percent higher than the national mean and with greatly disproportionate representation in numerous high-profile occupations. The average IQ for American Jews is at least 115, probably closer to 120. In any population, there are any number of subpopulations, and those that place great faith in learning will clearly raise their IQ over time.

One must also wonder what effect events such as the Spanish conquest of the Inca civilization or the Mongol conquest of the Islamic civilization had on destroying the intellectual elites of these cultures and possibly reducing the average intelligence and cultural level for these groups. The precise roles of intelligence, ecology, and cultural practices, as well as the feedback among them, in influencing societal achievement are yet to be determined. This critical topic is certainly worthy of intense investigation.

## POLICY IMPLICATIONS

Daniel Seligman closed his book *A Question of Intelligence* this way: "One major message of the IQ data is that groups are different. A major policy implication of the data, I would argue, is that people should not be treated as members of groups but as individuals."

In this regard, we agree with the individualistic perspective of Murray and Herrnstein and of Seligman. But we realize that many do not and that the meritocratic society we favor is not without its drawbacks. In the next and final chapter, we examine the implications of the reality of race for the future.

CHAPTER NINE

# Learning to Live with Race

*We explain here why we took the time and effort to write this book. We believe that it is not only appropriate but important to study race. Why? Because it helps us to apply the evolutionary perspective to the analysis of human variation generally. Variation, in both body and behavior, both within races and between, is the norm, not the exception. However, recognition of average race differences, in our opinion, does not inevitably lead to racist attitudes or policies.*

*We present three scenarios of how we think America and the world might deal with race in the years ahead: The Meritocracy in the Emerging Global Economy; Affirmative Action and Race Norming; and Rising Resegregation and the Emergence of Ethno-States. We describe the costs and benefits, and the dangers and opportunities, of each. We also examine the feasibility of a worst-case scenario posed by ethnically targeted weapons.*

*We remain guardedly optimistic about our ability to recognize the reality of human differences, because the only alternative is to give in to despair. Were that our natural inclination, our lineage would have perished long ago.*

The scientific study of race, no matter how loaded with the onus of past events and politically unpalatable at the present time, is not only appropriate but necessary. It provides a case study for the necessity of applying the evolutionary perspective if we are to comprehend the meaning of human physical, behavioral, and body-chemistry variation. Unless we pursue such study, our understanding of our species, our origin, and our place in nature will remain captive to religious or political dogma. Widespread rejection of the evolutionary perspective by religious zealots, whether humanist or fundamentalist, and by political partisans, whether liberal or conservative, does not bode well at a time when the issues of environmental preservation, interethnic conflict, and inequalities in the distribution of wealth and status have taken center stage.

The key concept here is *variation*. Human races are not, and never were, distinct, mutually exclusive, Platonic entities into which every living person, unearthed skull, or set of bones could be pigeonholed. Races represent variations on the basic human theme, each containing its own subthemes, that mix and intertwine over the course of time. It is only by using a select set of morphological characteristics or 50–100 genetic markers that one gets anything approaching clear-cut separations. Those markers are also important because they measure the tempo of the theme of human evolution. But just as we can recognize themes and subthemes without performing an analysis of a musical score—or even knowing how to perform one—so too ancient non-European civilizations and contemporaneous hunter-gatherer societies sorted humans into groups that correspond with those revealed by the latest DNA studies. So could we contemporary humans—at least until propagandized by colleges, universities, or PBS. And so too could a visitor from another planet should one ever arrive. The attempts to prove that race is not a biological reality but a mere social construction, even when penned by such authorities in their respective fields as Jared Diamond (evolutionary biology), Alan Goodman (physical anthropology), Richard Lewontin (population genetics), or the late Stephen Jay Gould (paleontology), simply do not hold up when one examines the converging lines of evidence detailed in this book. These and other statements and manifestos from lesser lights range from the truly heartfelt but misguided to the pathetic to the absurd.

As we have shown, the morphological differences between human races can exceed those found between subspecies, or even species of our nearest relatives, the chimps and gorillas, and other nondomesticated animals. Yet, as Lewontin rightly pointed out, the genetic differences between human races are small. We must look to our best friend, the domestic dog, where breeders have exercised extreme selection to find a level of variation equivalent to that found in humans. Canine differences in physique, behavior, and body chemistry have been produced in a very short time (for the most part, a few hundred years). Yet, despite the vast morphological and behavioral variation among dog breeds, we are only beginning to able to distinguish between them, or even between dogs and wolves, using the latest DNA evidence.

How much time is required to produce such variation? It depends on the heritability of the trait, the strength of selection on it, and how much of an advantage the difference confers on an individual. For example, if the heritability of IQ is .5, as the data suggest, this implies that half of the individual differences within the population results from genetic variation. Now, if we suppose that parents on average have an IQ one point greater than the population mean for the previous generation, then IQ can change by one-half point per generation, two points in a century, and ten points in 500 years, assuming increased intelligence advantages an individual.

Unlike for dog breeds, no one has deliberately exercised that level of selection on humans, unless we exercised it on ourselves, a thought that has led evolutionary thinkers from Charles Darwin to Jared Diamond to attribute human racial variation to a process termed "sexual" rather than "natural" selection. Natural selection is differential survival of traits, and the genes responsible for them, based upon the demands of the environment. In a classic example, there was natural selection for dark-colored moths when the English landscape was darkened by the smog of the first industrial revolution. Under these circumstances, the dark-colored moths displaced light-colored moths because they were able to blend into the darkened tree trunks. Recently, there has been selection for light-colored moths as the trees have lightened in color because of the demise of smokestack industries.

Sexual selection, in contrast, is based upon which partners we find most attractive because of their appearance, not necessarily their survival value. Here the classic example is peafowl, where the hens prefer to mate with elaborately plumed male peacocks even though their tail is of no use apart from attracting females and may attract predators as well. Sexual selection is survival of the fairest in the land, not the fittest. However, no one has yet provided any hard evidence showing that process has produced racial differences in our species.

The latest evidence from the recent synthesis of nuclear DNA, mitochondrial DNA, and Y-chromosome studies, along with the archeological and paleontological records, is now consistent in showing that no human racial lineage dates back more than 50,000 years, and many, perhaps most, can be traced back only 20,000 years. The out-of-Africa model of human evolution does not support Gould's well-known argument that there simply has not been sufficient time for human races to have evolved. Rather, the recent-origin/out-of-Africa model, not some form of parallel evolution of long-standing lineages, means that racial differences are (or were) more significant functionally, not less so. This is so because the amount of time allowed for the process of race formation is much smaller, whereas the degree of racial differentiation is obviously the same and, for human morphology, large. The shorter the period of time allowed in which to produce a given amount of morphological difference, the more selectively/adaptively/functionally important those differences must be. The 20,000–50,000-year model increases that significance well beyond anything previously contemplated. Further, there is no good reason to think that behavior should somehow be exempt from this pattern of functional variability—if anything, the opposite is the case. But there is more. During the past 10,000 years, human cultures have differentiated to a much greater extent with respect to achievement than was the case previously. Thus, not only was the time involved in raciation brief, but also the selective demands on human cognitive capacities may well have differed regionally to a substantially greater extent than could have been the case previously.

For most abilities, both mental and physical, in which we are so interested and on which we place so much value, there is tremendous overlap between the races. Even when the differences among racial mean values for some salient feature of the human condition are relatively small, as they usually will be, statistical reality will exaggerate the effects of those differences at the more visible tails of the distributions involved, and it is the tails, not the means, that drive our perceptions, feelings, and policies. The relative proportion of individuals capable of performing at the highest level is, by definition, exceedingly small in any group. But a small difference between the average of two groups results in a greater representation of certain groups than others at both the high and the low ends, along with the recognition and

monetary rewards that accompany achievement in a society organized like ours. In the real world, it is impossible to have the Lake
Woebegone scenario in which "everyone is above average"—or
even one in which everyone is equal.

The issue before us, then, is how and to what extent we deal with
these differences. From the general to the specific, consider now
three examples where the recognition of the reality of race makes a
difference. Recognition of the biological reality of race can be a life-
and-death matter in prescribing the most appropriate medication.
(Awareness of differential reactions in dog breeds has become standard veterinary practice, as described in *Veterinary Drug Handbook*,
the analogue to *Physicians Desk Reference*.) Our understanding of
the racial factor in medicine is only just emerging and will require
constant monitoring and revision, but there is no reason to brush it
under the carpet of political correctness unless our society has
reached the point where we exercise greater humanness and intelligence regarding our pets than our fellow man.

Another area in which the reality of race becomes a life-and-
death matter is the criminal justice system. The latest DNA
methodology is as capable of identifying the race of victims and
suspected perpetrators of crimes as standard DNA analysis is of
making individual identification. Naturally, all forensic methods
call for corroboration, and fortunately our legal system provides
for questioning of evidence and cross-examination of expert witnesses by the defense. It should be noted that had the DNAPrint
method been available for use in the Baton Rouge serial-killer
case (the necessary database became available only recently), it
would have spared a number of individuals from having to go
through police questioning. In that case, the search was shifted
from white to African-American suspects, but individual DNA
matching has also been used as grounds for appeal on behalf of a
number of black Americans apparently wrongly convicted.

Some controversy has arisen over the role of race in medicine, and much exists regarding its role in our legal and criminal justice systems, but the most inflammatory matters have involved the issue of genetically influenced racial differences in intelligence, educational achievement, and financial success. Relegated to the margins of the scientific arena after World War II, the topic returned to center stage with the publication of Arthur Jensen's 1969 *Harvard Educational Review* article, "How Much Can We Boost IQ and School Achievement?" and again in 1994 with the publication of *The Bell Curve* by Richard Herrnstein and Charles Murray. Although the task force appointed by the American Psychological Association to investigate the question of a genetic component in the mean difference in IQ between blacks and whites concluded that "There is certainly no support for a genetic interpretation" (p. 97), no one has demonstrated a method of compensatory education that produces relatively permanent increases in mental ability, as opposed to learning how to answer specific test items correctly. The term "ability" is often taken to mean a quality that is inborn and immutable, but we use it to mean the result of the interaction between each individual's genes and environment, including the biological environment, in which the individual has developed. Twin and other kinship studies have established that there is a significant heritable component to virtually every human ability, and despite the assertion of the APA, there is substantial evidence for some genetic component in average group differences.

There is suggestive evidence that some biological, but not genetic, factors, such as breast feeding and vitamin supplements, can have a small but significant role in increasing cognitive ability, at least among certain subjects. The efficacy of such approaches can only increase as we obtain greater knowledge of both individual and group variation. The critical point here is one of cost-benefit analysis, also known as opportunity costs. Every dollar and every man-hour spent on method A means an offsetting dollar and man-hour that cannot be spent on method B. It is our considered opinion that the biological approaches provide promise of much more cost-effective methods, particularly for diagnosing and treating those most at risk.


## THREE SCENARIOS

The three scenarios of how our nation and the world might live with race have been selected not because others could not be envisioned, but only to illustrate that if there is a given set of desired outcomes and changing one of them affects the others, only one of them can be maximized at a time.


### Meritocracy in the Global Marketplace

We use the term "marketplace" rather than "global village" because no matter how widely the latter term is accepted, what is emerging is anything but a village where everyone knows everyone else—and everyone else's business—where status is ascribed rather than achieved, and where there is little mobility, up or down the social hierarchy. Rather, what we see in the emerging global economy is that whether it's baseball, Broadway, ballet, or biotechnology, barriers based upon racial membership continue to erode. The best and the brightest move to the top—and to the United States.

The meritocracy is a positive-sum game in which everyone and every group benefits, on an absolute scale. The mean level of performance in any field rises, so all benefit, but the variance also rises. Although the overall average goes up, the gap between the top and the bottom, whether between individuals or between group averages, increases even more. Many people feel they are being left further behind. As disproportional representation becomes evident, resentment toward certain high-performance groups increases.

In the global meritocracy, the best and the brightest have never had it so good. They form a sort of international elite and often marry with those of other races. Their common feature is their status among members of different racial groups. Nonetheless, there is no reason to assume that the racial appearance of vast areas of the world, including China, India, sub-Saharan Africa, and the Middle East, which have not changed in recorded history, will change any time soon. This is not the case in the developed world, however, where birthrates have been plunging for the past two centuries to the point that they are currently below replacement level, except among certain religious groups. Barring some major change in ideology and consequent policy, it seems likely that the United States and Western Europe each year will see an increasing percentage of the population composed of first- and second-generation immigrants, increasingly from the underdeveloped countries of the Third World.

The ultimate evolutionary irony lurking on the horizon is that having conquered and colonized the world in the previous two centuries, Europeans and their descendants became so wealthy that they brought about their own extinction. The only exceptions are the subgroups (fundamentalist Christians, traditional Catholics, Latter-Day Saints, Orthodox Jews) that are most hostile to acknowledging the evolutionary perspective. But this has not stopped them from operating according to its dictates. To the contrary, they do so with an unconscious vengeance.

Even in utopia, the one good that can never result from a positive-sum game is status. This does not produce insurmountable problems when the differences are among members of the same group. Here, evolution has equipped us to expect and to accept such differences. Few of us resent a rich kinsman or coethnic. When the differences, even if relative rather than absolute, are associated to some degree with group markers such as race (and to a lesser extent sex, age, or religion), however, overcoming envy becomes more problematic. The examples of basic military training, sports teams, music groups, and successful businesses show that it can indeed be overcome. But doing so requires in a sense creating a new identity by to some extent stripping away the old. Eventually, the individual is able to identify with several different groups. Increasing societal complexity, by definition, means increasing the number of groups in that society to which a given individual can belong. This process tends to mitigate exclusive group identification and the associated resentment toward other groups.

The meritocracy resonates quite well with a major tradition in American history, and the United States is probably better positioned to choose this option than any other. But it is not the only tradition. On the one side, our nation's record of racism and discrimination is long and powerful; on the other, the pull of egalitarianism and leveling, though much more recent, is also strong. If we opt for greater equality, particularly group equality, it will bring with it lower levels of achievement. It can also lead to a backlash among the majority group and high-achieving minorities, including some Asian Americans and Jews.

One strong argument in favor of the meritocracy is that over the course of American history, it has worked for the most part. Starting with the Irish, the Chinese, the Jews, and going up to the Vietnamese and people from the former Soviet bloc more recently, groups have entered the United States, and many of their members have "made it."

The obvious cases in which this hasn't been true are African Americans and American Indians. But here a closer look is required. First, an increasing number of African Americans were improving their lot even before the civil rights movement, let alone affirmative action, because of the overall economic growth following World War II. The alternative strategy of setting aside reservations for American Indians can hardly be called a success—rather it has stood in their way. Of course, a bit of perspective is always required in addressing racial and ethnic questions. The obvious physical differences between blacks and whites in the United States and the history of slavery and Jim Crow should be compared against cases such as the former Yugoslavia or Ireland where physical and genetic differences are minimal, yet ethnic conflict has raged for decades, even centuries. Brazil, once thrown up as an alternative to the United States, increasingly appears to be a worst-case scenario, not a best-case one.

The meritocracy need not mean insistence on rigidly selecting *only* on the basis of some predictor of job success such as SAT scores for college applicants or strength and agility tests for firefighters. We believe that race (as well as sex and age) can, and in certain cases should, be used in a mix of factors for selecting from among a pool of qualified applicants provided

- It is demonstrably relevant;
- It can cut both ways; and
- The bar is not lowered just to meet a quota.

A few examples will better explain this:

Among a pool of applicants to college or graduate school, all of whom have met the minimum SAT or GRE score required, race, along with sex, age, citizenship (i.e., foreign students), and economic background can all be considered factors in creating a diverse student body, as this is part of the educational experience.

In selecting candidate firefighters, all of whom have met the required level of performance on a test of strength and agility, it may be desirable to match as closely as possible the ethnic composition of the community in order to facilitate better interaction and participation. Certainly, language is a factor to be considered here, and in certain areas, sexual orientation may even be relevant. All members of a community have a vested interest in seeing that their city doesn't burn down.

In selecting an instructor for an educational program for largely minority youth, it may be desirable to select a qualified candidate from that race because arguably the person might establish better rapport. But under the principles of the meritocracy, the argument could also be turned around: The world of work still remains largely one of white, male bosses, and thus it might be preferable to select such an applicant so that the students learn as soon as possible to deal with what they are likely to face in the real world.

These and many other possibilities can be imagined, and we would hope that the institutions involved would use their imagination, experiment, and report their results. The one policy that is not acceptable under the meritocracy is to continue lowering the bar until some racial (or other) quota, however much it is euphemized as a "timetable" or a "goal," is met.

Other policies totally compatible with a meritocratic society include searching vigorously among minority groups for promising candidates and providing remedial training when there is evidence that it is likely to pay dividends.

## Affirmative Action, Race Norming, and Quotas

How far we have come from judging individuals based on the content of their character rather than the color of their skin can be seen from the example of race-norming, quota-driven treatment for academic admissions at the University of California at Berkeley.

From about 1984 until 1996 (when affirmative action was ceased), a substantial percentage of freshman admissions (up to about 40 percent) was reserved for "underrepresented minorities," and race, ethnicity, and gender became major determining factors in the hiring of new faculty. This approached produced, though perhaps with the best of intentions, an apartheid-like situation—two student bodies separated by race/ethnicity and performance who wound up, in the main, in different courses, pursued different majors, and had minimal social interactions but maximum resentment. That was only to be expected when the difference in average SAT scores between the white and Asian students on the one hand, and black and Latino students on the other, was about 270 points (1,270 versus about 1,000). This difference is not trivial but rather is equivalent to about three to four years of academic achievement, and Berkeley is no place to play catch-up. As far as anyone knows (there are no published studies on the matter), no catching up, as measured by objective test scores, in fact took place.

Rather than achieving greater integration or even color-blindness, the Berkeley campus became a place where the association between race/ethnicity and performance was real, obvious, and of ever-increasing strength. The result was to produce two communities, separable on racial/ethnic grounds and increasingly divergent from one another academically, socially, and in ethos—an outcome desired, presumably, by no rational soul. It is, frankly, difficult to imagine policies that could have been more deliberately crafted or better calculated to exacerbate racial and ethnic tensions, discourage individual performance among all groups, and contribute to the decay of a magnificent educational institution.

The message of the evolutionary perspective is that any group-based policies are bound to have effects of this sort, because the evolutionary necessity of individual variation almost always will lead to group variation, and statistical realities require that group differences in any measurement of performance are exaggerated as one approaches the ends of the bell curves involved, where the high-visibility action is taking place. Thus when we assess group representations with respect to the high-visibility pluses (e.g., high-paying jobs) and minuses (e.g., criminality) in any society, it is virtually guaranteed that they are not going to be equal—and that the differences will not be trivial. The problems then come in recognizing and adapting to those realities.

The meritocracy recognizes that there are certain harsh realities in life. Society is not omnipotent. It can provide opportunity, but it cannot mandate that individuals will make equal use of those opportunities. It can in no sense make groups equal. It cannot level up—only down—and any such leveling is necessarily at the expense of individual freedom and, ultimately, the total level of accomplishment.

## Rising Resegregation and the Emergence of Ethnopolitics

Despite or perhaps because of government-imposed quotas, society becomes increasingly polarized along racial lines. A large number of white Americans harbor the suspicion that all minority members in high-status positions are there only because of affirmative action and not because of ability or achievement. And whenever a minority member is shown to have been at fault, as in the case of *New York Times* reporter Jayson Blair, who was fired when it was revealed he was guilty of plagiarism, it is seen as confirming those suspicions.

America increasingly resegregates itself. This trend can already be seen in housing, enrollment in private schools, racial composition of public schools, and political affiliation. Racial interaction becomes largely pro forma rather than a matter of choice. The

extent to which America has already become two (or more) nations can be seen in the results of the 2000 presidential election
in which the overwhelming majority of white Americans voted
for George W. Bush, whereas blacks and Hispanics largely opted
for Gore. If this trend continues—and projections are that it will
only accelerate—no matter which side wins an election, at least
one racial group will feel disenfranchised and alienated. As
shown by the county-by-county map of the Gore-Bush election,
or the differential reactions of black and white Americans to the
verdicts in the O. J. Simpson criminal and civil trials, America
has become Balkanized, a model to be avoided, not emulated.

In the television documentary *Beyond the Glory*, former heavyweight boxing champion Mike Tyson says, "I'm a nigger. I'm a big
strong nigger that knocks out people and rapes people and rips off
people and bullies people." (Tyson was convicted and served time
in prison for raping a black Miss America contestant and later bit
off part of the ear of opponent Evander Holyfield, also African
American, when he was losing their boxing match.) Later in the
two-hour rant filled with rage and remorse Tyson says, "I'm gonna
live my life. I understand this society that I live in hates me" but
then defiantly adds, "I'm gonna live it 'til they kill me."

This feeling of alienation and glorification of violence in response to perceived and, in many cases, real injustice is by no
means unique to the United States. Another TV documentary,
*Mike Versus Tyson*, shows that the boxer drew a larger and more enthusiastic crowd when he visited Brixton (a black ghetto in southcentral London) than did Nelson Mandela, whose message of
peace and reconciliation has probably done more to eliminate
racism, open up opportunities, and raise the status of people of
African descent in the eyes of the world than anyone since the late
Martin Luther King Jr. The fact that the words and deeds of a thug
like Tyson, whatever his one-time boxing prowess, resonate more
strongly with so many in the black underclass than do those of a

Nobel Peace Prize winner who endured years in prison to bring down the most repressive racist regime of recent years suggests that these individuals have only contempt for the meritocracy.

The black underclass is not unique in seeing itself as victimized and shut out by the global marketplace. An ever-increasing proportion of the Arab and greater Muslim world is becoming worked up into a frenzy of terrorism, even to the point of suicide bombing. And every predominantly white nation has its share of lunatic-fringe skinheads. All around the world, downwardly mobile males who perceive themselves as being deprived of wealth, status, and especially females by up-and-coming members of a different race are ticking time bombs.

Despite the rise of the global marketplace, in many places the world is fragmenting along ethnic lines, and often violently so. Rwanda and the Congo (formerly Zaire) have been ripped apart by genocide. Nor is this process confined to the Third World and people of color. The former Soviet Union and Yugoslavia readily come to mind. Perhaps nothing can illuminate more clearly the reality of race than the horrific prospect of ethnically targeted weapons. Knowledge is always a two-edged sword, or perhaps better, a surgeon's scalpel that can save lives or a serial killer's shiv that can take them. The very technology that allows ethnic identification by DNA to assist law enforcement and that allowed us to trace the origin of our species has potentially opened the door to selective extermination of portions of it.

## DYING, NOT LIVING, WITH RACE: THE POSSIBILITY OF ETHNICALLY TARGETED WEAPONS

Over 2,000 years ago, Scythian warriors dipped their arrowheads in manure and rotting corpses to increase their deadliness. By the fourteenth century, Tatars reportedly catapulted the dead bodies of plague victims over the walls of fortresses they were besieging. In at least one case, the British gave smallpox-infested blankets to hostile Indians during the French and Indian War. In World War II, the Japanese dropped plague-infected fleas on Chinese cities.

Allegations of the use of biological warfare before the twentieth century are difficult to confirm. Advocates on either side have an interest in promoting or discrediting the charges. Further, the conditions of war provide a breeding ground for disease. In colonial wars, the indigenous people or, more often, the colonizers may have been exposed to a disease long enough to have developed some form of immunity, to which the other side has had no previous exposure. Even if one accepts that all such pre–1900 incidents were deliberate, the unintentional transfer of disease has been overwhelmingly more lethal.

Using the most stringent set of criteria, however, scholars have corroborated at least two incidents of the premeditated use of biological weapons against members of a different racial group: the catapulting of plague-ridden cadavers into the Crimean seaport fortress of Caffa (then under control of Genoa and now in Russia and known as Feodosia) by the Tatars in 1346, and the intentional transfer of smallpox-infected blankets by the British at Fort Pitt to the temporary alliance of North American Indian tribes that had joined in what has been called "Pontiac's Rebellion."

Proof of the latter event comes from the journal of William Trent, a partner in the trading firm of Levy, Trent, and Company and commander of the fort's civilian militia, dated June 23, 1763: "Out of our regard to them, we gave them two Blankets and a Handkerchief out of the Small Pox Hospital. I hope it will have the desired effect." The transfer is confirmed in the ledger of the fort's military commander, Captain Simon Ecuyer, which under an entry "Sundries got to Replace in kind those which were taken

from people in the Hospital to Convey the Smallpox to the Indians" is listed two blankets and one silk handkerchief and their
prices. The archives have also revealed an entry in the journal of
General Jeffrey Amherst (who preceded General Gage as British
commander-in-chief in North America): "Could it not be con-
trived to send the *Small Pox* among those disaffected tribes of Indians? We must on this occasion use every stratagem in our
power" (emphasis in Amherst's original). A leading authority,
Mark Wheelis of the University of California–Davis, concludes
that although the use of smallpox as a biological weapon at Fort
Pitt "is indisputable," its actual effect (as opposed to the natural
spread of the disease) is "impossible to determine."

There is also evidence that the British used smallpox against
the Continental forces in the American Revolution by releasing
slaves who were infected by the disease. In July 1781, General
Alexander Leslie wrote to the British commander, General Corn-
wallis, that he would send pox-ridden black slaves who had come
over to the British side back to plantations owned by revolution-
ists. The earliest alleged use of biological weapons in North
America, however, was by the Iroquois in 1710 against the English, with whom they were in an uneasy alliance of convenience
against the French. In this case the Indians spent an entire day
hunting animals, flayed the bodies of the ones they had caught,
and threw the rotten flesh into a river to contaminate the water
that flowed downstream to the British encampment. The biological attack had the desired effect, and the British were forced to
retreat, burning their fort and their canoes.

The ultimate in biological warfare, however, would be the development of ethnically targeted weapons—biological weapons
that selectively attack members of a certain race or races but, like
the Death Angel in the book of Exodus, ignore members of the
attacker's race. Such "race bombs" would consist of three compo-

nents: (1) a biological weapon (of which there are many, such as sarin and anthrax now in existence, most particularly, a pathogen to which members of the targeted ethnic group are more susceptible than those of the aggressor); (2) a set of genetic markers (which as noted previously is now available) that distinguish between races; (3) an interface mechanism that would "marry" the first two components, activating the bioweapon when it encounters a suitable target.

The possibility of such weapons was noted as early as 1970 by Carl A. Larson, head of the Department of Human Genetics at the University of Lund in Sweden. His article in *Military Review*, which is published by the U.S. Army Command and General Staff College at Fort Leavenworth, Kansas, pointed out that heritable differences between populations (races) in body chemistry could serve as the basis for a new generation of biological weapons. Then in 1972, the *Defense News* carried a report that through genetic engineering it might be possible to "recognize DNA from different people and attach different things that will kill only that group of people. . . . You will be able to determine the difference between blacks and whites and Orientals and Jews and Swedes and Finns and develop an agent that will kill only [a particular] group." The 1993 *Stockholm Peace Research Institute's Yearbook* answered the question of whether "genetic weapons'" could be developed by stating that if "investigations provide sufficient data on ethnic genetic differences between population groups [which in 2003 we now have], it may be possible to use such data to target suitable micro-organisms to attack known receptor sites for which differences exist at a cell membrane level or even to target DNA sequences inside cells by viral vectors." The article also concluded that the "genetic differences between human groups [that is, races] may in many cases be sufficiently large and stable so as to possibly be exploited by using naturally occurring, selective agents or by genetically engineering organisms and toxins with selectivity for an intended genetic marker."

A report of the British Medical Association entitled *Biotechnology Weapons and Humanity*, written by Malcolm Dando, concluded similarly: "If there are distinguishing DNA sequences between groups [the DNAPrint methodology has demonstrated there are], and these can be targeted in a way that is known to produce a harmful outcome, a genetic weapon is possible." Dr. Vivienne Nathanson, chairman and organizer of the BMA project, stated that "With an ethnically targeted weapon, you could even hit groups within a population. The history of warfare, in which many conflicts have an ethnic factor, shows us how dangerous this could be."

In fact, research and development of such "race bombs'" have already taken place in at least two different countries. In 1998, *The Sunday Times* (London) reported that both South Africa (under the former apartheid regime) and Israel have worked on ethnically targeted weapons. In testimony before the postapartheid Truth and Reconciliation Commission, Dr. Daan Goosen, head of a South African chemical and biological warfare plant, said he had led a research team that was ordered to develop a "pigmentation weapon" that would "target only black people" and that could be spread through beer, maize, or even vaccinations.

Western intelligence sources have reported that Israel has also been trying to develop such a weapon. *Foreign Report*, one of Jane's security and defense publications, reported an unnamed source as saying that Israeli scientists have used some of the South African research. William Cohen, secretary of defense in the Clinton administration, confirmed that he had received reports of countries working to create "certain types of pathogens that would be ethnic-specific," and an intelligence source stated that Israel was one of those countries.

Developing a weapon that would target Arabs but spare Jews would be much harder because the two groups are exceedingly alike genetically. However, a scientist working at Israel's biological research center in Nes Tziyone said the team had "succeeded in pinpointing a particular characteristic in the genetic profile of certain Arab communities, particularly the Iraqi people." Dedi Zucker, a member of the Israeli Knesset, denounced the project: "Morally, based on our history, and our tradition and our experience, such a weapon is monstrous and should be denied."

The end of apartheid put an end to research and development on the South African race bomb, and the removal of the regime of Saddam Hussein in Iraq has probably eliminated any sense of urgency on the part of Israel to develop such weapons. But we must recognize, first, that ethnic conflict exists both within and across national borders around the world and, second, that unlike ICBMs with warheads, biological race bombs can be developed by small terrorist groups. Indeed, such groups have developed and used simpler biological weapons.

The technological capability for developing the ethnic identification module, the bioweapon module, and the interface needed for joining the two will only increase over time, become less expensive, and open to more groups. As is always the case, the technology for developing a defense against a weapon system is the same as that used in creating one. As the 2003 war against Iraq showed, the demand for monitoring can itself be the flash point that ignites conflict. Even if a weapon is built, mutation might eventually produce immunity against the biological bullet. And even if race bombs do not have the pinpoint accuracy desired, they have the potential to do great harm to people of all races and ethnic groups. Rather than technology, we must rely on our ability to overcome ethnocentrism, envy, and xenophobia, and these are thin reeds indeed on which to lean. Any extremists crazy enough to attempt to use such weapons would be crazy enough to view large numbers of dead among their own nation, race, or ethnic group as "acceptable losses" in some unholy holy war to save their own group.

Are racially targeted weapons really feasible? The methodology for identifying race from DNA is now commercially available. Important racial differences in susceptibility to disease are also now well documented. Exploitation of these technologies is not financially out of range for some terrorist organizations. The most difficult part is developing the interface needed to join the two other components (assuming that hasn't already been done). Nor does the required technical expertise pose an insurmountable hurdle. Some of it can be obtained, for a price, from biological weapons scientists from the former Soviet Union desperately short of cash and even more so of conscience. More difficult is finding a safe haven in which to develop the race bomb.

It is therefore worthwhile to examine which countries are most at risk from the use of such weapons. Most clearly endangered are ethnically homogenous nations with low populations in which, in effect, everyone is part of an extended family. Iceland is one such example, as is Estonia; both have agreed to have their entire national genome mapped. Fortunately for them, neither of these countries has any major adversaries. Both Israel and the Palestinian Authority meet the criteria of homogeneity, low population, and ethnic hostility, and as noted, there is evidence that work on such weapons has been performed by at least one nation in the volatile Middle East. A major mitigating factor against the possibility of the use of race bombs in that region is the genetic similarity between the adversaries. The same would hold for the Serbs, Croats, and Bosnians in the former Yugoslavia; the Irish Catholics and Ulster Protestants in Northern Ireland; North and South Korea; and Pakistan and India. In the case of Pakistan, and even more so India, there is probably greater within-borders genetic diversity than across their frontier. Nonetheless, as the power of genetic racial markers to discriminate between groups increases, the problem posed by relative genetic similarity between groups will be reduced. The long, ongoing genocidal war in Sudan between the racially mixed Islamic north and the black African Christian and traditional-religion south is a likely prospect for this risk.

Perhaps the most immune to attack by race bombs from an outside source are nations like the United States that have a large, racially diverse population. However, these factors do not provide protection against the use of such weapons by terrorist groups within our country. The best defense here would be provided by an increased rate of racial intermarriage, which we are indeed seeing. But paradoxically, intermarriage, particularly of females of the majority group with males of a minority group, is the factor most likely to cause some extremist terrorist group to feel the need to launch such an attack.

In this arena, the evolutionary perspective has not been so kind. Although one male can produce almost uncountable offspring, the reproductive capacity of females is very limited. The all-time champion in this regard seems to be the Mongol emperor Genghis Khan or, more likely, his paternal grandfather. A Y-chromosome study, which tracks inheritance along the male line only, shows the Great Khan has 16 million male descendants living across the expanse of Asia surrounding Mongolia and stretching from Uzbekistan to Manchuria—one in every 200 males alive today. Since the average male alive at that time has only twenty descendants living today, the Universal Ruler, the name he adopted after uniting the various Mongol tribes in 1206, was 800,000 times more successful than his contemporaries. And that's only the male line.

Females provide the gating factor. Over the course of a lifetime, it will be the rare female who can give birth to rear as many as fifteen children. Indeed, the average for females across all cultures and history is six to seven children, not all of whom will reach maturity. Viewed from the racial solidarist perspective, intermarriage is an act of race war. Every ovum that is impregnated by the sperm of a member of a different race is one less of that precious commodity to be impregnated by a member of its own race and thereby ensure its survival.

When there is conflict between two ethnic groups, even the highly technical question of the degree of genetic similarity between them can become incendiary. In 2001 a very technical, scientific journal, *Human Immunology*, published an article entitled "The Origin of Palestinians and Their Genetic Relatedness with Other Mediterranean Populations" by Antonio Arnaiz-Villena and eight other authors. Arnaiz-Villena is an established authority in the field, whose publications have appeared in *Nature* and *Science*, the two most prestigious science journals in the United Kingdom and the United States, respectively. The article concluded that Jews are genetically exceedingly close to Palestinians and that the source of their present troubles is based "in cultural and religious, but not in genetic differences." But it also included a number of extraneous, gratuitous political comments, with references to Israeli "colonists" rather than "settlers" in the Gaza strip and Palestinians living in "concentration" rather than "refugee" camps. Dedicated to "all Palestinians and Jews who are suffering war" (the less than perfect English is also relevant), the paper also challenged the "claims that Jews are a special, chosen people and that Judaism can only be inherited."

After a deluge of complaints and the threat of mass resignations from its New York staff, Elsevier, which bills itself as market leader in "the publication and dissemination of literature covering the broad spectrum of scientific endeavours," reacted in a manner more like that of the Inquisition or the propaganda ministry of a totalitarian government. A notice was sent to subscribers, almost all of whom are academics or libraries, telling them to ignore or "preferably to physically remove the relevant pages." The article was also removed from the journal's website and from subsequent printings. Arnaiz-Villena was fired from the editorial board.

A defender of Arnaiz-Villena went so far as to say that if he "had found evidence that Jewish people were genetically very special, instead of ordinary, you can be sure no one would have objected to the phrases he used. . . . This is a very sad business." Robin McKie, science editor of *The Observer* (London), called Elsevier's act of ex post facto self-censorship "drastic" and "unprecedented," generating fears of a precedent for "the suppression of scientific work that questions Biblical dogma."

*Skeptic* covers scientific controversies as well as the usual debunking of psychics, faith healers, and claims of the paranormal, and does so with an edge. A major part of my (Miele's) job as senior editor, and Vince's, as a member of the editorial board, along with the other editors, is to catch and delete or rewrite howlers before we go to press. In the *Human Immunology* case, no matter how inappropriate the article was for a scientific journal rather than an op-ed piece, or even how offensive, the fault lies with not with Arnaiz-Villena, who, though grudgingly, acknowledged his poor choice of words. The journal's editors and the publisher, Elsevier, acted irresponsibly, first in accepting the article without requiring Arnaiz-Villena to remove his extraneous and gratuitous remarks, and then in trying to place all the blame on his shoulders. Rather, they should have acknowledged their own responsibility, issued a mea culpa, urged readers of the journal to concern themselves only with the article's scientific content, and promised to exercise the highest level of scrutiny in searching for and removing any political special pleading, regardless of point of view, from a respected scientific journal.

## RACE INTO THE NEW MILLENNIUM

In the previous chapters we have presented the evidence and the arguments that prove that race is not, as claimed by the PBS *Race* documentary, "an illusion." Neither is it, as anthropologist Ashley Montagu titled his book, published in countless editions, "man's most dangerous myth." The task that lies before us is to ensure that race does not become "man's most dangerous millstone." Doing so calls for recognizing reality, not attempting to hide from it.

Table 9.1 summarizes what we believe are the relative advantages and disadvantages of the three scenarios of the future of interethnic relations, both nationally and internationally. We fully recognize that the first law of economics, "you don't get something for nothing," applies. The critical point of *Race* is that evolution is dependent on variation, with which few would disagree. The consensus in the media and the social sciences would disagree, however, with our argument that finding group differences in any one trait implies that there will be group differences in other traits. For example, given the substantial morphological differences between human races (exceeding those seen in nondomesticated animals), it is more likely than not that racial differences will also exist in body chemistry and behavior.

We also believe that recognizing the reality of race means realizing that Arthur Jensen's "Laws of Individual Differences" apply to groups as well. Namely:

- Individual differences increase as task complexity increases;
- As the mean increases, the variance (the gap between the top and the bottom) also increases; and
- Individual differences increase as tasks are practiced over time.

TABLE 9.1    Three possible scenarios for race in the new millennium

|  | Meritocracy in the Global Marketplace | Affirmative Action and Race Norming | Resegregation and the Emergence of Ethno-States |
|---|---|---|---|
| **Advantages** | Highest economic growth, average economic level, and productivity.<br><br>Maximum individual opportunity and mobility up and down the socioeconomic scale.<br><br>Most conducive to individual rights.<br><br>Most able to adapt and change quickly. | Decreases feeling of minority groups that they are being left out.<br><br>Produces a greater number of positive role models.<br><br>Increases interracial contact, thereby eroding old barriers rooted in unfair practices. | Maximizes sense of community.<br><br>Maximizes security by having a fabric of society rather than just a socioeconomic ladder.<br><br>Maximizes true global cultural diversity and preservation of historical traditions. |
| **Disadvantages** | Greatest variation between individuals and groups; gap between rich and poor is maximized, leading individuals and groups to feel they are being left out while others prosper.<br><br>Most dependent on individual accepting and exercising personal responsibility.<br><br>High rate of change produces feeling of instability. | Lowers level of economic growth and mean economic level of society.<br><br>Increases resentment on part of high-performing groups.<br><br>Results in a certain number of unqualified minority members being promoted ahead of more qualified members of other groups. | Lowest level of economic growth and social mobility for out-group members.<br><br>Lowest ability to change reduces survivability in the face of changing conditions.<br><br>Maintenance of ethnic homogeneity requires highest level of internal enforcement. |

*continues on next page*

TABLE 9.1    (continued)

| | Meritocracy in the Global Marketplace | Affirmative Action and Race Norming | Resegregation and the Emergence of Ethno-States |
|---|---|---|---|
| Disadvantages (continued) | Existence becomes atomized and sense of belonging to a community is lost.<br><br>Popular culture becomes aimed at the lowest common denominator. | All minority members, whether qualified or not, may be stereotyped as "affirmative action" cases.<br><br>Some minority members may be placed in positions in which they fail or from which they cannot advance.<br><br>Can lead to creation of "apartheid" campuses and Balkanization of society, moving it toward Resegregation and the Emergence of Ethno-States. | Maximizes probability of interstate violence. |

For example, consider a sport at which neither of the authors is adept and compare our hypothetical performance to that of the best golfer in the world, arguably of all time. (The same principles would hold for playing violin or doing crossword puzzles.) The greater the difficulty of the golf course, the greater the difference between the score of either of the authors and that of Tiger Woods. Our best hope is to play miniature golf, although even here, Tiger might sink every hole in one shot. Second, as overall average performance in golf (or any other sport or activity) increases, the gap between the best golfer in the world and the worst also increases. Finally, assuming that one of us took up golf at about the same time as Tiger Woods, the more we all practiced, the greater the difference between us would become. Jensen's three laws also apply to average differences between groups.

The take-home message is that no amount of training, money, or boost to self-esteem can achieve a Lake Woebegone equality where "everyone is above average." The only way to achieve equality is by leveling down, not up. In our hypothetical golf match, we would have to tie one hand behind Tiger's back or blindfold him, although it is not even certain that this would guarantee our victory. Another bitter reality, as Richard Herrnstein pointed out in 1971, is that the more we continue to remove artificial barriers and equalize opportunity, the more differences in performance will be based on genetic differences. This is because once all the environmental differences are removed, only genetic differences remain. Herrnstein originally considered only individual differences within a given race, but the same principle applies to average racial differences if they have any genetic component. Jensen's laws and Herrnstein's syllogism are the bitter facts of life that come with meritocracy. That is one reason so many people find it ethically unacceptable.

We recognize these harsh realities, but our sympathies remain clearly with the meritocracy. We take this position on both ethical and economic grounds. First, it most clearly corresponds with what both of us were taught was "the American way," however much we have learned of our nation's failure to live up to that goal. Further, it has produced the greatest economic gain for the greatest number of people in the history of the world. Items that were luxuries of the rich only a decade or two ago, such as VCRs and cell phones, are commonplace today, even among the underclass. In the process, our civil liberties have also expanded, not constricted.

We believe that recognition and study of racial differences are not racist if we insist on the realization that everyone can gain on an absolute basis even as differences between individuals and between groups might remain the same or even increase. In our view, the most important thing government can do is to remove all reference to group identity from both statutory and administrative law and to focus instead on enhancing the potential for achievement by individuals.

Imposing equality requires the use of government force, thereby reducing individual freedom. This is not only ethically unacceptable, but it also hamstrings individual initiative and the intellectual and economic growth that come with it. It also means insisting on maintaining a lie and thereby eroding freedom of speech and academic inquiry when research suggests otherwise.

But we also recognize that there is no such thing as a free lunch or even a free lunchroom. The meritocracy has its costs. As evolutionist Ernst Mayr noted, "Equality in spite of evident nonidentity is a somewhat sophisticated concept and requires a moral stature of which many individuals seem to be incapable."

Around 5 million years ago, out on the African savanna, our ancestors separated from the apes. Since that time, our cranial capacity has increased threefold. One would have to assume a concomitant, if not necessarily commensurate, increase in our cognitive ability. Around 50,000 years ago, modern *Homo sapiens* started to diverge into the racial lineages that definitely still exist and that are readily recognizable today. The task that lies before us in this millennium is to see how realistic, sophisticated, and ethical we humans can be in the minefield that is race, while coming out alive having traversed it.

# Notes

## PREFACE

For a popular presentation of the contemporary scientific and ethical consensus in both the media and the social sciences regarding race, a consensus we challenge in *Race: The Reality of Human Differences*, see the PBS documentary *Race: The Power of an Illusion* and the accompanying website (http:www.pbs.org/race).

## OPENING STATEMENT: THE CASE FOR RACE

The sources for the quotations from U.S. presidents are, respectively: Thomas Jefferson, *Notes on the State of Virginia* (New York: Harper Torchbooks, 1964), p. 134; R. Current, ed., *The Political Thought of Abraham Lincoln* (New York: Bobbs-Merrill, 1967), p. 105; Theodore Roosevelt, "Review of *Social Evolution* by Benjamin Kidd," in *The Works of Theodore Roosevelt* (New York: Charles Scribner's Sons, 1926), vol. 13, p. 240; and John Ehrlichman, *Witness to Power* (New York: Simon and Schuster, 1982), p. 223.

Darlington quoted in C. Coon, *Adventures and Discoveries: The Autobiography of Carleton S. Coon, Anthropologist and Explorer* (Englewood Cliffs, NJ: Prentice-Hall, 1981), p. 371.

## CHAPTER 1: RACE AND THE LAW

The discussions of *Rice v. Office of Hawaiian Affairs* and *Haak v. Rochester School District* are taken from http:www.versuslaw.com.

The use of the DNAPrint methodology in identifying the Baton
Rouge serial killer is described in Dana Hawkins Simons, "Getting DNA
to Bear Witness: Genetic Tests Can Reveal Ancestry, Giving Police
a New Source Of Clues," *Silicon Investor*, Science and Technology section, 6/23/03 (http:www.siliconinvestor.com/stocktalk/msg.gsp?msgid=
19042492); Josh Noel, "Florida Lab Pointed to Race—Serial Killer
Search Changed Course" (http:www.2theadvocate.com/cgi-bin/print
me.pl); ABC News, "Racial Profiling—Will a New DNA Test Shatter
Serial Killer Profile?" (http:abcnews.go.com/sections?GMA?Primetime/
forensics_serialkiller030613.html); Nancy Touchette, "Genome Test
Nets Suspected Serial Killer," *Genome News Network* (http:
www.genomenewsnetwork.org/articles/06_03/serial.shtml); "Law Enforcement Independently Validate DNAPrint's Forensics Tests," *Forensic
Nurse* (http:www.forensicnursemag.com/hotnews/31h2272358.html).
The underlying methodology of DNAPrint is described in *DNA Witness
2.0 Validation Studies* (Sarasota, FL: DNAPrint Genomics in conjunc-
tion with National Center for Forensic Science and San Diego Police
Department Crime Lab, no date). Descriptions of the methodology that
have appeared in peer-reviewed scientific journals include Michael
Bamshad et al., "Human Population Genetic Structure and Inference
of Group Membership," *American Journal of Human Genetics* 72
(2003):578–589; and M. D. Shriver et al., "Skin Pigmentation, Biogeo-
graphical Ancestry, and Admixture Mapping," *Human Genetics* 112, 4
(2003):387–399.

The research on how children develop the concept of race without
being taught can be found in Lawrence A. Hirschfeld, *Race in the Making: Cognition, Culture, and the Child's Construction of Human Kinds*
(Cambridge: MIT Press, 1996), pp. 97, xi.

CHAPTER 2: RACE AND HISTORY

The view of early anthropologists on Egyptian art is from Alfred C.
Haddon, *History of Anthropology* (London: Watts, 1934). Information
on the concept of race as shown in the art and literature of ancient

Egypt, Greece, and Rome (including Table 2.1 comparing the African traits in *The Moretum* with those identified by contemporary anthropologists) can be found in Frank Snowden Jr., *Before Color Prejudice: The Ancient View of Blacks* (Cambridge: Harvard University Press, 1983); and Snowden, *Blacks in Antiquity: Ethiopians in the Greco-Roman Experience* (Cambridge: Harvard University Press, 1934).

The sources for ancient India are R. Craven, *Indian Art* (London: Thames and Hudson, 1997), p. 9; L. Torday, *The Mounted Archers: The Beginnings of Central Asian History* (Edinburgh: Durham Academic Press, 1997), p. 39; and R. Goring, ed., *Larousse Dictionary of Beliefs and Religions* (New York: Larousse, 1994), p. 64. For the Islamic period, a wealth of information, including plates of art pieces showing different races, can be found in B. Lewis, *Race and Color in Islam* (New York: Harper & Row, 1970). For ancient China, see E. Barber, *The Mummies of Ürümchi* (New York: Norton, 1999), p. 18.

## CHAPTER 3:
## ANTHROPOLOGY AS THE SCIENCE OF RACE

This chapter is adapted largely from Frank Miele (the junior author), "The Shadow of Caliban: An Introduction to the Tempestuous History of Anthropology," *Skeptic* 9:1 (2001):22–35. Our source for *Federalist* Number 10 is Alexander Hamilton, James Madison, and John Jay, *The Federalist Papers* (New York: New American Library, 1961), p. 78.

For more information on the early history of anthropology, see Haddon, *History of Anthropology*.

The definitive work on the American School of Anthropology is W. Stanton, *The Leopard's Spots: Scientific Attitudes Toward Race in America 1815–59* (Chicago: University of Chicago Press, 1960). John S. Haller Jr., *Outcasts from Evolution* (Urbana: University of Illinois Press, 1971), also supplies useful information.

For Franz Boas and the Boasian school of anthropology, see Marshall Hyatt, *Franz Boas, Social Activist* (New York: Greenwood Press, 1990); and Regna Darnell, *And Along Came Boas: Continuity and Revolution in*

*Americanist Anthropology* (Philadelphia: John Benjamins Publishing, 1998).

For the role of Cold War politics and the concept of race in social science, see Thomas Borstelmann, *The Cold War and the Color Line: American Race Relations in the Global Arena* (Cambridge: Harvard University Press, 2001).

Carleton Coon's major works on the subject of race are *The Races of Europe* (New York: Macmillan, 1939); *The Origin of Races* (New York: Knopf, 1962); and *The Living Races of Man* (New York: Knopf, 1965). Ashley Montagu's book, *Man's Most Dangerous Myth: The Fallacy of Race* (New York: Columbia University Press, 1942), has since appeared in numerous revisions.

For the debate between Ashley Montagu and Carleton Coon, see Coon, *Adventures and Discoveries*; Pat Shipman, *The Evolution of Racism: Human Differences and the Use and Abuse of Science* (New York: Simon and Schuster, 1994); and Milford Wolpoff and Rachel Caspari, *Race and Human Evolution: A Fatal Attraction* (Boulder, CO: Westview, 1998). The hostile reviews of Coon's *Origin of Races* by Theodosius Dobzhansky and Ashley Montagu, as well as Coon's responses to them, appeared in *Current Anthropology* 4, 4 (October 1963):360–365.

Jensen's article that brought the discussion of race back into the mainstream of behavioral science is A. R. Jensen, "How Much Can We Boost IQ and Scholastic Achievement?" *Harvard Educational Review* 39, 1 (1969):1–123. He was interviewed about the current status of the controversy by the junior author in F. Miele, *Intelligence, Race, and Genetics: Conversations with Arthur R. Jensen* (Boulder, CO: Westview, 2002). For a detailed presentation of Rushton's r/K theory of race differences in a matrix of more than sixty behaviors, see J. P. Rushton, *Race, Evolution, and Behavior: A Life History Perspective* (Port Huron, MI: Charles Darwin Research Institute, 2000).

CHAPTER 4: RESOLVING THE PRIMATE TREE

Chapters 4 and 5 are largely the senior author's (Sarich's) personal story of the effort to develop the molecular clock for primate evolution in general and human racial evolution in particular; included is discussion of some of the ramifications of that effort. The references given here begin with the precursors to the initial work in the Anthropology Department at the University of California, Berkeley, and continue from there.

Morris Goodman, "Evolution of the Immunological Species Specifity of Human Serum Proteins," *Human Biology* 34 (1962):104–150; Emile Zuckerkandl and Linus Pauling, "Molecular Disease, Evolution, and Genetic Heterogeneity," in Michael Kasha and Bernard Pullman, eds., *Horizons in Biochemistry* (New York: Academic Press, 1962), pp. 189–225; Morris Goodman, "Serological Analysis of Recent Hominoids," *Human Biology* 35 (1963):377–436; Morris Goodman, "Man's Place in the Phylogeny of the Primates as Reflected in Serum Proteins," in Sherwood L. Washburn, ed., *Classification and Human Evolution* (New York: Aldine, 1963), pp. 204–234; Morris Goodman, J. Barbanas, and G. W. Moore, "Man, the Conservative and Revolutionary Mammal: Molecular Findings," *Yearbook of Physical Anthropology* (1973), pp. 71–97; Emil L. Smith and Emmaneul Margoliash, "Evolution of Cytochrome *C*," *Federation Proceedings* 23 (1964):1243–1248; Elwyn L. Simons, *Annals New York Academy of Science* 167 (1969):330; John Buettner-Janusch, *Transactions New York Academy of Sciences* 32 (1969):132–133; Vincent M. Sarich, "A Molecular Approach to Human Origins," in P. C. Dolhinow and V. M. Sarich, *Background for Man* (Boston, MA: Little, Brown and Company, 1971), p. 76; Sherwood L. Washburn, "The Study of Human Evolution," Condon Lectures Committee, Oregon State System of Higher Education (1968), reprinted in Dolhinow and Sarich, *Background for Man*, pp. 82–117; R. Lewin, *Bones of Contention* (New York: Simon and Schuster, 1987), pp. 105–127; B. G. Richmond and D. S. Strait, "Evidence That Humans Evolved from a Knuckle-Walking Ancestor," *Nature* 404 (2000):382–384.

CHAPTER 5: *HOMO SAPIENS* AND ITS RACES

Important research papers for the application of the molecular clock to the origin of races include W. M. Brown, M. George, and A. C. Wilson, "Rapid Evolution of Animal Mitochondrial DNA," *Proceedings of the National Academy of Sciences* 76 (1979):1967–1971; W. M. Brown,

"Polymorphism in Mitochondrial DNA of Humans as Revealed by Restriction Endonuclease Analysis," *Proceedings of the National Academy of
Sciences* 77 (1980):3605–3609; R. L. Cann, W. M. Brown, and A. C.
Wilson, "Mitochondrial DNA and Human Evolution," *Nature* 325
(1987):31–36; K. L. Knight, *Mortal Words* (New York: Pocket Books,
1990), p. 212; T. D. Kocher and A. C. Wilson, "Sequence Evolution of
Mitochondrial DNA in Humans and Chimpanzees: Control Region
and a Protein-Coding Region," in S. Osawa and T. Honjo, eds., *Evolution of Life, Fossils, Molecules, and Culture* (Springer-Verlag, 1991), pp.
391–413; A. DiRienzo and A. C. Wilson, "Branching Pattern in the
Evolutionary Tree for Human Mitochondrial DNA," *Proceedings of the
National Academy of Sciences* 88 (1991):1597–1601; L. Vigilant, M.
Stoneking, H. Harpending, K. Hawkes, and A. C. Wilson, "African
Populations and the Evolution of Human Mitochondrial DNA," *Sci-
ence* 253 (1991):1503–1507; P. A. Underhill et al., "Y-Chromosome Se-
quence Variation and the History of Human Populations," *Nature
Genetics* 26 (2000):358–361; M. Ingman, H. Kaessmann, S. Paabo, and
Ulf Gyllensten, "Mitochondrial Genome Variation and the Origin of
Modern Humans," *Nature* 408 (2000):708–713.

The most important work on tracing human racial differentiation
through the Y-chromosome appears in "Population Genetic Implications from Sequence Variation in Four Y-Chromosome Genes," by
Peidong Shen, Frank Wang, Peter A. Underhill, Claudia Franco, Wei-
Hsien Yang, Adriane Roxas, Raphael Sung, Alice A. Lin, Richard W.
Hyman, Douglas Vollrath, Ronald W Davis, L. Luca Cavalli-Sforza,
and Peter J Oefner, *Proceedings of the National Academy of Sciences* 97
(2000):7354–7359. It was Underhill's talk based on the article that we
attended and is mentioned in the text.

CHAPTER 6: THE TWO
"MIRACLES" THAT MADE HUMANKIND

For the possible role of the development of spoken language from
gestural language, see J. A. Iverson and S. Goldin-Meadow, "Why
People Gesture When They Speak," *Nature* 396 (1998):228; Michael

Corballis, *From Hand to Mouth: The Origins of Language* (Princeton, NJ: Princeton University Press, 2002).

## CHAPTER 7: RACE AND PHYSICAL DIFFERENCES

Materials on the rate of evolutionary change are Motoo Kimura, "Evolutionary Rate at the Molecular Level," *Nature* 217 (1968):624–626; Jack L. King and T. H. Jukes, "Non-Darwinian Evolution," *Science* 164 (1969):788–798; Jon Entine, *Taboo: Why Black Athletes Dominate Sports and Why We're Afraid to Talk About It* (New York: Public Affairs, 2000); Vincent M. Sarich, "The Final Taboo: Race Differences in Ability," *Skeptic* 8, 1 (2000):38–43.

The material on differences in susceptibility to disease and the effectiveness of dog breeds is from Donald C. Plumb, *The Veterinary Drug Handbook*, 4th ed. (Ames: Iowa State University Press, 2002).

The materials on racial differences in susceptibility to disease, the effectiveness of pharmaceuticals, and the ethics of using race in medicine are from Richard S. Cooper, Jay S. Kaufman, and Ryk Ward, "Race and Genomics," *New England Journal of Medicine* 348 (March 20, 2003):1166–1170; Troy Duster, "Buried Alive: The Concept of Race in Science," *Chronicle of Higher Education*, September 14, 2001; Jane Kaye, "Genetic Research on the U.K. Population: Do New Principles Need to be Developed?" *HMS Beagle*, September 14, 2001; Neil Risch, Esteban Burchard, Elad Ziv, and Hua Tung, "Categorization of Humans in Biomedical Research: Genes, Race, and Disease," *Genome Biology* 3, 7 (July 1, 2002):1–12 (http:genomebiology.com/2002/3/7/cinnebt/2007); and Sally Satel, "Medicine's Race Problem," *Policy Review Online*, December 2001 (http:www.policyreview.org/DEC01/satel.html).

## CHAPTER 8: RACE AND BEHAVIOR

The research on behavior differences between the four dog breeds and between Caucasian and Chinese neonates is in Daniel G. Freedman, *Human Biology: A Holistic Approach* (New York: Free Press, 1979), pp. 144–161. A wealth of information on breed differences can also be found in J. P. Scott and J. L. Fuller, eds., *Genetics and the Social Behavior of the Dog* (Chicago: University of Chicago Press, 1998). For Freedman's "discomfort" with race research, see Freedman, "Is Individuality Possible?" in Nancy Segal, Glenn Weisfeld, and Carol C. Weisfeld, *Uniting Psychology and Biology: Integrative Perspectives on Human Development* (Washington, DC: American Psychological Association, 1997), p. 61.

The summary of the evidence for the role of some genetic factor in race differences in average IQ and the validity of the sub-Saharan IQ score is from J. P. Rushton and A. R. Jensen, "Thirty Years of Research on Race Differences in Cognitive Ability," *Psychology, Public Policy, and Law* (in press). The association of average national IQ and economic prosperity is described by R. Lynn and T. Vanhanen, *IQ and the Wealth of Nations* (Westport, CT: Praeger, 2002).

The discussions of African IQ with Henry Harpending, Richard Lynn, and J. P. Rushton are from their personal communications with Frank Miele and are used with their permission.

### CHAPTER 9: LEARNING TO LIVE WITH RACE

The best source for the early history of biological weapons is Mark Wheelis, "Biological Warfare Before 1914," in Erhard Geissler and John Ellis van Courtland Moon, eds., *Biological Toxin Weapons: Research, Development, and Use from the Middle Ages to 1945* (New York: Oxford University Press, 1999), pp. 8–34. The alleged use of smallpox by the British against the American Indians has been the subject of much debate. The original documents establishing that this occurred during the siege of Fort Pitt can be found at http:www.nativeweb.org/pages/legal/amherst/lord_jeff.html.

The background on the post–World War II research and development of ethnically targeted weapons can be found in Malcolm Dando, *Biotechnology Weapons and Humanity* (Amsterdam: Harwood Academic Publishers, 1999). For the two known attempts to develop such weapons, see Oread Daily, "No One Looking for Racist Bioweapons," http:southafrica.indymedia.org/news/2003/05/4008.php; Uzi Mahnaimi and Marie Cohen, "Israel Planning 'Ethnic' Bomb as Saddam Caves In," *Sunday Times* (London), http:www.the-times.co.uk/pages/sti/1998/11/15/stifgnmid03004.html; and Steve Russell, "Iraqis and Palestinians Facing Israeli Ethnic Bullets," http:www.yowusa.com/Archive/June2001/Ethnic2/ethnic2.htm. For the role of competition for women from members of another race as a powerful factor motivating racism, see Pierre L. van den Berghe, *The Ethnic Phenomenon* (New York: Elsevier, 1981).

The depublished research paper by Antonio Arnaiz-Villena et al. is "The Origin of Palestinians and Their Genetic Relatedness with Other Mediterranean Populations," *Human Immunology* 62 (2001):889–900. The affair is described by Robin McKie, "Journal Axes Gene Research on Jews and Palestinians," *The Observer* (London), November 25, 2001; and in Oasis TV Library, "World Peace and Genetics: Why Not?" December 6, 2001 (http:www.oasistv.com/news/12–6-01-story–2.asp).

For a popular account of Genghis Khan's genetic progeny, see Steve Sailer, "Genes of History's Greatest Lover Found?" June 2, 2003, http:www.upi.com/view.cfm?StoryID=20030205–100301–1566r.

# Index